THE BLACK SCORPIONS

THE BLACK SCORPIONS

Serving with the 64th Fighter Squadron in World War II

GENERAL JAMES A. LYNCH AND GREGORY LYNCH JR.

CASEMATE

Philadelphia & Oxford

Published in the United States of America and Great Britain in 2023 by
CASEMATE PUBLISHERS
1950 Lawrence Road, Havertown, PA 19083, USA
and
The Old Music Hall, 106–108 Cowley Road, Oxford OX4 1JE, UK

Hardback Edition: ISBN 978-1-63624-306-1
Digital Edition: ISBN 978-1-63624-307-8

A CIP record for this book is available from the British Library

Printed and bound in the United Kingdom by CPI Group (UK) Ltd, Croydon, CR0 4YY

Typeset in India by Lapiz Digital Services, Chennai.

For a complete list of Casemate titles, please contact:

CASEMATE PUBLISHERS (US)
Telephone (610) 853-9131
Fax (610) 853-9146
Email: casemate@casematepublishers.com
www.casematepublishers.com

CASEMATE PUBLISHERS (UK)
Telephone (0)1226 734350
Email: casemate-uk@casematepublishers.co.uk
www.casematepublishers.co.uk

All photographs from author's collection unless otherwise credited.

Contents

Preface

Whenever the Lynch family gathered in numbers beyond the immediate family—whether it was back in Melrose, Massachusetts, with my uncle and cousins or up in San Francisco with my Great Aunt Ida—and tales were told of our family history, occasional mention was made of my paternal grandfather James Lynch's memoir about fighting in World War II. I vaguely knew my grandfather, or Papa as he preferred to be called, fought in World War II. There were artifacts around the house pointing to his service. I used his wartime duffel bag on many camping trips; that bag was tougher than Kevlar and basically unmarred despite its age. There were a few khaki side caps stuck in a drawer. My father showed me some handkerchiefs Papa had had made from parachute silk. That was about it.

Furthermore, my connection with Papa was tenuous at best. Our family moved away from Massachusetts, where Papa lived in Medford, when I was six. I was told he used to take us to Jordan Marsh at Christmas to meet Santa and pick out a toy. I know that because there are pictures and stories from my sisters. One of the solid memories I have of him is that he was a superhero who took nitroglycerine pills to help with his heart. Another is that I was at his house once in Medford and we watched the funeral of General Dwight Eisenhower. That is about it as far as the memories go. Sadly, he died in 1975 at the young age of 69 before I got the chance to know him.

Whenever his name was mentioned afterwards, it was coupled with the book. The book that detailed his experiences in World War II. The book that was never published.

That wasn't the biggest travesty. That was the loss of the photos that accompanied the book. According to my father, the pictures were what really made it. Papa was the company security officer for his unit. During his service, it was his job to collect any and all pictures found on the men and destroy them. You weren't supposed to have pictures of the unit in case they fell into enemy hands. It was a security no-no and Papa took the job of rounding up those contraband pictures seriously. The only problem: he never destroyed them. He kept them. After the war was over, supposedly, he had a great stash of pictures to illustrate his exploits.

When Papa died, my father went looking for the photos. They were always kept in a desk drawer in a folder next to the one that held the manuscript. The picture folder was empty, and no one knew where the pictures had gone. My father thought Papa might have sent them off with the manuscript to a publisher and the pictures were never returned.

That is where the story stood for decades. Whenever I met up with the cousins or my Uncle Jimmy and the talk would turn to Papa's book, the inevitable question would be, "Where are the pictures?" At some point, Uncle Jimmy started to think the pictures might be lost somewhere in his basement. When Papa passed, a lot of his old keepsakes and memorabilia ended up in Uncle Jimmy's basement. That's how the photos might have ended up there. The family just had to find them. For years after that revelation, I would ask my Uncle Jimmy or my cousins whether they had found the photos. The answer was always no. The nadir of the story came when the basement flooded. The pictures, if they existed, might have been ruined by the water and most likely tossed out with the rest of the mess.

Now, this hunt for the missing pictures doesn't take into account the state of the actual manuscript. My father felt Papa's manuscript needed someone to go through and edit it. Papa barely graduated high school and my father thought the language of the book was a bit basic. In the same breath, my father would also declare he didn't want to do too much to the writing so as not to destroy Papa's voice. The goal was to find someone to take on the task of going through the manuscript and make it ready for publication. There were no takers. There were a few writers in the family, me included, but none of us had any interest in the project.

The book sat unremarked for decades, only spoken of in passing. My father hoped someone would jumpstart this project and get Papa's book out into the world.

In the late 2000s, I decided I would finally do something. I did it for my father's sake. At some point, I think everyone wants to do something for their parents to show them how much they mean to them. This was my opportunity to show my father how much I appreciated him. It was his dream to have the book published. He just didn't know how to do it. I felt it was something I could help him with. In order to do that, the first thing I would have to do was at least put the book into an electronic format so editing could take place more easily.

My first day typing, I could see one of the reasons why the book had been rejected by publishers. Papa had written the book in all capital letters. I was so used to texting and writing in online forums by this point, where "all caps" has a particular significance, I felt like Papa was shouting his story at me. The style was a bit awkward as well. Papa was used to writing military reports and that's how the book came across: one long military report. It took months, but eventually the manuscript was in a manageable form.

As I went through the book, I became enthralled by Papa's exploits. I finally learned he was with an air combat squadron. Though he was not a pilot, he made sure the pilots had everything they needed to do their jobs. He traveled across the globe to give assistance to the British Army when they needed it most. Papa and the 64th

Fighter Squadron of the 57th Fighter Group fought General Rommel across the top of Africa. When that job was finished, they fought the retreating Germans up through Italy. The squadron flew sorties almost every day. If they weren't fighting, they were on the move to the next airstrip. There were quiet times as well. There were booze runs to Malta and a hunt for musical instruments to start a band. Papa described a side of the war that's not often depicted, the everyday events of military life.

My grandfather supplemented his story with a lot of additional material to give his story context. Not only were there pictures, but Papa also added news articles of the time to show what was happening beyond the 64th Fighter Squadron. There were messages from Generals Eisenhower and Montgomery. He included bulletins from the Eighth Army about troop movements and strategic battles. There were documents that explained pivotal battles like the Mareth Line and Wadi Akarit. He also reached out to his former comrades to have them share their tales. Some of the men were captured after being shot down and their exploits were recorded. All these additional elements, along with Papa's narrative, provided a unique and richly detailed story.

After I finished typing the manuscript, I was very pleased with the story, but I could tell it needed work. Sadly, I didn't really have the time to give the book the thorough editing it needed. I figured I would get to it eventually.

Over in Massachusetts, my cousin Chris was very excited when he learned I was working on Papa's book. He spent a lot of time with our grandfather growing up. Of all the grandkids, he had the closest bond to Papa. That bond probably helped convince Chris to join the Army himself. Chris would always pester me whenever we communicated. "Have you finished Papa's book yet?" And I would always ask if he had found the pictures. That would quickly bring the conversation to a close. It had long been decided that without the pictures there could be no book. Over time, I started to think I could probably put the book together with pictures from other sources. There is an online forum dedicated to the 57th Fighter Group that has a lot of pictures from the people in the squadron. I even found one of Papa in the collection. I guess my grandfather wasn't as successful at rounding up the forbidden pictures as he thought. If I couldn't find Papa's pictures, I could certainly use these.

The narrative changed in 2022. Both my Uncle Jimmy and my Aunt Eileen had passed on and Chris lived in their house in Melrose. He and his two brothers and two sisters were going to sell the house as part of their inheritance and were in the process of clearing out the myriad material scattered throughout. Everything had to be sorted, either saved or thrown out. Out of the blue, I received a text from Chris saying they had found Papa's pictures. "Surprised" didn't really encompass my reaction. I believed the pictures had long since vanished from the house. They were found tucked away in a bag in some dark corner of the cellar. They hadn't been destroyed in the flood. After years and years, I no longer had the excuse of not having the pictures I needed to finish the book. Chris boxed up the album and sent it to me. I started fixing Papa's book.

Now, it is done and ready to be shared. The more I read the book, the more I got to know this relatively young man and the job he did serving his country. In the end, his story is an amazing one. I hope Papa likes the way his book turned out.

Gregory Lynch Jr.
Raymond, CA
January 2023

A map showing the movement of the 57th Fighter Group from 1942 to 1945

For my father who would have loved to see this book.
My grandfather would dedicate this book to his sons Greg and
Jim for whom he wrote the book.

Members of the 64th Fighter Squadron celebrating VE-Day.

Introduction

In 1942, the eyes of the world were focused on the battles taking place between General Erwin Rommel's *Afrika Korps* and the British Eighth Army on a piece of property called the Sahara Desert which embraced Egypt, Libya, and Tunisia. I read the daily reports of this action in a faraway land but gave little or no attention to it. The papers were full of war news in those black days of early 1942.

In August 1942, I found myself living in a British-issued tent not far from where the Eighth Army made its last stand during its last retreat. This spot was called El Alamein and I doubt we will ever be able to forget this spot. Historians are still writing stories about this battle of battles.

A fighter squadron equipped with desert pink Warhawks (P-40) from Boston, Massachusetts, was my outfit. I was the adjutant and, later, executive officer. This squadron, after a few months in the desert, selected the name "Black Scorpion Squadron." They had good reason to select this name. We fought those scorpions and the enemy at the same time. The black scorpion had as deadly a sting as the P-40 did and became part of our official insignia.

We were told our squadron was to be a mobile organization. There was no Army manual to tell us how to run such an outfit. We made up our own plan and went about the business of implementing what had never been tried before and probably will never be tried again. We felt it was a good plan and we used it for the next 33 months until the squadron completed its assignment in the Po Valley in northern Italy.

During all this action, I kept a diary, which was not permitted,

64th Fighter Squadron members out in the desert. (57th Fighter Group website)

and collected daily intelligence reports, newspaper stories, souvenirs, pictures, and letters from home. I saved all the letters I wrote my wife and two sons. After the war, I pasted all the pictures in an album. The letters and other material were filed away, forgotten.

A few months after the war, I joined the Medford Post No. 45 of the American Legion. I later became commander of this post. I rejoined the Malden, Massachusetts, post of the Veterans of Foreign Wars (VFA). I had been member-at-large of the VFA since the battle of El Alamein when an old soldier from World War I signed me up. I also joined the famous Ancient and Honorable Artillery Company of Massachusetts. In 1947, I went back to my old National Guard outfit, the 104th Anti-Aircraft Artillery Brigade of the Massachusetts National Guard.

Being a member of these various military organizations gave me a chance to meet and swap war stories with many of my old buddies who had been away for several years to all parts of the world. After a few years, I gave some thought to putting on paper the experiences and incidents I viewed during my six years of active duty.

The Black Scorpion Squadron was one of the three squadrons that made up the 57th Fighter Group. Upon our arrival in the Middle East, we were made part of the Ninth Air Force. Our assignment with the Eighth Army was to supplement the British and Commonwealth air units, known as the Desert Air Force, to deny Rommel's *Afrika Korps* in his advance towards the east. The officers and enlisted men of the 64th Fighter Squadron had many years of service and were experienced technicians in the various sections that made up this outstanding squadron. Most of the pilots were young but they had many hours of flying in the States. The balance of pilots was just out of flight school. In one case, a boy went back to high school to pick up his diploma after he received his wings. The ground officers in most cases were in the Army a few months, being called to active duty from the reserves. Their only experiences as officers were in college during their time in the Reserve Officers' Training Corps. All members of this squadron rose to the occasion and performed in an outstanding manner. This was a team effort and no one man or section could be singled out as the hero of this activity.

The pilot was the man that was up in the air bombing and strafing enemy positions and taking lots of flak from the anti-aircraft guns of the very efficient *Afrika Korps*. Many times, a pilot was called a "glamor boy." We had very few of them in our squadron. The pilot always remarked that he knew it took a team effort to keep his plane flying.

I have tried to put on paper my personal experiences that I lived with during my 33 months with the Air Corps. I feel it was a privilege to serve with such a group of dedicated men who had one objective: service.

It has been said you need a reason to write a book. I think I have cited my reasons. The following chapters should prove my point.

PART I

The African Campaign: Massachusetts to Tunisia

CHAPTER I

Boston

On **July 5, 1942**, I arose from my cot in the cantonment area of Wood Island Park, in east Boston. This had been the living quarters of the 64th Fighter Squadron for the past few months. This area was just over the hill from what is now Logan International Airport. It was 3:00 am. Little did I know that morning what was ahead of me for the next three years. The first order of business was to see 200 men and officers had their breakfast, followed by the packing of their gear for the move to the South Station in Boston at 5:30 am.

The movement went off as planned and we boarded a special train bound for Fort Dix, New Jersey. The troops were not told our destination. In fact, I had been walking around for about ten days with the movement order in my pocket and instructions from higher authority not to even mention the move. We were rushed in the side door of the station and boarded the already spotted train. There was no fanfare for us. In fact, there was no one to see us off, not even the higher headquarters people that had issued the orders for this move.

The men had known something was going on for the past week. All we could tell them was we were changing stations. That was all I knew. I had no orders other than we were going to Fort Dix. We all felt this was the move to an overseas assignment. After the train pulled out, and I settled down in my seat, I had some time to think for the first time since I woke early that morning. My thoughts went back to what brought me to this spot.

In 1928, I enlisted in the 241st Coast Artillery Harbor Defense Regiment of the Massachusetts

Me in my truck in East Boston before heading back to service.

National Guard and served as a battery clerk, supply sergeant, and sergeant major. I went to the Massachusetts Military Academy in 1935 and was commissioned as a second lieutenant in the same unit. I was called to active duty in September 1940 and served with the same regiment until midnight of December 6, 1941. After midnight, I was out of the Army due to a War Department ruling called "over age in grade." There were many officers in the same boat as I was. I had some leave coming to me and I went back to my old job as a band organizer, which included selling musical instruments to school children.

For the 30 days prior to December 6, I was busy with my work, but my mind was on the previous 18 months when I trained new enlisted men and selectees that had been assigned to our outfit. On Sunday, December 7, I was out working on some business calls; the radio in my car was not working. For a few hours, I was out of contact with the news. In the early afternoon, I arrived at the home of Mr. Charles Cavanaugh, the bandmaster of the American Legion Band of Wilmington. Just as I entered his home, his wife asked if I had heard the news. They told me all about the bombing of Pearl Harbor. I really was shaken up. I had been in the service since 1928 and the day the Army says "You are too old," a new war is on.

I returned home immediately and listened to the news broadcast until early the next morning. The next few weeks were rough on me as I wanted to be back in the

```
      4. a    Under the provisions of par. 6,
   contained in War Dept. letter, file AG 210.31
   (7-31-41) OB-A, Sept. 5, 1941, subject: "Service
   with truop units - Maximum age of commissioned
   officers", as amended, the following named
   officers having been relieved from further duty
   in the active military service of the United
   States are assigned to the STATE DETACHMENT,
   MASSACHUSETTS NATIONAL GUARD:

   Capt. ROBERT H. ANDERSON, effective Nov. 28,1941
   Capt. SYDNEY B. BURRELL,        "     Nov. 26,1941
   Capt. NORVILLE L. MILMORE,      "     Nov. 28, 1941
   Capt. ARTHUR A. WHALLEY,        "     Dec. 6,1941
   1st Lt. CONNELL ALBERTINI,      "     Nov. 26,1941
   1st Lt. HOWARD P. DAVIS,        "     Dec. 8, 1941
   1st Lt. JAMES E. O'NEILL,       "     Nov. 14,1941
   Staff Sgt. JAMES A. LYNCH,      "     Dec. 6, 1941
        (2nd Lt., C.A.C., N.G. of U.S.)
```

The notice informing me I was being discharged from duty.

service. I made a trip to Washington, but they gave me little or no assurance as to what would happen to me as far as being recalled. My wife was happy I was home with the children. She wanted no part of the war. In the middle of January, she called me at the office and said there was a big fat envelope from the War Department and she would not open it. I rushed home. The letter said I was being recalled, not to my own outfit but to the Air Corps.

I reported to Mitchell Field and was assigned to a room in the Telephone Building on 14th Street in New York City. My job was a dull one, but I enjoyed the difference from the coast artillery. The room I worked in plotted the seaward flights coming into New York. In this room was a plotting board showing the direction of the flights. If an unidentified one showed up, my job was to alert the proper authorities. We all had a status board which showed the number of fighter aircraft available to attack any enemy intruders. This board was pathetic as, many days and nights, we only had a few aircraft that could fly.

I remember one night when a report came in that 50 planes were coming down the Hudson River. When this was reported to the colonel in charge, his remark was, "They must be the enemy as we do not have that many aircraft." The report turned out to be the action of a crank.

The status board was always the center of attraction when we had visitors in the room. I suggested to my commanding officer that it be removed and instead have a small board placed on the desk in front of the operator running the room. He accepted the recommendation. This reduced the gossip about how many planes we had.

The Navy also had a spot in the room. They had operators standing by radios tuned to the SOS band around the clock. During February and March 1942, we had a lot of ships torpedoed off our shores and around the world. When reports came into the room, we would record and pass on the information to the intelligence officer at First Army Headquarters in New York. Often, when I purchased a newspaper, I would look for the report of the sinking of the ships we had heard about on the Navy radio; not once did I find one.

Despite this important work, I was anxious to return to an organization with troops. My wish was granted when I was assigned as adjutant of the 64th Fighter Squadron, 57th Fighter Group, stationed at East Boston. Here I was, back home only a few miles from where I started in 1940. This was a different assignment, and it took a little time to get acclimated to a new type of operation. The squadron was equipped with P-40 Warhawks, but only a few of them. Early in April, we received 25 more and a new group of pilots. Training was in full swing. Boston and Cape Cod was the training area for the officers who would later fight over the sands of the Western Desert many thousands of miles away.

During this training period, we lost a few fine young men in crashes. That will always happen with an extensive training period like they had. As the weeks went by, we continued to receive many new men and officers. By June 1, we had enough to make two squadrons.

We received orders to make up one squadron of officers and 249 enlisted men from this large group. We were told to select the most experienced men for our squadron and the remaining officers and enlisted men were to be shipped to what is now known as Hanscom Field in Bedford, Massachusetts. Those officers and enlisted men later formed the 79th Fighter Group.

A few days after we had our squadron all set up, without any fanfare, the planes took off one morning and didn't come back. Headquarters had tight lips. We were in the dark as to what to expect next.

As always, the grapevine produced some information: our boys were flying around Mitchell Field, New York, in new desert pink Warhawks. Within a week, all was silent again. We heard the planes had left for parts unknown. We never heard where they went until we met up with them two months later.

In the middle of June, the call came from headquarters for all our crew chiefs, engineering, and armament officers to travel to Florida. During this activity, we were told nothing. Of course, we wondered just what the true picture was. On June 20, I was given the secret orders to prepare to move to Fort Dix, New Jersey, on July 5. I had to carry these orders around with me for the next two weeks. No talk about the move was to be made.

At this time, I had a death in my family, and I did not have a lot of time for the service. The funeral proved very difficult for me due to the silence of the coming move. There was lots of work to be completed before leaving the cantonment area. We even had a man in the guard house, and we had only one 2½-ton truck to take care of all our needs for the upcoming move.

Headquarters seemed to have forgotten us. I had to put some pressure on them to release our prisoner from the guard house. I also had a meeting to discuss giving us enough transportation to move out. The most important thing to do was to assign someone to take over all our buildings and the property in the buildings, which was worth hundreds of thousands of dollars. We always felt someone at headquarters, who was staying behind, was angry because they were not going overseas with the 57th and couldn't care less about taking over after we left.

The men were not told of the move until the day before we were to leave East Boston. This was rough on some of them, but the orders stated this procedure. Also, they were confined to the area on that final night. We doubled the guard, but I knew some of the men found a way to get out. I had a busy week prior to our departure taking care of paying bills with the local merchants who supplied us with part of our rations. The merchants all asked lots of questions as they were told this would be the last of the purchases.

I had a visit from the local police captain about a complaint concerning some of our boys. I told him, if any of our boys were involved, they would not be in this area much longer. He pressed me for further information but that was all I could say. He accepted this and left shaking his head.

We had a local Catholic priest, Reverend Father McCarthy, pastor of the Star of the Sea Parish in East Boston, who said mass in the area on Sundays. He called up on Saturday as usual and wanted to know what time to come for mass. I just said there would be no mass. I later wrote Father McCarthy from New Jersey and tried to explain. He answered my letter and wanted to visit with me at Fort Dix. I did not get the letter for two months; by that time, I was in Egypt. I wrote and told him I was sorry we could not get together due to the distance.

He was a grand man and really enjoyed saying the mass for the squadron. He was beyond the age to be in the service, but felt he was doing his part by serving our boys for their spiritual needs.

We arrived at Fort Dix at 4:00 pm at a siding not far from the barracks. This would be our home until we received new orders. We all marched to our assigned barracks and the work was poured on immediately. We had all kinds of meetings, but nothing was said about where we were going. Our 210 officers and enlisted men needed all kinds of inoculations. Some of the men required physical examinations.

I will always remember one young man who did not act normal. I sent him to the hospital for a physical examination. He was returned as ready for overseas duty. I called the hospital and had a talk with the doctor and told him I wanted the boy to have a mental examination. He requested we send him back the next morning. The boy never went overseas as the mental examination proved he should have not been in the Army let alone prepared for shipment to an overseas station.

We could not make or receive any phone calls. Our mail was dropped in a box and held until a further date.

I had another young man come into my office. If we were going overseas, he said he wanted to get married before we left. At that point the date for departure was not set. We had a long talk. I found out the young man had made his wedding plans a long time before

Reverend Charles Louge, chaplain for the 64th Fighter Squadron.

this move. I told him to see me later in the day. I went to work and made all the necessary plans with headquarters, such as the chaplain and the chapel and getting the young lady into the area. This was a problem as we were restricted to the area.

It all worked out and we had a nice wedding for the young man and his sweetheart. We arranged a little reception off post and permission was given for him to stay with his wife for a short honeymoon at the Pig and Whistle Inn just outside the gate. The young man was grateful for what we did for him.

Another incident involved a young wife of one of our boys who came to my office with a baby in her arms. She stated she was stranded without funds and her husband had none. Her husband was the big shot gambler of the 64th and had lost all his money the night before. I don't know how she got into our area. We were forbidden to go out or have anybody come in. But she was there, and something had to be done.

The Red Cross representatives were only a few blocks from our area. A short visit to them produced the necessary funds to send the young lady on her way with her child.

During this time our new chaplain, Reverend Charles Louge, a captain from Cleveland Heights, Ohio, reported in. He came to squadron headquarters instead of the group headquarters. He stated he just wanted to make a quick report and would be on his way for a few days of leave. This was at 11:00 am. I told the good father that at 2:20 pm he would be on his way to a train which would take him to a boat going on a long trip overseas. He was quite surprised. He had to contact his old outfit at Fort Hamilton in New York for someone to pick up his car.

On August 13, I had a meeting with the group headquarters acting commanding officer. He informed me we would leave Fort Dix on August 15, load on a boat in New York Harbor and head to a port on the Red Sea. This took me by surprise. I had to do a lot of thinking to remember where the Red Sea was. Again, I could not discuss this move with any of my officers or enlisted men. As of this date, we could not use the name of our squadron. The name would be lost until a further date. Our squadron was now known as "9141B."

During our days of preparing for movement overseas, we received new men to fill in some gaps that showed up when headquarters came up with a new table of organization. We received all our replacements except for several radio repairmen. I kept bugging headquarters for the men. The usual response was they were on their way, and we would receive them before we left.

On the day before we left, I received a call that the replacements were coming to our headquarters that morning. We received the 10 men we were short. They were the same truck drivers we had left in Boston when they changed to the new organization tables. What could you do?

They came with us and were a happy lot. They served us well, but we never did receive the radio repairmen. We just had to work with what we had.

Before leaving Boston, we received our share of the profits from the Coke machines. This money came in very handy as we planned a party for the boys on their last night before going to a foreign land. These funds also helped to give us each a good-sized box lunch to take with us to the boat as no meal would be served on board until the morning after loading.

The party turned out to be a successful one. The boys let their hair down. They had the right to do this as this was the last party they would have for a long time.

By midnight, we had all the boys in their bunks. On the morning of July 15, we had an early call. This was a busy day for all of us. We had an excellent breakfast and there was plenty for all. It was prepared by our excellent mess section.

After breakfast, the bunks had to be broken down as we would not be sleeping on them again. We all had lots of gear to be packed, which was the first order of business after the bunk break down. We had our last meal at noon; then the rush was on to clean out the barracks and mess hall and stand by for the usual inspection. I had been through these many times. We received a real nice compliment from the inspectors. One of them stated the barracks was the best they had seen.

One of the inspectors told us of a kitchen they had visited. They found the fires still in the stove and food in the oven. Our departure from our area in Fort Dix

---

A note from President Roosevelt upon the 64th Fighter Squadron's departure to the Middle East:

The White House
Washington

TO MEMBERS OF THE UNITED STATES ARMED EXPEDITIONARY FORCES:

You are a soldier of the United States Army.

You have embarked for distant places where the war is being fought.

Upon the outcome depends the freedom of your lives: the freedom of the lives of those you love—your fellow-citizens—your people.

Never were the enemies of freedom more tyrannical, more arrogant, more brutal.

Yours is a God-fearing, proud, courageous people which, throughout its history, has put its freedom under God before all other purposes.

We who stay at home have our duties to perform—duties owed in many parts to you. You will be supported by the whole force and power of this Nation. The victory you win will be a victory of all the people—common to them all.

You bear with you the hope, the confidence, the gratitude and the prayers of your family, your fellow-citizens, and your President.

Franklin D. Roosevelt

was without fanfare. The men lined up, went into the waiting trucks at 2:20 pm, and were off to the entraining area.

At 3:30 pm, we boarded the broken-down coaches of the Penn Railroad. Since I was the military train commander for this move, I was the last to board the train. Just before the train pulled out, a jeep rushed towards the platform looking for me to sign some papers. The papers turned out to be for the young man we had sent for a mental examination at the base hospital. The signed papers assigned him to the hospital for further treatment. I was very happy he was not going with us. The spot we were headed to would be no place for him.

The train was a long one. It moved slowly. Its destination was Jersey City; we arrived at about 7:00 pm. After disembarking, we marched with all our luggage to the Penn Ferry. The ferry dock was alive with military activity. Many troops had to be ferried across the Hudson River to Pier 90 in New York City. This was an exciting experience for all of us. As the ferry approached the pier, we saw our ship with many soldiers lined up waiting to board. The name on the stern and bow of the ship was covered. Everybody wanted to know the name of the ship. The reason for it being covered, of course, was for security.

CHAPTER 2

At sea on *Pasteur*

Shortly after our ferry tied up, we lined up, waiting for the word to embark on a trip that would bring joy and sorrow to many. We had a short wait. Our call was made to line up at the base of the gangplank. The usual system was in order. When the last name of the man was called, he answered by giving his first name and middle initial. The first three grades and officers were assigned to staterooms. The rest of the squadron was assigned to a particular deck.

The staterooms left something to be desired. All were made over for military transport. A room that normally took care of one person had four people in it. This was understandable as a war was on; they had to make the most of all the space.

Shortly after disembarking, I went and found out we were on *Pasteur*, a ship built by the French for the South American cruise trade. It was 29,300 tons. This ship was known as the ship with the huge smokestack. Early in the war, *Pasteur* carried French gold reserves to the United States and was escorted by the Aircraft Carrier *Bearn*. It also made numerous Atlantic crossings with troops and prisoners during the war.

On March 2, 1942 a plan to take over the ship by German prisoners of war, who also were on *Pasteur*, was detected when a British sailor who understood German, heard a group of Germans singing a song which had a message about the takeover. Each man received a ditty bag from the American Red Cross as he went up the gangplank. Each bag contained writing paper, cards, pencil, and the soldier's best friend when away from home, a sewing kit. Each kit had the name of the person that made it. I remember my kit came from a party in Colorado. Many of us wrote a thank you note for this useful equipment.

Information was passed around that we would not sail until the next morning. The room was hot, as all ships without air conditioning are, especially tied up at a pier in overcrowded conditions.

Everybody was tired by the time we were all checked in and settled. I had a meeting with my officers and first sergeant as to the schedule of messing for the following morning. After the meeting, I thought I would take a stroll out on the dock, but I soon found out that, once on the ship, there was no leaving.

I don't think anybody had trouble sleeping after such a busy day. Our stateroom was quiet. Everyone was asleep when I arrived back after my short walk to the gangplank area.

The next morning, everybody was up early and off to breakfast. The enlisted men were fed on the lower decks in very crowded conditions. It was reported there were 6,000 men on the ship. The officers ate in the ship's main dining room in conditions I would say were excellent for a troop transport. We even had a printed menu.

At 8:30 am, *Pasteur* slowly backed out of the pier with the help of a few tugs and started on a trip that ended 32 days later.

As we left our pier, we could see the French liner *Normandie* lying on its side at Pier 89; a sad sight of what was once a beautiful ship.

Slowly, we moved down the Hudson River and out into the Atlantic Ocean. We all had been issued life jackets and instructed to always keep them with us. We also had to wear our web belts with our canteens filled with water.

We picked up a destroyer as escort shortly after entering the ocean. My scheduled time for lunch was 1:00 pm. Just after being served my soup, the ship seemed to lean over. I left the dining area to investigate. A short walk brought me out on deck. The ship turned in a constant circle and our destroyer escort traveled at great speed and dropped depth charges. I believe B-25 Mitchell bombers were in the air dropping bombs in the same area the destroyer dropped its charges. No general alarm was given on the ship. After about a half hour, things went back to normal.

At 4:00 pm, we had a repeat of the action we had at 1:00 pm, only that time the destroyer remained behind to work over the area. We proceeded along with the escort of a couple of bombers overhead. We followed a course where the ship would make a small half circle, then a larger one and then a final, very large half circle.

The ship moved along at the rate of 25 knots, which is considered a good rate of speed.

The following morning, as I arrived on deck, we still had the destroyer and the bombers as escort. About 1:00 pm, the destroyer dropped off. The bombers left shortly thereafter. We now had a PBY flying boat for an escort. During the morning we had our boat drill. This was followed by a very interesting talk by Colonel

---

A note from the Navy about the minesweeper activities around the Pasteur:

At 1335 on July 16, 1942 the destroyer minesweeper STANSBURY (DMS-8) while accompanying the PASTEUR, at 39° 52' N Longitude and 73° 13' W Latitude dropped four depth charges upon receiving a sound contact. At 1711 on July 16, STANSBURY, at 39° 14' N Longitude and 72° 11' W Latitude, dropped thirteen depth charges upon receiving a sound contact. In both cases there was no evidence to indicate the nature of the contact or the effect of the depth charging.

Jackson of the British Army. His subject was ship movement and the importance of a strict blackout.

During the colonel's talk, he gave us no information as to where we were heading for or why. I will always remember our room steward, a man that had been at sea for many years; his home was near London. He claimed we were heading for England.

Saturday, July 18. We moved along at a fast clip on a smooth sea. We still had the PBY flying boat for our escort. We moved into a new time zone and turned our watches ahead one hour. We had the usual boat drill and the meeting with the members of the squadron was held on our assigned deck area. Setting-up exercises were scheduled by units. When this took place, other units would have to move out of the area. Conditions on deck were beyond overcrowded but the men took it in stride. They were glad to be out in the fresh air. During the nights, there was a schedule of sleeping in the open on deck as the sleeping below decks was getting hotter every night.

Sunday, July 19. The sea was as calm as a mill pond. We moved along at the same fast clip. The flying boat is still with us. Religious services were held by the chaplains for all faiths. Shortly after noon, the weather closed in and that was the last we saw of our PBY escort. We were on our own for the rest of the trip. Watches were turned again.

Monday, July 20. A nice day and the sea was still calm. I conducted a rifle inspection this morning after the boat drill. The men of the squadron had followed the instructions we had given them back at Fort Dix of how important it was to keep after the rifles, especially at sea. They all seemed to understand what the salt air did to the barrels. We found practically every rifle in excellent condition. During the afternoon, all the anti-aircraft guns were test fired. This helped break up the monotony of the day. Most of the crews on the anti-aircraft guns were American boys assigned to our ship. Some of them had even made a few trips on this ship.

Tuesday, July 21. We still enjoyed a calm sea. We had the usual activities such as boat drills and meetings with our men. There was a constant check by military police on all members of the ship to see every man wore their web belt with canteen and had their life preserver with them no matter where they went. Watches moved again one hour.

Every day, a group of officers was assigned as blackout officers. The duty consisted of checking the port holes all over the ship. On this night, it was my duty to do some checking and I found very few infractions of the rules. The checking was always carried out before dark. One port hole left open with lights on could be seen for miles. That was explained during the talk given by Colonel Jackson a few days previously.

Wednesday, July 22. Another calm day with the usual duties such as roll call of the men and officers. Boat drill.

Thursday, July 23. We had rifle inspection this morning. During the inspection, we had a good rainstorm, the first rain since leaving New York. This pushed the men under cover, which was not good as the days were really becoming warmer. We received information we were off the coast of West Africa and would stop at Freetown. This made for good conversation about the hopes of getting off the crowded ship.

Turned the clocks and watches ahead another hour today. We saw a freighter not too far from us. This is the first ship we have seen since the destroyer left us on the 17th.

A large school of whales were seen not too far from ship. This was a quiet night, as all have been on this trip. I walked along the deck and observed the stars which are quite a sight when we are in complete darkness. Observed the Southern Cross for a few minutes.

I went back down to my crowded stateroom and, along with my fellow officers, censored mail for an hour. Most of the men observed the security rules for writing. We had to return a few letters to boys for naming the ship and other incidents that were not permitted.

Friday, July 24. All you could hear over the ship this morning was that we were stopping today at Freetown, West Africa. We thought it would be a good idea to have a pool on the time the *Pasteur* would drop anchor at Freetown. This was accomplished by a chart and having the boys select the time. Lieutenant Pete Mallet of Portland, Maine, adjutant of the 66th Squadron, was the lucky winner of the pool of $23.00. We dropped anchor at 4:37 pm.

Freetown is on a plain surrounded by a succession of wooded hills. It is the administrative headquarters for the Sierra Leone Peninsula and the offshore island. It is considered the best harbor in West Africa. From this port ginger, kola nuts, gold, platinum, chromate diamonds and palm oil are exported. They manufacture soap and the port has a ship repair works. Freetown was founded in 1788 and practically destroyed by the French in 1794 but quickly recovered.

We were told we were the first American troops to arrive at this port. We had many unhappy soldiers on board when the announcement was made no one would leave the ship at this port. One of the reasons given was it would be not advisable for the health of the command. Another was we would be on our way in 24 hours. We had many visitors alongside the ship. The natives with their small boats paddled around us until it was dark. Many cigarettes and candies were tossed to these natives. We never did tie up at the dock. Oil and water tenders came alongside and pumped all night.

Saturday, July 25. Oil and water barges are still alongside. We left Freetown at 5:45 pm and headed in the direction of Cape Town. Shortly after we cleared

Freetown, we met a large convoy of ships heading for England. As darkness took over, we headed for our quarters, always mindful of the blackout regulations. The room we had was crowded. In order for some of the boys to play bridge, a couple would have to climb to the upper bunks and watch. We had a few sharp bridge players in our outfit. One I remember very well was Lt. John H. Miller III from New York. He was the group adjutant.

Sunday, July 26. This is our second Sunday at sea, and the religious services were held by the chaplains of the various faiths. After services, we held a meeting of the men and conducted setting-up exercises on the sports deck.

This evening we had a session with our room steward, Pat. All the way, his story was that we were going to England. Even with the direction we are heading, we still can't get him to change his mind. I think he was just hoping for England as he had not been home for some time. Pat had been through some hair-raising experiences during his many years at sea and enjoyed telling us about them. He was a faithful and hard worker. He had many staterooms and gangways to take care of and did them in an efficient manner.

Monday, July 27. We passed over the Equator at 4:30 am. I have never been on a ship that passed over the Equator. I was told a ceremony would take place on that day. This did not happen as the crowded conditions would not warrant the festivities that normally take place. A few days later, I received a certificate.

I, Neptunus Rex, Son of Saturn, of Jupiter: Ruler of the Seven seas and of all living things therein: Lord of the Wind and Waves, and tides do hereby issue this Proclamation.

All ye Men of Earth, ye Mariners who sail the Seven Seas and Ye Denizens of the Deep; Know ye: That on this 27th day of July on the good ship "PASTEUR" **James A. Lynch** in the course of crossing that fabled line that doth my domain around its middle, has been duly instructed in the mysteries of my realm and subject to arduous tests and trial by my good and faithful servants of **The American Republics Line** and having proved a worthy shellback, is hereby declared duly initiated into the solemn mysteries of the Ancient and Honorable Order of Neptunia, and forthwith elevated to the exalted office of a **Good-Neighbor-In-Waiting** in my royal equatorial court and is entitled to all the nautical rights, privileges and obeisance pertaining thereto.

Attest T. A. Fraser Captain SS Pasteur   Neptunus Rex
Custodian of the Royal Pin

Tuesday, July 28. We still head south, out of sight of land. The rumor of the day was the *Pasteur* had been torpedoed a day out of Freetown. The bridge game was in full swing this evening.

Wednesday, July 29. Still heading south. This was the day we had lots of talks with the men covering subjects of military courtesy, guard duty, and we read the Articles of War. A meeting was called by Captain Chandler, our group intelligence officer. We were informed we would be permitted to go ashore. The captain gave the men a talk on intelligence duties. He talked further about the trip ashore, and the conduct expected there. During the afternoon, it was announced over the ship's public-address system that we were passing the island St. Helena. This island owes its fame to the fact that, from 1815 to 1821, Napoleon was in exile there. This is the island he died on in 1821.

Thursday, July 30. This was a routine day which included the regular exercises on the sports deck, and the inspection of rifles and mess gear. During the afternoon, we were told that we passed the Tropic of Capricorn. This belt of the earth's surface is known as the Torrid Zone.

Friday, July 31. Another routine day but the boys are all talking about going ashore in Durban. They are made happier by a talk about Durban by Colonel Jackson. He also gave word about the disembarking. Clocks ahead one hour today.

Saturday, August 1. This was my day to eat all my meals with the men on C deck. The men had complained many times about the food and, after eating three meals with them, I could understand their complaints. It was difficult for the men, after being used to good American food, having to almost overnight make a big change to British food, which is prepared altogether different than our food. The job of feeding so many men three times a day and under conditions that left a lot to be desired was also a challenge.

I found that the boys were not obtaining enough food to satisfy the appetites that were created by the sea. I filed a report with the commander of troops and a few recommendations I made were put into effect.

One interesting thing was we had a few boys on KP (kitchen patrol/police). After talking with them, I suggested they be relieved and replaced by a new set. The people on KP all agreed they were very happy. The reason was they had plenty to eat.

For the first time on this trip the weather was rough; the ship was really rolling. We had a few seasick boys. We changed into woolen clothes. We set the clocks ahead another hour today.

Sunday, August 2. We woke up this morning to angry seas. Church services were held for the third Sunday at sea. The big job of the day was to have all our men take their physical examinations. My thoughts went back home today as this was my son James A. Jr's 12th birthday.

Monday, August 3. We arrived outside the breakwater of Durban at 9:32 am. There was still a long way to Durban, and we proceeded slowly and finally arrived at the pier at 6:00 pm. There was more sad news for all. No passes until tomorrow.

As the ship edged into the pier, the docks were crowded with the dark natives of Durban. They were a happy lot, and they sang songs for a couple of hours. The harmony of this large group is something one would never forget. When they would stop a song, the boys would yell for more. The singing was helped along by the tossing of coins, candy, and the ever-popular American cigarettes.

It was a quiet night, and we moved the clocks ahead one hour.

Tuesday, August 4. Everybody up and ready to go this morning. The weather was ideal for a day on dry land after 19 days on an overcrowded ship. All the enlisted men were given passes which allowed them to say ashore until midnight. I was not so lucky. I drew officer-of-the-day until 6:00 pm.

My duties, along with several other officers on the various decks, pertained only to the U.S. military personnel left on board as guards. We had no troubles with our troops but there had been some rumbling among the crew for a few days before we reached Durban.

During the mid-afternoon, trouble really broke out. One of the crew got out of hand and wanted to see the ship's captain. He took on several of the crew. They had a free-for-all for a few minutes and tried to have the American guards and officers break it up. We felt this was the duty of the ship's security guards. Within a short time, the fight was broken up and the crew members returned to their quarters.

My room steward, Pat, always kept us posted on the activities of the crew. In a conversation with him later in the afternoon, he told me the story of what caused this crew member to get out of line. He had been given disciplinary action for some infraction of the ship's rules and had been forced to stay on board for the rest of the trip. Also, he would lose his pay for this period. This crew member was trying to go ashore to file a protest. Pat felt the man had been given too much punishment for the infraction.

The rest of the afternoon moved along, and I was relieved at 6:00 pm. After cleaning up, my first thought was to find a good place to eat and have a drink. I made for the center of Durban and found a spot called the Playhouse. It was nice to get away from the mutton we ate so many times in the past 18 days. It was a funny feeling sitting in a restaurant so many miles from home.

All my friends who went off at the ship in the morning were nowhere to be found. After a leisurely meal, I stepped out into the dark of Durban. No one told us about a blackout. So here I was in a strange city in a strange country trying to find my way around. My first thought was to get back to the ship. I finally found a set of car tracks and remembered I saw tracks along the dock near where the ship docked. I was lucky and made it back to the ship.

The reports of the officers and men of their day on shore made good conversation until late. The treatment of our men by the Durban folks left a lasting impression.

Wednesday, August 5. Passes were in effect for the whole day up until midnight. We were told the ship would leave on the morning of the 6th. A group of us went off the ship and into the center of Durban.

Not seeing the city in full swing due to my duties yesterday, I was amazed at this modern city with a population of 262,765. Durban was full of modern buildings, fine stores and beautiful beaches. In the center of Durban, the main attraction for all of us were the rickshaws (a small two-wheeled carriage drawn by the native Zulus who were garbed in colorful costumes, their head dress was something to write home about). Each driver tried to outdo the other. They were doing a rushing business with the boys from our ship. The people of this city opened their hearts to all our boys. They told us we were the first American troops to go through this port. A tour through the countryside arranged by an owner of the Studebaker agency on West St made the day one to remember. This gentleman even invited us to his home for cocktails and an evening at a beautiful night club.

At 11:30, we had to report back to the ship. Many failed to meet the midnight deadline. Letters of "reply by endorsement hereon why you did not report on time" were passed out at the gangway by a duty officer.

I can't remember any disciplinary action being taken for those who failed to arrive on time. I went off to bed with thoughts of leaving this beautiful city and wonderful people.

Thursday, August 6. Up early this morning. The ship moved away from the pier at 7:45 am. A check of our men showed all were accounted for. There were rumors around the ship some boys from other groups were left in Durban. After we were underway for about a half hour, a speed boat could be seen coming towards our ship and finally caught up with us. The crew opened one of the entrances on the lower deck. The boat came alongside with a young sergeant who had been detained in Durban. I understand his commanding officer met him and greeted him with "Good morning, private."

After the excitement of leaving Durban, we got down to business and had a rifle inspection. Most of the men appreciated the good equipment they had been issued and were taking good care of same. The morale of the men was very high. Up to this time, we had only one incident which caused us any trouble.

A report was passed on to me that one of our men had been turned in for some remarks he had made about this wasted trip we were making. The report stated he said the German Army was moving in all directions and we would be defeated. This boy happened to have German parents. An investigation was conducted and completed without any proof this man made the statements as reported.

In reading the news bulletin posted each day, some of use wondered why we were heading towards Egypt when it looked like the old "Desert Fox," Rommel, would be at the dock to meet us in Egypt.

Friday, August 7. We now head east, and the reports are we are off the island of Madagascar. We gave this island a wide berth as the French and the British are fighting there. Exercises were held on the sports deck, and we had some movies.

Saturday, August 8. Going northeast and still off Madagascar. We are now in the Indian Ocean. Pat, our room steward, is now convinced we are not going to England. We questioned Pat about the black eye the ship's captain showed up with this morning. His only remark was he had an accident in Durban. It was rumored a few of the crew ganged up on him.

Sunday, August 9. This is our fourth Sunday on board *Pasteur*. We still head northeast. Church services were held for the various denominations.

Monday, August 10. We are heading north this morning and it is getting warm. A routine day with an inspection of rifles and mess gear.

Tuesday, August 11. We woke to a very warm morning. We did our morning setting-up exercises on the sports deck. This was my day to take my turn on the bridge for watch duty. I had the 8–10:00 am, 2–4:00 pm, 8–10:00 pm and the 2–4:00 am. This duty consisted of reporting anything out of the ordinary. We passed over the Equator at noon today for the second time in 14 days. This incident passed without any comment; in reading the new bulletins, the war in Egypt wasn't going too well.

Wednesday, August 12. I came off watch at 4:00 am this morning and slept a little later this morning. Most of this day was spent with the men in the mess hall on C deck doing drill instruction. We had a good group of men in our squadron. Most of them knew their rifles inside and out. At this meeting, we had one man who did not show up. We had this man paged over the public-address system without any response.

Thursday, August 13. Another warm morning and we are in the Gulf of Aden. This is the southern end of the Red Sea and is about twelve hundred miles long. At its greatest width it is about two hundred miles wide. During the morning, we sighted land for the first time since we left Durban. We purchased a world map in Durban, and we are tracing our steps along this route to a strange land.

The first sergeant reported that one of our men was still missing this morning. He reported some of the men had seen him during the last 24 hours, but he was not answering to the paging and not reporting to our scheduled formations. Although this man was on the ship, we carried him on our morning report as absent without leave due to the fact he failed to appear.

Late this afternoon, I found a group of soldiers waiting outside my stateroom. One of them stated that his group had been informed by our missing boy that I was holding a large sum of money belonging to the missing boy and this was the day I was going to the hold of the ship to open our safe and return his money. I informed them I held no money of his. This young man had apparently been doing some gambling and owed this group money. They soon left, very dejected.

Earlier in the day, we sighted the shores of Somaliland. This was the hottest day we have had since leaving New York. I stayed up on deck late tonight as the area below decks was like a furnace. A rotation system was put into effect for the boys on the lowest deck to come up on deck tonight to sleep. The rotation system was carried out each night thereafter so that all the boys had a chance to get a good night's sleep, if that was possible with the crowded conditions.

Friday, August 14. Up early this morning after a rough night. It was like sleeping in a pool of water. The staterooms were boiling. With the ship sealed at night for blackout, this made below decks hot as a jungle.

We entered the Red Sea this morning. For the first time since leaving New York, we see plenty of ships. The Red Sea is actually red at times. I am told this is caused by thousands of tiny sea animals. At times there are reddish streaks in the water due to the hot winds blowing the sand from the desert.

All during the trip we had a guard placed alongside a large vault outside the dining room. Why? We never could find out. During the noon meal, we heard about six shots ring out and we were all startled. It turned out that the guard, who carried a loaded .45 machine gun while on guard at the vault, had not had his safety on and just pressed the trigger and out came six rounds. Fortunately, he was holding the gun facing the ceiling and the six rounds went up into the structure without injury to anyone.

We later found out what was in the vault. A few Norden bomb sights.

We spread canvas over the sports deck today as the sun was too hot.

Saturday, August 15. Four weeks ago this date we left New York. This was a long time to be crowded on a ship with not much room to roam. We had a swimming

---

The 64th Fighter Squadron received this message from headquarters prior to disembarking in Egypt:

Memorandum to: All officers

1. The end of the sea journey is approaching

2. It is proper that the officers and enlisted men of this detachment be commended for their cheerfulness, soldierly conduct, and discipline under the trying and crowded conditions ancient to such a movement in time of war.

3. I desire to thank both officers and non for their fine attitude, so in keeping with American Army tradition.

THOMAS H. MORROW
Lieut. Colonel, AAF
Commanding

pool on this ship, but the pool had no water in it. Instead, it was loaded with equipment. After another night in the boiler-like stateroom, we proceed with a routine day except for a talk by our chaplain, Father Louge.

Our missing young man was finally found. Disciplinary action was taken, although not for being absent without leave. He failed to take care of a brand-new .45 Tommy gun which had a barrel rusted beyond repair.

We were told we would come to the end of our boat trip sometime tomorrow morning. The weather was the hottest I have ever experienced. This was forgotten when we were told today would be our last day on this hot box of a ship. We were issued a supply of toilet paper and a beef ration this afternoon.

CHAPTER 3

Palestine

Sunday, August 16. Six weeks ago, today we left our home station in East Boston, Massachusetts, and this was the fifth Sunday on board *Pasteur*. We dropped anchor at 11:45 am in a spot called Port Tawfiq, Egypt. We were briefed on the unloading procedure. Since the ship had no dock to tie up to, we went ashore in small boats.

We were cautioned about our baggage. The attendants had a system of pushing baggage overboard and their Arab friends would trail the boat to pick up anything pushed over. There were many oil tanks around this port and the smell of oil was nauseating. There were many barrage balloons in the area of the oil tanks. A very dirty harbor with lots of barges with war equipment. One thing I remember were the many barges loaded with Canadian Black Horse Ale.

Our squadron started to disembark at 3:45 pm and it took quite a bit of time to unload all the boys as the boats were small. It took about an hour to reach the landing area. We were then taken to a tent area a few miles inland.

These tents were in an area not far from the mountains. There were no floors, and the sides were tied up for ventilation. The red sand of Egypt was the only cot to sleep on. We were fed by a British unit. The meal left something to be desired.

The boys, believe it or not, were in a happy mood and sang songs until a late hour. Not much sleep tonight as the sand was hard and dirty.

Monday, August 17. Up early after a rough night sleeping on the hard sand of the Egyptian desert. The breakfast was served at an early hour, and we had the day to roam around the area. We could not go far as there was no means of transportation. We did find a YMCA Club and they permitted us to have a swim. Later in the day, we received information we would move out of this area for a spot kept under wraps.

Tuesday, August 18. We were up at dawn this morning. We were all happy with the thought of leaving this dirty and uncomfortable so-called camp. We marched to a train depot along the Suez Canal not too far from the camp.

We boarded trains at 6:45 am and left the area at 8:10 am. These trains were as rundown as any train we had ever seen, and we were packed in.

At noon, we stopped at El Qantara, Egypt, at a NAAFI, which means Navy, Army, and Air Force Institutes, run by the British, similar to an American Canteen. They served us a good meal and we had the opportunity of exchanging the little money we had.

We were on our way again about 1:00 pm. Within a few miles, the baggage car that carried our luggage came up with frozen brakes. We had to leave the baggage car on a siding, unload all the baggage, and store it in the cars with the troops. This made the crowded conditions more unbearable.

This operation took about an hour and off we went on this so-called train. We now moved along the Sinai desert. The view was wonderful with date trees and the

As part of the disagreement between the 64th Fighter Squadron and the suppliers in the British Army, the following list was prepared detailing our daily requirements:

		Equivalents when Basic items are not available
1.	Beef Fresh or Frozen with Bone or Mutton Frozen.	14 ozs.
2.	or meat boneless.	10.5 ozs.
3.	Tinned Bacon.	2"
4.	Fresh Eggs.	1 Egg. 4.7 ozs. T/Herring or T/Salmon
5.	Dried Peas, Bean or Lentils	1/2 ozs. Peas beans or Lentils
6.	Rice.	1/2"
7.	Oatmeal.	1 1/2"
8.	Fresh Vegetables (incl 2 ozs. Onions).	18" (Onions 2 ozs. and Rice 2 1/2 ozs.)
9.	Fresh Potatoes.	10" (OR T/Potatoes 6 ozs.
10.	Fresh Fruit.	9" T/Fruit 2 ozs. or Dried fruit 1 1/2 ozs.
11.	Jam or Marmalade.	1 1/2"
12.	Coffee.	2"
13.	Tea.	1/2"
14.	Fresh Milk.	10" Tinned Milk 4 ozs.
15.	Cotton Seed oil.	1/2"
16.	Butter.	1"
17	Margarine.	3/4"
18.	Bread.	12"
19.	or flour.	9"
20.	Flour (culinary).	3"
21.	Macaroni.	1/4"
22.	Cheese.	1/4"
23.	Sugar.	5"
24.	Pepper.	1/25"
25.	Mustard.	1/100"
26.	Pickles.	1/10"
27.	Salt.	1/2"
28.	Syrup.	1/2" Sugar 1/2 oz.

occasional sight of camels. The heat was something we had never experienced, and the crowded conditions did not help.

On each platform between the train cars, there was a can of ice. We took turns leaving our canteens submerged to cool the water a little. We moved on through the night with little sleep. The train made many stops. On several occasions, it had to back up and start again to move over the slight grades along the route.

Wednesday, August 19. We were still on this train, but we were not moving. The engine broke down and we waited for a new one. We were finally on our way again and arrived outside Haifa, Palestine, at about 2:00 pm.

Colonel Barnum's Report

This is a report of the Black Scorpion Air Echelon after they left East Boston to parts unknown on June 25, 1942, supplied by Lt Col. Robert A. Barnum. Barnum was a flight leader at the time mentioned above. Bob flew over 100 combat missions, went home, and returned as the commanding officer of our squadron when we were stationed in Corsica.

The group arrived at Hempstead, Long Island, New York, home of Mitchell Field at 4:20 am. For the next couple of days, we attended lectures and drew equipment, but no one was telling us where we were going. When they showed us the pink P-40s on the flight deck and remarked that these are the ships that you are going to fly, with all the news in the papers about Rommel sweeping to within 80 miles of Alexandria, Egypt, we guessed that we would probably head to that area.

On June 29, we started flying and were instructed by Lt. Comm. Ottinger from the aircraft carrier *Ranger* as to how to take off and land on the deck of a carrier. We were still kept in the dark as to whether or not we were going over on a carrier. With the officers from the carrier around, we figured it out that we would go over from some east coast port such as Quonset Point or Norfolk,

Major Robert Barnum (right). Commanding officer of 64th Fighter Squadron, December 16, 1944–August 7, 1945.

Loading the P-40s onto USS *Ranger* before heading to Africa. (57th Fighter Group website)

Virginia. This afternoon we were all given an extra $750.00 with our June pay, but still no more information.

On June 30, we were told that we would have a dry run tomorrow. This dry run worked out to be the real thing as we took off at 6:00 am on the morning of July 1st and flew to Quonset Point, Rhode Island and landed very close to the aircraft carrier *Ranger*.

It seemed in minutes after landing the *Ranger* had slings on the P-40s and by 10:00 am 75 planes of the 57th Fighter Group were on board of this large carrier.

General Cannon, who would go to Africa by air later, was on hand to bid the group farewell. At 12:30, we pulled away from the dock and proceeded to the mouth of the Narraganset Bay. Five destroyers, one heavy cruiser (*Augusta*) and the light cruiser *Juneau* were waiting for us and away we go.

On the morning of July 2, we were around the ship and shown our General Quarters Station, Ready Room and Abandon Ship Station. The ocean was a beautiful blue and the flying fish added to the splendor of this great Atlantic Ocean.

July 3. We are about 120 miles southwest of Bermuda and the mission for this date is to warm up our ships, check our guns which picked up some rust from the salt air.

July 4. Celebrated this holiday cleaning my guns and I will never complain about an armorer having a soft job. We had a sub scare during late afternoon and the destroyers spent some time over the suspected area and were back in regular convoy after about a 10-minute workout.

July 5. Cleaned the guns and laid around the deck. At 6:00 pm, one of the destroyers picked up four sailors from a raft.

July 6. This morning we are off Trinidad and of course we want to go ashore. At one time, the orders were no one goes ashore but later that was lifted and at 8:00 pm we were given three hours leave and that was to go the Naval Air Station only. This island with its towering peaks and low rain clouds and deep valleys awed me. The officer's club was a three-story building with a large court with a swimming pool that overlooked a narrow lagoon. The walls of the lagoon rise straight up from the water for about two hundred feet and are heavily covered with vegetation and tropical trees. At the end of the lagoon is a beautiful sandy beach. It is nearly everything one ever dreamed of. After a few drinks, most everybody went for a swim and then to supper in a beautiful dining room. A few drinks after supper and back on board the *Ranger* before 11:00 pm.

July 7. Still in port this morning so we have no General Quarters. The mission for this morning was to check our guns. We were told that we could go ashore again and although it was raining hard everybody took advantage of this short leave. Spent the afternoon at the Navy Club and had a nice dinner and back to the ship at 9:00 pm.

P-40s on the deck of *Ranger*. (57th Fighter Group website)

July 8. At 6:45 am the *Ranger* lifts anchors and proceeds to sea by the Gulf of Paria toward the Dragon Mouth. The mountains of Trinidad stood out distinctly against the blue sky. Our five destroyers went out ahead of us plus five other patrol boats to clear out any subs that may be waiting for us. We clear Dragon Mouth at 7:30 am and head out to sea.

An oil tanker has joined the convoy. We finally get the news as to where we are going when Col. Frank Mears, the Group Commander, told us we were heading for Cairo, Egypt. This was not a surprise as we had guessed correctly as to our destination.

July 9 and 10. Routine days with General Quarters and still working on the machine guns and the running up of our P-40s. A lot of boys are promoted by the way of a wireless message.

Colonel Frank Mears, CO 64th Fighter Squadron, August 19, 1941–June 28, 1942. (57th Fighter Group website, Frank Mears Collection)

July 11. General Quarters as usual. At 6:00 pm, a meeting is held in the ready room and the maps of the area we will travel over after we reach our destination are brought out. At 7:30 pm, we have General Quarters and two of the destroyers are off our port side and they are dropping depth charges like mad. Each can had 12 ash cans within it and they were dropping the cans very deep. This action lasted for about one hour and then things returned to normal.

July 12 and 13. We get our guns back into our ships and we have a movie and bull session about the Curtiss P-40. Still going over the maps.

July 16. We are 315 miles from Africa this morning and we run up our ships and started packing the equipment that would go in the plane. (The Ground Echelon left New York this date and headed for the same spot that the Air Echelon heads for)

July 17. Meeting this morning in the Ready Room on radio procedure and the ships are filled with fuel.

July 18. Well this is our last day on the *Ranger*. Spent some time packing my clothes in my ship. The P-40s were all spotted on the flight deck, and everything is set for the big show. We are 90 miles from the Equator, and it is cold on deck today. The ship's band play a concert for us after a wonderful meal.

July 19. This is our big day. We are all up at 5:15 am. Breakfast at 6:00 am and finish packing my ship and also go to the parachute loft for my chute. At 7:00 am, I am all ready to go and, at 7:30 am, the Navy scouts take off and they are followed by Colonel Mears, the Group Commander. I am No. 6 for takeoff, and I am in the air before I reach the end of the deck.

Boy, this is a thrill. I mean it is really something. Everything happens so fast you don't have time to be scared. We got about a 300-foot run and that is all. But we had a 30-knot wind over the deck. It has been 19 days since I have flown and sure feels good to be in the air again. We buzz the carrier, destroyer, and cruiser and when 18 of us are in the air, we head for land which was about 50 miles away. We hit Accra, (Ghana) Africa, on the nose and go into land.

Accra has only one good runway and that is into the prevailing winds. Made a good landing and taxied to our parking spot and there waiting for us is Master Sergeant Buck Rivers and Staff Sergeant Herman Zubkoff of Hartford, Connecticut,

P-40 taking off from the deck of *Ranger*. (57th Fighter Group website)

and many other crew chiefs of the squadron. (These men had been flown over from there after the Air Echelon left).

We went for a briefing at the headquarters and were informed that 12 ships must leave before 12:00 noon and our destination would be Lagos and Kano, which is inland from the coast of the Gold Coast of Africa. Three flights of 12 each are off the ground, and they are convoyed by A-28A and A-20As. The rest of us hang around until tomorrow.

July 20. We must stay for another day as some of the ships are having engine or radio trouble. Thirty-six ships are off this morning from the other units, so we make a trip into the city of Accra which was three miles from the landing strips. This is an experience I will never forget.

First, we went to the food market, food, or stuff that resembles food, was all over the place. People lying around and children and grown-ups running around with little or no clothing on. The smell was terrific. One of the finer foods of the market was dried fish. They look and smell like some of the fish that was washed up on the shore at home after a storm.

I took a few pictures and some of the sights we saw were unbelievable. Young girls ran around with little or no clothes on. They seemed to be proud of their bosoms.

After the market, we took a tour around the town and took a lot of pictures. At one time, when we stopped to replace a roll in the camera, we had a mob of about 75 natives around us and they all wanted to have their picture taken. We finally made it to our bus and departed for the airfield. Some of the boys threw out some money from the bus and what a scramble ...

July 21. We are off the ground this morning with a convoy leader from the RAF [Royal Air Force] who is flying an A-20 and we start out for Lagos, Nigeria. We went along the coast of Vichy France and into Lagos and to Ikeja, which is 10 miles North of Lagos. It is a runway cut out of the bush (jungle). Landed at 9:00 am, reported in to the RAF Headquarters for something to eat. We will spend the day in this far away spot. Some of the missions that had been ahead of us had taken off before we arrived and had to return due to bad weather conditions.

We are put up for the night by British Imperial Airways. Very good food and the ... [locals] are doing some laundry for the boys. A few of the boys and myself got to the Palace Hotel for a few beers. Lots of girls around and they want to Jig-Jig for love.

July 22. Left Akeja at 11:45 am, delayed due to convoy plane had trouble and had to wait for another ship to come in. Our destination this morning is Kano and on the way one of the planes from another squadron developed engine trouble and crashed somewhere in the bush. We circled but didn't locate him. We landed at Oshogbo and reported the crash. Within a short time, this RAF post reported that this downed pilot was found, and he was burned seriously but will be OK. Plane burned up. Lucky boy to make it.

It is raining and the ceiling is very low, so we stay in the bush country. Went in town to a spot called the European Club and had a few beers (A bad beer dive in the states). The club membership is made up of two Free French, two Englishmen, One Turk, two Greeks, and a Medico, etc.

We could hear the native drums pounding most of the night.

July 23. A house boy brings us our tea. These boys are paid 12 dollars per month. We take off at 9:00 am with a 500-foot ceiling and about 40 miles out it is down to nothing, so we turn around in a valley and come back to Oshogbo.

It clears up and we take off again and have a good trip to Kano, Nigeria. The city of Kano is all made of red mud bricks and has a large wall around it. Airport fairly good. This trip from Oshogbo took two hours and on the edge of the runway is a crashed plane but the pilot was in the hospital and will make it.

July 24. Up before dawn this morning but had to wait as the convoy ship's radio is out and we hang around until 1:00 pm. We take off for Maiduguri which is 300 miles away. We give the city of Kano a real buzz job and at 2:45 pm, we are at our destination.

July 25. Up at dawn and wait for five B-25s to take off. A good take off and good buzz job and we are on our way to Free French Fort Lamy. A short hop of 200 miles and then a long hop to El Geneina, Sudan, which is 525 miles away. Had a nice flight. Landed with lots of gas left. Made it in two and a half hours. This country is very desolate, neither desert nor bush. Just hell.

July 26. Up at dawn at El Geneina and a short hop to Al Fasher, Sudan. Gas used at El Geneina must be carried by camel from Al Fasher. We land in Al Fasher at 8:30 am. We are held up with some of the boys needing some propellers adjusted. We take off at 11:25 for Khartoum, Sudan, via El Obeid, Sudan, 560 miles away. At El Obeid at 9,000 feet on schedule I used 87 gallons to gas up to El Obeid. Everything OK up to 85 miles southwest of Khartoum. At about 2:00 pm at 8,500 feet, my motor cuts out dead. I immediately fell out of formation and started looking for a forced landing field. I saw the Nile but thought it was a mirage, but I saw a small water hole and headed for it. I found a large open space beside it that looked level and prepared for a wheels-up landing.

As I approached the field, it looked pretty good, so I put my wheels down and made a normal landing. I had landed near a small native village. A PAA (Pan American Airlines) captain told me later that they were "Fuzzie-Wuzzies," the gang that broke the British squadron. About 30 or 40 natives gathered around the ship and they looked friendly. Before I got out of the ship I snapped a picture of them, then I got out and tried to talk to them. One of them, who appeared to be the Big Shot, beckoned me to come with them (about 50 or 60 now) to the nearby wadi and to a mud hut to meet a very old man who I figured was the local King.

First, they offered me dirty desert water. I refused because I had my canteen. Next came tea in a dirty little glass. Refused. About five minutes later came some kind of hot coffee. I sipped a little with the King and all was well. We looked at each other's knives. I showed them my compass, then the King and relatives posed for me while I took their picture. Then I went back to my ship.

On the way back, I took a picture of a little stray camel. About 2:45 pm, I saw an A-20, but he didn't see me. About 5:15 pm, a B-24 came by and found me after a few circles, he dropped some food and fruit and then a note and said a DC-3 was coming out from Wadi Senia and would land if I thought it OK.

About 15 minutes later, a DC-3 and B-24 came back, and the DC-3 circled a couple of times and then landed. I ran back to my ship and got what I could get and back to the DC-3 and we took off. By this time, it was dark. We flew over to the Nile and Khartoum and Wadi Senia. I sure was glad to get some civilization and some water. I went to bed at 9:00 pm and was wakened shortly thereafter by a real cloud burst. Most of the boys were at Khartoum for the night.

July 27. Everything flooded. Most of the fellows had to stay in Khartoum because the wadis along the Nile were flooded. Roads are bad. No bus for Khartoum tonight so to bed early.

July 28. Took off for the spot where I had to force land my plane in a DC-3 with a couple of crew chiefs. They went over the ship and found that the parts could be installed tomorrow (automatic boost), met some of my friends near my plane and the guards that were placed around the ship were not needed as not a bit of clothing or equipment had been touched. The heat in this area was terrific. Back to Khartoum and a good meal and off to bed.

July 29. Back to the ship and the boys put in a hot day working over the broken part. The guards that were left to guard this airplane told some tall stories about their night in the desert. We took off at 6:00 pm and back to Khartoum.

July 30. Up at 4:30 am and repack my ship. At 7:30, we put up a flight and headed for Wadi Halfa and Luxor. At Wadi Halfa, it is a few buildings and the desert and the airfield all in one. It is 110°F in the shade and no shade. No gas trucks and they fill the plane from five-gallon cans. After filling up at Wadi Halfa, we are off to Luxor. We have a sandstorm, and it is hot as hell. Our accommodations at Luxor are pretty good with good meals and beds and some good beer.

A group of the boys hired a two-horse carriage to see the temples around Luxor. First, we went down the Nile one-and-one-half miles from that hotel and saw Karnak. Then, we went to the Avenue of the Sphinxes, Hypostyle Hall, Statues of Thutmose II, the Sacred Lake, Cleopatra's Needle, and the Grand Gateway. Took a lot of pictures and then back to the horse and carriage and then down to the Luxor Temple. I saw the forecourt, Ramses III, and his best wife etc. Then a snake charmer found us some huge scorpions and a six-foot cobra. A very good show. Back to the hotel and dinner.

July 31. Up at 5:30 am and out to the field, took off at 7:00 am and gave the field a good buzz. We had a B-25 for convoy leader this morning and we are headed for Cairo, Egypt. We flew up the Nile and flew over Thebes and on to Landing Ground 224 which took us over the three huge pyramids.

We could see the bomb craters that the bombs left after the Jerries' bombing mission of yesterday. We went to the officers mess for a briefing for our next stop which would be Haifa, Palestine. We left L.G. 224 at Noon and across the north side of Cairo, then across the Suez Canal at Ismailia and across to Beersheba, up to Gaza and our new home, Muqeibili, Palestine, which is on the plain of Esdraelon about 30 miles southeast of Haifa and just 10 miles from the Jordan river.

We landed about 2:30 pm and it was good to see lots of the crew chiefs and many men from our squadron and the other squadrons who we had not seen since leaving the *Ranger* on the 19th of July.

We found that there was a swimming pool not far from the camp and this was a welcome spot for all. There were many Arab villages nearby and we were told that they were far from friendly. There is no electricity in this camp, and we have to get by on kerosene lamps.

August 1. We are trying to make our quarters livable and spent most of the day cleaning up the rooms and grounds around the area.

August 2. We have a truck this morning and a group of us set out for Haifa. On the way we visit Mount Carmel and then to the finance officer for the British and exchange our money from U.S. dollars into Palestinian money. Had a swim in the Mediterranean. The water was really salty, but we had fun. Back to the field at 6:30 pm and shortly thereafter I got the "Runs" or the "Screaming Meemies" and was very sick all night.

August 3. Still very sick this morning and old Doc Meyers is around to everyone with the Sulfanilamide about noon. Stayed in bed all day as the weird sickness called Sand Fly Fever leaves me very weak. To bed early with the thought of going out to the "Blue" tomorrow for some operational training. (The blue is known as out in the desert.)

August 4. Up at 7:00 am this morning and we were informed that we would go to Cairo at 9:00 am for some training in the desert. We took off in a DC-3 with all our gear such as parachute, pistol, gas mask, steel helmet, clothes, and oxygen mask. We landed at Heliopolis Aerodrome and proceeded to the Heliopolis Hotel, and we had to wait until the squadron commanders returned from a meeting with General Strickland and General Brereton. At 5:00 pm, we have a meeting where we are told we would not go out to the "Blue" until Thursday. We all take off for Cairo and a trip to the Pyramids and to Mary's Home around 11:30 pm

August 6. Up at 6:00 am this morning and this to be the big day. We head for the desert at 8:00 am. All the groups met at the famous Mena House which is just across from the pyramids. We drive out into the desert for one-and-one-half hours to the half-way house. We stop for a stretch and then proceed to our new home and arrive there about 12:30 pm. There are 11 of us and we are split up between the

British and South African squadrons. I am assigned to 2 Squadron, South African Air Force (SAAF). This squadron is commanded by Major Joseph Reynolds, a young man of 25 years old. This squadron is flying the same P-40s as we have, only they call them Kittyhawks or Kittybombers

They feel that the P-40 is not the plane to fight the Jerries' ME-109s and Macchi 202s. We pay a visit to the operations tent and the various shops that are set up in this sandy desert with loads of sun and blowing sands. After supper, they throw a beer party for us, and it looks like these boys are going to be good to work with.

August 7. Well, our first night in the desert wasn't so bad. Our Batboy (orderly) woke me up at 7:00 am, gave me hot tea and warm water to wash with. We find out we are not going to work today and look over the squadron set up and have tea at 11:00 am and lunch at 1:30 pm. During the afternoon, we learn that 4 Squadron SAAF commander had been shot down by a German ME-109 and killed about 10 miles from our spot. During the night, we could hear the explosion and rumblings in the vicinity of Cairo. The desert is a cold spot at night and with proper equipment it is good sleeping.

August 8. Up at 7:00 am. The flies won't let you sleep. The daytime is fly time, and they work you over good. At night they disappear. We received our "Baptism of Sand" today. It blew most of the day. At 5:00 pm, Bilby and myself team up with the squadron leader and take off for a training flight. We flew their tactical formation of line abreast or Co. Front. They say that this is the only formation they can use against the German ME-109s.

A pilot by the name of Stewart from 2 Squadron was shot down this morning. He was lucky in that he bailed out and landed inside our lines. Colonel Strickland is out for lunch and there is some mix up over our flying operation. There is some talk about us going back to Palestine unless we do some operational flying.

August 9. This morning a big bomber show came off. A squadron of Bostons and a squadron of Baltimores, plus 2 Squadron and 260 fighter squadrons as escort, went over at sun up. I assumed that they would work over some Jerry aerodrome. They all return safely without mishap. Six ME-109s followed the Kittyhawks back to the field but stayed up pretty high. These shows are early in the morning cause the sun is in their favor. The Bostons and Baltimores fly a close formation which is a pretty sight.

August 10. Col. Strickland and a British War Correspondent from London drop in this morning. Lots of pictures taken as we are news in that we are the first American pilots in the desert. The colonel says we are going to do some operational flying. The nights are something in the desert and it is easy to get lost unless you are careful. Many of us have been lost for a while just going from the mess tent to our own.

Some excitement around the field when one of the SAAF boys comes back from a mission with part of his tail shot off and only two strands of his rudder wire left. He made a crash landing and walked away from his ship OK. After dinner, we have a show by a South African swing band and a few beers. It made for a pleasant evening.

The squadron has four mascots: two small dogs, a monkey, and a canary. The monkey is a real showman. His name is Jocko, and his big job is taking care of the collie puppy named Gambert. The monkey has been with the squadron since the Ethiopian Campaign.

August 11. I have the runs this morning and the crapper seats were damp and that did not make me feel any better. When the sun comes up it seems to bring the flies with it and then the sand starts to blow and today I can't see 20 feet ahead of me.

Some of the boys are going on a mission today; it is called a fighter sweep. We are about 80 miles from Cairo and 35 miles from Alexandria. We can hear gunfire all day today and the anti-aircraft fire unit just north of us was throwing up a lot of lead. We could not see any planes.

CHAPTER 4

Haifa, Palestine

Wednesday, August 19. After a slight delay, we proceed to the Haifa railroad station; we were further delayed when the train separated, and we had to back up and pick up about half the train that became uncoupled. We finally arrived in the station and proceeded to unload after 30 hours in broken-down trains that only covered 315 miles. There were not many people around the station, and we proceeded to buses that were waiting.

Haifa had a population in the vicinity of one hundred thousand. It had the only deep harbor in Palestine. The oil lines from Iraq terminate at this port and at the time of arrival we witnessed a busy port with oil lines all around the port.

This port was used as a naval base during the war. After loading our buses, we headed out through the beautiful rolling hills of this strange country. Our destination was 30 miles away to a British camp called Muqeibila, Palestine. For the first time since the middle of June all the members of the 64th Fighter Squadron are together. We spent most of the rest of the day and evening swapping stories of our trips.

The pilots came over on the deck of the U.S. aircraft carrier *Ranger* and then took off from the carrier near the Gold Coast of Africa and, after several stops for fuel along the way, put their planes down on this field.

This camp was made up of brick buildings with plenty of room for everybody. The camp had an excellent kitchen which we missed when we left this spot.

Thursday, August 20. This was a day of rest for all, and it was welcomed as the effects of that train ride from Suez left us in a very tired state.

Friday, August 21. The food situation was not to our satisfaction, so I had a meeting with the British catering officer who had charge of supplying us food. A trip to Haifa was necessary to visit the British DID (Daily Issuing Depot) They proved to me that they were doing their best with what they had to work with. In fact, I found out they were giving us a little better food than they were giving their own troops.

During my short stay in Haifa, I was able to send a cable home. We'd had no communications with home since leaving the States in July.

We were all briefed on a possible parachute attack and posted guards all over the area tonight. We had reports the Germans had bombed Haifa but never did obtain verification of same.

Saturday, August 22. The camp was hit with what was called Sand Fly Fever; this was accompanied by diarrhea. Fevers ran up to as high as 104°. This gave our medical officers some busy hours as no one that I could remember was spared this uncomfortable situation. The shortage of latrines made matters worse. Many of the boys waiting their turn had some washing to do when nature would not wait. To make matters worse, we had a practice alert tonight for a parachute attack. Many did not answer the call as they could not get out of bed. This fever just sapped your strength. In most cases, it lasted for about forty-eight hours.

CHAPTER 5

Edku, Egypt

Wednesday, August 26. This morning we prepared a group of enlisted men and officers for a move to set up a camp in Edku, Egypt. We were assigned, for the move, the good old workhorse of World War II, the C-47 transport airplane.

We loaded two of these with kitchen stoves, mechanic kits, personal equipment, and about thirty men in each plane. The pilot, in talking about the weight, said he had just come from China where he had been flying loads of rice for the Chinese. He thought we could make the trip as long as the engines did not fail on take-off.

We had a successful flight which took a couple of hours. After we finished unloading, our next job was to obtain some tents because we didn't have any. The base commander was most cooperative. Later in the afternoon, we had tents and a few trucks.

We had our meals with the Royal Air Force (RAF) today and had a tour of this large base and its five airfields. One thing I always remember was, while I waited in the base commander's office, he tried to reach a party on the telephone and was told his party was not available. His remark to the party he had on the line was to tell him to "Give me a tingle on the blower."

This had me confused for a moment and I asked him about the remark. He explained that he wanted his party to call him back. This was the first of many experiences we had with the British and their slang.

Along with the tents and trucks, we drew our open-air latrine, which consisted of four large metal buckets with wooden seats, complete with covers and a screen and poles.

What our desert latrines looked like. (57th Fighter Group website)

Our desert pink P-40s came in this afternoon, and we are ready for operations. We drew some rations, and the mess boys are preparing to serve meals starting tomorrow morning.

Thursday, August 27. The mosquitoes had a feast during the night which had us really worried. We had been told that the Anopheles Mosquito was in this area. They carried malaria so some action had to be taken.

A trip to Alexandria was necessary to obtain nets. The depot that issued them had to look up the area on their maps to verify whether or not we could have them issued to us. I remember the British sergeant saying it was OK for us to have them. I said, "Well, let's have them." He replied that the requisition must be signed by the major in charge. He told me that the major was having a nap and to come back in a couple of hours. My reply was to wake the major as I had come quite a ways and wanted to return to camp as I had many duties to take care of. His reply was no one wakes the major until 4:00 pm. So, I waited until the major woke up, obtained the nets, and headed back to camp.

Monday, August 31. I received a report early this morning that one of our master sergeants was in the Mustapha Barracks, a British jail, for some incident that occurred outside the Cecil Hotel in Alexandria.

Upon my arrival at the barracks, I was ushered into the office of the head of the British "Red Caps," which are the same as our Military Police. He read to me a long statement of his authority and also informed me, in view of the fact we were the only Americans in this area, he had jurisdiction over us. He then proceeded to read the charges against our sergeant.

It seems the sergeant decided to go into the Cecil Hotel for a drink and was informed the hotel was out of bounds to enlisted men. He then tried again to gain entrance and was ejected. The sergeant could not understand this and decided to seek revenge which amounted to urinating all over the front steps of the Cecil Hotel.

After this action by the sergeant, the Red Caps were called in and the sergeant spent the night in the brig. Upon the release of our sergeant, I observed this brig was not the place for anyone to spend a night.

The colonel was very insistent the sergeant be court-martialed for this affair. The sergeant was an old timer in the Air Force with an outstanding record. It was decided the punishment for this deed was time served in the brig at the Mustapha Barracks, a real Bastille.

Tuesday, September 1. Some of the pilots moved to the desert area to assist a South African fighter unit that had many losses in planes during what they called "the flap" (moving back).

This would be the first time that an American fighter pilot would be flying combat missions against the enemy in the Western Desert. All of our boys returned safely.

Today we received mail. It was the first time we had mail since leaving Fort Dix on July 16. The morale of the outfit was in high gear after the mail call.

Wednesday, September 2. Most of the pilots went off this morning to assist the South Africans. All returned after a day of flying with some real veterans of desert warfare.

We are moved to the further end of this large airdrome to make room for another squadron. We did not need so much room now that our boys and planes would stay out with the South Africans starting tomorrow.

A group of American bombers were now on this airdrome. I watched the first loading of bombs to be dropped tonight on the troops of the "Desert Fox," Rommel.

I had a visitor today. He was the farmer who ran a fruit produce store in the village of Edku. We came to an agreement: he would clean out our latrines and pay the squadron fund the sum of $12.00 a week or 3 Egyptian pounds. He informed me he would use this human waste as a fertilizer. We had heard about this system the farmers in this area used. For this reason, we were forbidden to buy any vegetables from them.

Thursday, September 3. Our pilots were off again this morning to fly combat missions with the South African fighter pilots. All returned safe. This was a real experience for our boys. They are flying with experienced fighter pilots; at the same time they are giving the enemy a hard time each time they fly a mission.

Friday, September 4. American bombers are now on the same field with us. I spent some time with these boys as they load bombs for some missions coming up.

Thursday, September 10. Took a ride to Alexandria and visited our American consulate. The prime purpose of my visit was to try to obtain an American flag to fly over our area at the camp at Edku.

A meeting was set up for me to see the consul the following day with a sort of promise he may be able to obtain a flag for us.

Friday, September 11. Returned to Alexandria and obtained the American flag with a promise

I'm adding a message to our munitions. (57th Fighter Group website)

I would return it when I received one through the regular issue. This promise was not kept as we never obtained one. The flag stayed with us.

This was our first pay day since we left East Boston in July. We were paid in Egyptian money. We had a difficult task trying to make the amounts come out correctly. The Egyptian pound was worth four dollars in our money, and we received pounds and piasters. The pounds came in one, five, and tens. Some of the piasters were in paper and some in metal.

The boys had a real hard time at first in figuring out the value. I remember the 50-piaster piece was the size of our 50-cent piece. At times you would forget it had the value of $2.00. The piaster was pegged at four cents.

In the afternoon, I spent some time out in the desert paying off the pilots and men working with the South African squadron. Their No. 2 Squadron, who our boys worked with, had a pet monkey by the name of Jocko and he gave me a hard time. Jocko kept trying to steal the money from the pay table.

On several days, while stationed at Edku, many planes from the desert were forced to land at our base due to sandstorms at their respective bases. The pilots on some occasions reported sand blowing as high as 14,000 feet. This was hard to believe but we found out for ourselves later in the campaign.

Saturday, September 12. This was a routine day. The boys put together some old metal pipe we found on the airfield so that we could have a flagpole. The pole was finished late in the day.

Sunday, September 13. For the first time, I believe, an American flag flew over Edku, Egypt. It was a wonderful sight to see the Stars and Stripes flying so far from our home station in Boston.

A detail saw to it that, when we moved, the pole would come down and be erected again at each of the fields we were on in Egypt, Libya, Tunisia, Malta, Sicily, Italy, and Corsica.

Tuesday, September 15. A German reconnaissance plane was over our area for the first time since we arrived. He flew at a very high altitude and the British anti-aircraft guns just could not reach him. His vapor trail was something to watch. He made a few trips during the day.

We received some American trucks. It was a welcome sight to see them roll in as we had been getting along with some old British ones since our arrival at this base.

The orders to move came out today. That was very welcome as well because it meant that our squadron would be together for the first time since leaving home.

CHAPTER 6

Landing Ground 174, Egypt

September 16–October 26

Wednesday, September 16. We broke camp and proceeded to a spot called Landing Ground 174. LG 174 was just off the main road that runs from Alexandria and Cairo. We were about thirty-five miles from Alexandria and about sixty-five miles back of El Alamein.

The Qattara Depression marked the southern end of the El Alamein line, 436 feet below sea level. This is the second-lowest elevation in Africa. Virtually impassable by tanks and similar vehicles, it is said this area saved the British from defeat when they selected the El Alamein line for the last line of defense during the retreat in 1942. The landscape helped defend their flank.

I must relate an incident that took place a few days before leaving Edku. Our so-called latrine with the four large buckets with wooden seats, surrounded by a canvas screen,

Our tents at Landing Ground 174 in the Western Desert.

was in the rear of our camp area close to a wire fence. I made an early visit to the latrine and found nothing but the four buckets. The seats and canvas screen were gone and a hole in the fence had been cut by someone with good wire cutters.

During the night, we were told, a British tent was stolen while four British officers slept in it. An investigation was conducted. During that, I was briefed on the thievery of the Arabs. The information proved to be so true, as we found during our travels across the desert of Egypt, Libya, and Tunisia.

This was a day of reunion as the boys from our first base in Palestine, and all the squadron, was together again. We had some new faces assigned to the squadron.

I met our new squadron commander, Major Clermont E. Wheeler of San Antonio, Texas. Our squadron commander, Lt Col. Frank Mears, who left us in East Boston, was now the group commander.

Most of the day was spent setting up our new camp. The tents were all British and I must say they were of superior quality. They were made of extra heavy cloth and each tent came rolled in a heavy woven rope which was used as flooring. The tents were of different sizes, some for two men, four men, and a large tent for 12 men. These 12-man tents were also used as mess tents and club tents for the officers and enlisted men.

Each tent had two pieces and, when set up, there was a space in between for the air to flow through which was a godsend with the terrific heat of the desert.

This area was a new experience for all of us as we were out in the open desert with only our tents for shelter. There was no water on this so-called air base. We had to depend on three British water bowsers which made daily trips to a water point many miles away.

We felt that the water had been chlorinated a few times before we received it. And if you have ever drunk water chlorinated a few times you know what I mean. The men soon became acclimated to this new taste.

To set up a camp to house 249 enlisted men and about sixty officers, along with tents for operations, intelligence, transportation, engineering, armament, ordnance, quartermaster supply, technical supply, medical, orderly room, mess hall, and two club tents for the officers and enlisted men, was no meager task.

Everybody pitched in and by nightfall we were set for a good night's sleep.

On our first airfield in Egypt, known as Landing Ground No. 174, back of the El Alamein line, we had our first experience with the scorpion. We found them in our shoes, our mosquito nets and most of our clothing that was not in use. We had been briefed many times by our medical people on the seriousness of the sting of the desert pest.

To the best of my knowledge, I cannot remember a member of our outfit receiving a sting. The first thing you did before you went to bed was to check your mosquito net for scorpions. When you arose in the morning you made sure you gave your clothing you were going to wear that day a good shake. A great place for the scorpion to park was in your boots.

The boys caught many scorpions. They had some fun with them by putting two of them in a glass jar with some sand and let the scorpions fight. Another sport was to put one in a jar and put a few live flies in with them. You would see quite a battle. Of course, the flies were no match for the scorpion, but they flew around for a while until the scorpion would attack with his stinger.

As darkness fell upon the camp, we had many experiences getting lost. We had no lights and very few flashlights, and the blackout restrictions were in earnest. Many officers and enlisted men were lost many times in this new environment. Most of the trouble was with the guards we had posted around our area. A few of the boys spent the night wandering around lost until daylight.

Thursday, September 17. This was the day we spent getting familiar with our new home. Our airfield left a lot to be desired. It was a long runway, but the sand stirred up by take-offs clouded the area with dust.

There were three squadrons stationed on this field. Our squadron, which was the 64th, and the 65th and 66th made up the 57th Fighter Group. We were under the command of the Ninth Air Force for administration but under the British Eighth Army for tactical work.

The group and its three squadrons were spread around the airfield and on one end of the field we had a company of Gurkhas. Their mission was to guard the airfield against paratroop attack.

These men left a great impression upon me in the way they conducted themselves. Real soldiers. The history of the Eighth Army victory in Egypt, Libya, and Tunisia should make for good reading.

They were commanded by a former tea planter from India by the name of Captain Macklefactor. We had many happy times with him while stationed on this field.

British anti-aircraft units were placed around the perimeter of the field. There was no tower for take-off instructions or radio communications with the planes. The take-offs were on a timed schedule which was given to the pilots at their briefing.

Training of the pilots was the priority of the day. Little did we know what was ahead of us.

Friday, September 19. This was another day to pull the loose ends of our new camp together. During the night, Jerry (the Germans) dropped bombs not far from our area.

Anti-aircraft next to Landing Ground 174.

Sunday, September 20. The first church services were held in the open desert.

Monday, September 21. Plans for moving were finally put on paper. There was nothing in any regulations that would tell us how to have a mobile squadron. We had to work out the plans ourselves.

In order for the squadron to function properly, when the time came to move from the field, we came up with this plan. When an infantry or artillery unit moves, it just packs up and moves out, but with airplanes you must move part of your unit forward and set up a base then be ready to receive the planes at the forward base. What we did is to split all the sections of the squadron into what we called A Party and B Party.

A Party would move out of the rear base and take with it all the members of their party and move to the new base. They would set up and be ready to receive the pilots and planes when they came in. When the forward base was ready, the planes would take off from the rear base. B Party would then move out and join up with A Party.

Tuesday, September 22. This was the day that we split our squadron up into two parties and broke down the A Party section. We loaded A Party on trucks for the practice move. The move went off very well. The men and officers witnessed a move repeated many times when the push started.

Thursday, September 24. We opened our officers' club tonight. It consisted of two of the big tents tied together with the heavy rope the tents came wrapped in as the floor. We had very little furniture, but it served its purpose. The pilots at times had many hours of waiting. Officers' clubs served for the passing of many lonely evenings. In this spot in the desert, there was no place else to go.

In the evening, we invited the officers from No. 2 Squadron, South African Air Force. There was a close feeling with these boys as they were the first that our boys met when we came into this area.

Members of No. 2 Squadron, South African Air Force, who helped our pilots learn to work "In the Blue."

We had beer for the opening which we purchased in Alexandria. A run was made daily for this beer. It was on the expensive side. It cost 10 piasters a can, which was 40 cents in American money.

It kind of burnt us up to pay this price, but what could you do? The store where we purchased the beer had a proprietor who couldn't care less when we complained about the price. To add insult to injury, the beer came from Brooklyn, New York. The enlisted men had a similar club. We pooled our money with them when the daily run was made for the beer.

Monday, September 29. The next three days were spent in Cairo attending meetings pertaining to the way they were going to feed us. The plans were never carried out. We were fed by the British for the next six months.

The food was not what we were used to, but we soon became acclimated to it. We had bread once in six months when we happened to run into a British field bakery on our move into Libya.

During my stay in Cairo, I had the opportunity to visit the shops and make a few purchases. You had to be sharp when dealing with these Arabs. They all felt that the Americans were millionaires. We had a few hours off in the afternoon and took a ride out to the pyramids and the Sphinx. We stopped at the Mena House, which is near the Sphinx, and had lunch. This is the spot where Roosevelt and Churchill met.

The flies on the outside veranda where we were served almost drove us crazy. You just had to keep brushing them off your food.

Before returning to our base, we visited the APO (Army Post Office) in Heliopolis just outside Cairo and picked up a lot of mail for the squadron. Mail was always the best tonic for the men.

The trip from Cairo to the camp was a hot one. We passed through the desert and only had one spot in the 70-mile trip to stop and refresh.

Friday, October 2. The boys did lots of flying today and lots of them buzzed the tent area before landing. The Germans dropped lots of bombs not far from the camp tonight. This was to be expected as this area was loaded with all kinds of troops and airfields. We had men from England, Canada, South Africa, New Zealand, Australia, India, Scotland, and our own group. All of us made up the British Eighth Army.

The only other Americans was a group of officers and enlisted men training the British on how to use our Sherman and Grant tanks. These tanks made a name for themselves in the battle to push General Rommel and his troops out of the Western Desert.

Saturday, October 3. This was an important day for us. We made a deal with a few

The Sphinx in Cairo.

Arabs to do our laundry. We set up a tent for them and supplied them with water and some tea and biscuits. We set the rate on each piece of clothing. It was very cheap. They did an excellent job and stayed with us for a couple of months.

The water problem was a little difficult. We had to truck the water some 40 miles each day. We also set up a shower for the squadron. We were able to obtain some lumber and built a frame to hold two 55-gallon gas drums. The boys in the welding section of our engineering section took care of this assignment. With an empty beer can for a shower head, and some tubing from a wrecked plane, we were in business.

The boys on the water run for the laundry filled the two drums each morning and by afternoon we had hot water in both drums. The heat was supplied by the red-hot sun, which pounded our area dally. This project was appreciated by all.

Sunday, October 4. We received a visitor from one of the nearby British units looking for a priest. One of their pilots had been killed and they wanted to bury him with a Catholic priest in attendance.

I contacted our group chaplain, Rev. Charles H. Louge, who was always willing to help. That afternoon, I drove him to a field not too far from ours. This was my first taste of death on the battlefield. Not giving much thought to the services Father Louge would conduct, we arrived at the British squadron and were directed to the post where the services were going to be held.

It was a spot in the desert. A hole had been dug and the young man's body, RAF pilot Quinn, lay alongside the hole wrapped in just a blanket. This sort of gave me a funny feeling because it was not what I expected for the burial. Little did I know I would be taking care of some of our own boys in the same manner at a later date.

A map was drawn of the spot of the burial, with grid quadrants marked, so later the body could be moved to a war cemetery.

Tuesday, October 6. We had our first real rainstorm. One thing about the rain in the desert was, shortly after it stopped, the soil would dry up quickly and then the sand would start blowing again.

We have often talked about the temperatures of the desert. A little research came up with some facts. In El Azizia, south of Tripoli in Libya, the highest temperature was recorded at 136.4°F. The Black Scorpion Squadron was stationed only a few miles from this spot at one time. The only spot in the world with a higher temperature is Death Valley, California at 137.0°F.

Friday, October 9. Our boys are out on another mission this morning. On any day when the boys return from a mission, we would listen in on the reports they would file with the intelligence officers who debriefed them on their return. This was a different day. The boys ran into some German ME-109s fighters. Captain Dick Ryan of Worcester, Massachusetts, Capt. George Mobbs of Little Rock, Arkansas, Capt. William Mount of Kansas City, Missouri, and Lt. Bill Beck of Nashville, Tennessee, shared the credit of shooting down the ME-109s. I believe that this was the first time an American pilot, flying with an American unit, shot down a German in the Western Desert.

We received a new crop of pilots today and plan for them to get some real combat training from our boys. These are hot days.

Tuesday, October 13. Our boys are out on missions again this morning. All return safe. They had three ME-109s to their credit. We have our first movie show in the desert tonight.

Wednesday, October 14. Lieutenant John Piasta of Webster, Massachusetts, our communications officer, installed a radio set from one of our wrecked airplanes in a panel truck and we listened to our boys out over the battlefield as they conducted their mission.

Thursday, October 15. We have on paper today the plans to move our squadron when the word comes. We are visited by Air Vice-Marshal Arthur Coningham, Commander, Desert Air Force. He gave us a real pep talk and stated how happy he was to have us assigned to support the British Eighth Army.

Friday, October 16. This was a day we all should remember. We were hit with a real sand and rainstorm along

Father Louge preaching to the men.

Captain William Mount, part of the first group of Americans to shoot down Germans in the Western Desert. (57th Fighter Group website)

with a severe thunder and lightning storm. We had most of our tents blown down and had little or no sleep. Many of the officers and men were lost trying to find their way around the area. Lieutenant Jay Wanamaker of Kansas City, our assistant intelligence officer, reported that he had seen a rainbow at midnight.

When the sand of the desert blows, especially with the velocity it blew that night, it cuts you. I was fortunate not to lose my tent but spent most of the night trying

Painting our famous Black Scorpion on a P-40. (57th Fighter Group website)

to keep it up. I had dug a hole and set my tent over the hole to give me some protection in the event of an air raid. By morning, this hole was almost filled with the sand of the Sahara.

This storm continued until about noon on the 17th. Then we had the job of cleaning up; tents had to be restocked and sand washed out of the planes and trucks. Operations were halted for the day until we got our camp back in action.

Tuesday, October 20. Boys are out today dropping bombs on Jerry camps. They all return safe.

A lot of thought was given about the squadron name from the day we started to operate out of the landing ground. Most of the squadron wanted a good name that would identify us because we had a great group of fine pilots. They were young and full of fight and wanted to fight. I am not sure whether this was the day the name was decided upon, but it was on this field that the name of "The Black Scorpions" came into being.

It was on this field the squadron really came to life. They received their first real combat training from here and, as we move through this story, you will understand what I mean.

Wednesday, October 21. This morning we had the first enemy planes over our field. It happened shortly after breakfast. Although 10 to 12 planes spent quite a bit of time over us, they failed to drop any bombs.

The British anti-aircraft opened up with all the weapons that surrounded the area. We just froze in our tracks but not for long as the area became littered with the fragments of the shells falling all over the camp. We also found out we did not have enough slit trenches. The project for the rest of the day was that everybody would have a slit trench.

Thursday, October 22. Pilots are out this morning on a bombing mission with 500-lb eggs, as we called the bombs. All back safe.

Friday, October 23. This is the day the British Eighth Army had been waiting for. All squadrons of the 57th Fighter Group were called together this morning, which totaled about one thousand officers and enlisted men, for a briefing.

A briefing crew from the British Eighth Army arrived in our area and it included many high-ranking officers. They gave us the real picture that would take place at 9:30 pm tonight. There were no secrets. This was the true story. It included the air and ground forces' missions. They had maps and charts showing the battle plan to drive Rommel out of the Western Desert.

Colonel Frank Mears. (57th Fighter Group website, Frank Mears Collection)

Colonel Frank Mears, the group commander, told us the part the 57th Fighter Group would play in this very important drive.

We all stayed up and, at 9:30 pm, the guns started. They could be heard all through the night. Thus started the Battle of El Alamein. We were told that over one thousand artillery pieces opened fire along the battle front.

The one thought I had that night was that I was glad we were on the right side and did not have to take the punishment the Germans and Italians were taking from this terrific bombardment.

We didn't get much sleep in the camp tonight as everyone was keyed up. We felt this was the beginning of the end of World War II.

Saturday, October 24. Our boys were out again on a mission and had good day. They shot down four Jerries.

Monday, October 26. Many enemy planes were over our camp through the night and early morning. The Germans bombers dropped many bombs but none on our camp.

CHAPTER 7

Landing Ground 174, Egypt

October 27–November 3

On October 27, 1942, Army Air Forces approved the emblem submitted showing the Black Scorpion and, from this date, we were officially known as the Black Scorpion Squadron.

Tuesday, October 27. This was the start of the dawn missions. I volunteered to wake the pilots for this very important mission. I arose at 3:00 am and checked with the guards to see the cooks had been awakened and then proceeded to the various tents of the pilots that would be flying this first dawn mission.

These young fellows really took some shaking to wake up. They slept very soundly for men that would be in a P-40 airplane in an hour or so.

The guards also woke the crew chiefs and other enlisted men who were assigned to planes on this mission. Within a half hour, we had a busy camp.

The cooks had some coffee ready. The boys were picked up in trucks and jeeps and driven to the operations tent for their final briefing. On this field we had no tower or landing lights to light up the runway. The night before, we placed trucks and jeeps all around the perimeter of the field and at a prescribed time all the lights of the vehicles would be turned on.

After the briefing, the boys were taken to their planes and, on a pistol signal from the operations officer, the truck lights were turned on. This gave the pilots some idea of what the field boundaries were.

We had 12 P-40s, which was the usual number on all missions. They were to take off, head out over the ocean

Taking time for a little coffee on the way to the next LG. (57th Fighter Group website)

and head toward the enemy lines. They would come in over the enemy camp just as the sun started to come up.

All the bombs were dropped but, before the mission was completed, a group of German ME-109s was in the air. The boys had quite a time. All our boys came home safe.

We put up another show this afternoon and the boys ran into some more ME-109s. After the prescribed flight time, which is the time that a P-40 could stay up (about three hours), all had returned but Lt. Lyman Middleditch of Highland, New Jersey.

None of the boys reported Middleditch was shot down because all the pilots were so busy trying to take care of the Jerries that jumped them. We understood.

We did not give up on Lyman. Within a short time, we saw a speck of something coming towards our field that looked like a P-40 and, sure enough, here is our last pilot of the mission on his way to land.

Lyman had quite a story to tell. He was jumped by a group of Jerries in their '109s and he had quite a time up there all alone. When he was finished, he had shot down three and damaged a few more. I can remember on many occasions Lyman saying the P-40 was a lousy plane. Every time I asked him how he felt, his comment was the same, "a lousy plane." He stated the pilots in the ME-109s just did not know how to fight with the plane they had (Lyman continued his comments about the P-40 after he went home and had some trouble with the Air Corps about his remarks).

Another first for this squadron was when Lt. "Babe" Ryerson came in for a landing, forgot to shut off his six .50-caliber guns and sprayed the area with gun fire. We were lucky no one was hit.

The penalty for this error was that Babe had to walk around the perimeter of the airfield with full equipment, including his parachute. He was a tired boy when he finished this task under the hot sun of the Sahara Desert. He did not complain; he felt he deserved it.

Lieutenant Lyman Middleditch hated the P-40. (57th Fighter Group website)

This same action happened a few times later, but I don't remember any of the boys repeating the Ryerson march.

Shortly after dark, we prepared for another first as the Indian Gurkhas, who were guarding our field against paratroop attack, had a dry run with all their troops and equipment. They went through our area waving their personal weapon, a knife called the Kukri.

All members of the command stayed in their tents during the

demonstration as they did not want to get in the way of these real fighting men from far off India.

As you can see, this was a busy day for the 64th Fighter Squadron.

Wednesday, October 28. Boys off on another dawn mission to bomb and strafe another German camp. These missions paid off as they caught many of the Jerries in their beds and destroyed many German planes before they could get off the ground.

Boys out on afternoon mission with some of the new pilots that had been training for a few weeks. Captain "Buck" Bilby from Skidmore, Missouri, shot down another ME-109. All return safe.

Thursday, October 29. This was a routine day with missions as usual. All boys returned safe.

Just after midnight, I was awakened by a rifle shot in our camp area. Upon investigation, our guard in the mess hall and officers' club reported he saw a soldier walking towards the latter. When he failed to clear this area, the guard investigated and heard someone in the tent of the club. He ordered him to come out, which he did, only he then ran away. He ordered the man to halt. Failing to respond to this order, the sentry fired at him and shot him in the leg.

The soldier, who happened to be one of our own, was taken to a British field hospital and treated for a flesh wound. This young man was lucky the bullet went through fleshy part of his leg.

We found money was missing from the club. The man was tried by a court-martial but found not guilty due to the lack of evidence. No money was found on him. His defense was he was just out walking. We had had several thefts in the squadron but could not pin it on anyone.

Friday, October 30. Boys off on early mission and run into some Jerries. Lieutenant Babe Ryerson, the young man who had to walk around the airfield a few days ago for failing to shut off his guns before landing, came in with his tail shot up. He had trouble landing and, rather than running into the enlisted men's camp area, put on hard brakes and tipped his P-40 over on its back.

When he was taken out of his plane, he was found to be wounded by a 20-mm shell which exploded in his cockpit. His left hand had quite a bit

Lieutenant "Babe" Ryerson with his flipped P-40.

of shrapnel in it. Ryerson was treated at the field and send to the British hospital in Alexandria.

Lieutenant "Rocky" Byrne of St Louis, Missouri, got a '109. Major Clermont E. Wheeler, better known as "Pudge," our squadron commander, Capt. Dick Ryan from Worcester, Massachusetts, Capt. Buck Bilby and Lt. Babe Ryerson claimed probables.

Saturday, October 31. This evening a few of us were invited to the Gurkhas camp which was only a short distance from our camp area. But we had trouble finding our way home. I believe I have mentioned what a difficult time it is in this area after dark to find your way.

Monday, November 2. Boys off on an early mission this morning. They worked over a dark airfield and destroyed several enemy aircraft on the ground. All returned safe but Capt. Marvin Lancaster of Vanceboro, North Carolina. None of the boys on this mission saw him go down. This, I believe, was the first officer we had to report "Missing in Action."

Movies tonight in the 65th Squadron area. They were put on by the British. I was promoted to captain today. I received the notice of promotion from the British radio unit assigned to our area.

Tuesday, November 3. Had to take a long trip this morning to pick up money for pay day. Still paying officers and men in Egyptian pounds and piasters. It's a difficult job converting from the payroll which lists the salaries in American dollars.

CHAPTER 8

Landing Ground 172 and 75, Egypt

Thursday, November 5. Our A Party move out to Landing Ground 172, which was about forty miles away. The move worked out very well and it gave the pilots a little more time in the air especially when the Jerries were on the run.

This was the first trial of our plan which would be used many times before we finished this mess.

Friday, November 6. B Party moved out to join A Party at Landing Ground 172. We arrived after dark and slept in the open for the night.

A group of P-40s on the flight line. (57th Fighter Group website)

Colonel Peter McGoldrick, who was to command the 79th Fighter Group, which is on its way over to Egypt, flew a mission with our boys and failed to return. I believe this was the colonel's first mission.

Captain Ernest D. Hartman of Indianapolis, Indiana, had a real scare when one of the Jerries put a bullet through his canopy; it passed in and out of same without hitting him.

Saturday, November 7. The push is going so well we are ordered to move again, this time we had quite a way to go to a spot called Landing Ground 75 (LG 75) which was beyond the El Alamein Line. A Party moved out. It was not long before we drove over the ground where the British Eighth Army had been when they put up the terrific bombardment on October 23.

We found a spot to camp for the night this side of El Alamein not far from the Mediterranean Sea. It was a cold night as we slept in the open. We listened for a while to the Army–Notre Dame football game from the States on a radio that one of our boys put together from some junk.

Sunday, November 8. Up early this morning and off to our new field. On the way, we pass through El Alamein. The sight I saw I will never forget. The area was covered with burnt-out tanks, trucks, and planes. We passed through a narrow area which was laid out with white tape telling us that this area had been cleared of mines.

In passing through, I still can visualize the piles of dead bodies along this small strip. We spent another night in the open and it was cold as are most of the nights in the desert.

We did not arrive at the spot we wanted to camp for the night until after dark and had to feed the officers and men. The cooks started our field ranges and one of them failed to close one of the bottom covers and it let out some light. This was

---

This was Hitler's answer to a message Rommel sent on November 2, 1942, informing Hitler that Rommel could not hold out any longer and he intended to withdraw while he could:

> It is with trusting confidence in your leadership and the courage of the German–Italian troops under your command that the German People and I are following the heroic struggle in Egypt. In the situation that you find yourself there can be no other thought but to stand fast, yield not a yard of ground and throw every gun and every man into the battle. Considerable Air Force reinforcements are being sent to C-In-C South. The Duce and the Commando Supremo are also making the utmost efforts to send you the means to continue the fight. Your enemy, despite his superiority, must also be at the end of his strength. it would not be the first time in history that a strong will has triumphed over the bigger battalions. As to your troops, you can show them no other road than that to victory or death.

our first experience of cooking in the open after dark. A group of British troops, who were putting up for the night, were soon on our backs about total blackout.

Our rations had been cut when we left Landing Ground 174; I visited with a British catering unit to file a complaint. They produced a letter from our Cairo headquarters which left no room for argument. From then on, it did not take long to prepare a meal. All we had was in cans

Time for some chow. (57th Fighter Group website)

and we had very few of those. We had to pull in our belts for quite a while from here on in.

The report we received about mines in this area showed the enemy had laid over 500,000. The casualties at El Alamein were over 75,000 Germans and Italians. Thousands of trucks and 500 tanks were destroyed.

Monday, November 9. Up at 5:00 and on the road by 6:00 am. Our next stop was Mersa Matruh where we would meet with a British liaison officer who would guide the convoy into Landing Ground 75.

Upon arriving in Mersa Matruh, a very small town which been shot up in good fashion by the Air Corps and artillery, all we found were burnt out tanks and bodies of Germans and Italians, but no liaison officer.

My convoy commander felt we should turn back. After a conference, he still insisted on turning back. I decided the powers-that-be knew we were on the road; I relieved the officer and took over moving the convoy forward.

I sweated for about ten miles as no one was on the road but us. I was relieved when I saw a group of British armored cars waiting for us.

They informed us enemy troops were in the area. They escorted us to the landing ground without incident and left us in this lonely spot. We were very low on water and gasoline and had to caution the men about waste. The orders on gas were that I would have to approve any drawings of gas from the small supply we had.

Within a few minutes, a British armored car came into our area looking for petrol, as the British called gasoline. We explained to the driver how short we were. He stated he had been chasing a German armored car and had to give up the chase for fear he would run out of gas.

I told the boys to fill his fuel tank. He was grateful and so were we as we had no arms to defend ourselves against tanks.

A short time later, a British convoy arrived with gas, bombs, and .50-caliber ammunition, but no water. This was the largest field that we had been at so far. We proceeded to set up for operations.

We found many booby traps around the area. After an hour or so, we started erecting our tents so we could be prepared for the planes from our rear base which would arrive later in the afternoon.

The water situation bothered me for a while. The nearest water point was many miles away. Later in the afternoon, my fears were washed away when a large British transport plane came and delivered water to us. The water was in two-gallon cans. It took some time to transfer this to our water bowsers.

The crew of the plane told us they would deliver us a supply of water as long as we needed it. They did a wonderful job and, although we were many miles from nowhere, delivered the water in a steady fashion.

This field became a busy spot later in the afternoon as many planes and convoys rolled onto this field.

During the night, we heard gunfire not far from our area.

Tuesday, November 10. Up early as usual. The sound of gunfire continued in the vicinity of our camp. The British transports delivered bombs and water all day. Our boys, who came in late on the 9th, were out on reconnaissance looking for some targets.

We received a report that "Mary's," the British whore house in Alexandria, had been bombed and several British officers were killed. The only comment I heard

---

The war engendered lots of forms of expression among the soldiers. Below is a poem written by an unknown British AA gunner.

A Soldier's Farewell to Egypt

Land of heat and sweaty socks
Sand, sun, and tons of rocks
Streets of which I give no name
Streets of sorrow, streets of shame
Streets of filth and stinking dogs
Harlot thieves and pestering Wogs
Hordes of flies that buzz around
Piles of Wog's shit on the ground
Clouds of dust that choke and blind
Driving fellows right out of their mind
Aching hearts, aching feet
Gyppo guts and camel meat
Arabs heaven, soldiers' hell
Land of bastards fare you well

came from a British officer who was in the group when the announcement was made: "What a wonderful way to die."

Wednesday, November 11. Boys out on missions this morning. All returned safe except for our squadron commander, Major Clermont Wheeler of San Antonio, Texas.

This was a day of crack ups on the field for all squadrons. This could be caused by the low-level strafing jobs they were performing. During this type of mission, the planes receive a lot of small-arms fire from the troops and the landing gears receive a lot of damage. When they return to base, they have their troubles. A Party moved out this afternoon for another lonely spot in the desert.

Thursday, November 12. B Party moved out after our planes took off for the forward base. On their way, the pilots carried out strafing missions. We traveled

The war had to be fought on many fronts. This article from the Young Catholic Messenger, *November 13, 1942, explains why the 57th Fighter Group was in Africa flying missions.*

Northern Africa is bristling with armaments and is ringing with the din of battle. More and more troops and supplies are being concentrated at different points. Aided by American bombers, the British have launched a fierce attack on the Germans and Italians under General Rommel in Northwestern Egypt.

American planes are bombing ships, bases, and docks in the Eastern Mediterranean. In the Central Mediterranean, the British, based on unconquerable Malta, are destroying Axis supplies and ships in Tripoli, Benghazi, Tobruk, and the parts of Italy and Sicily, and are hammering at General Rommel's supply lines. Vast British air fleets have come from England to pound the northern Italian cities at Milan, Genoa, and Turin.

In Western Africa, numerous bases have been established by the United Nations. Some are close to Dakar, the French-owned city which is only 1,800 miles from Brazil. The French Governor of Dakar has announced that that city of 100,000 inhabitants is ready to resist the capture by the United Nations.

If the Axis powers gain control of Northern Africa and the Mediterranean Sea, they will take the Suez Canal. The southern road to the oil fields of Iran and Iraq, and the road to the riches of India will open to them. Should they conquer the west coast of Africa, they could cut the American and British supply lines extending around Africa to the Red Sea and India. (Axis submarines are now sinking many United Nations ships west of Africa.) They might even invade South America.

Should the United Nations, on the other hand, be victorious in the struggle for Northern Africa and the Mediterranean Sea, all these threats would be removed. Supplies could be brought through the Mediterranean to the United Nations forces in Egypt, Iran, and India thus saving the long trip of 14,000 miles around Africa. Germany would be cut off from minerals and food which she now gets from French and Italian colonies in Northern Africa. The southern coast of Europe would be open to invasion.

Many military experts believe that the winning of Northern Africa and the Mediterranean will be a big step toward winning the war.

only 12 miles in the two hours since leaving LG 75 at 3:30 pm. Lots of trucks on the road as the Germans are on the run.

Friday, November 13. Off at 6:00 am after sleeping in the open on a cold and wet night. The men are in good spirits as usual, knowing every mile will bring them home sooner. We passed through minefields and lots of ruined German equipment.

Major Wheeler's plane was found. Foot tracks were traced for about two miles. This meant to us he was alive and probably taken prisoner. Passed into Libya at 2:00 pm. Water a problem on this trip. Glad to get out of Egypt.

CHAPTER 9

Gambut and Martuba, Libya

Saturday, November 14. Up at 5:00 am. Just as soon as breakfast was over, we are on our way to the first airfield in Libya. It is called Gambut.

Our boys flew out of the rear area and, after bombing the roads up ahead of us, they land and tell the stories how the Jerries are retreating.

General Lewis H. Brereton arrived to award the Distinguished Service Cross to our Lt. Lyman Middleditch (first Ninth Air Force Ace). Colonel Mears, the group commander, ordered everyone shaved for the occasion. I tried to talk him out of shaving as we were very low on water and were moving out at noon for another airfield without knowing about the water supply. He stuck to his guns, and everybody shaved.

When the ceremony was about to begin, our ace was not around. Lyman was quite a guy when it came to building things, such as a special heating unit for his tent. He also made up a special rig so he could have his pup tent in his plane. When he moved up to a forward field, he had his tent ready with special poles and rods that would take care of him until the tents from the rear base would arrive.

Someone reported Lyman had gone up to an area a couple miles from the field looking for some tubing for some project he was working on. We all waited until they located him. The general also waited. I believe we all waited about one-and-a-half hours.

The formation was set up and the adjutant read off the citation for the award. Lyman marched forward in his flying suit. Out of one of his map pockets some toilet paper unrolled as he marched forward. It made quite a sight, but this did not

Lyman Middleditch was quite the inventor. (57th Fighter Group website)

bother Lyman. He was a happy-go-lucky pilot, and he could not care less about a small incident like this.

In Brereton's published diary, the general makes note about the toilet-paper incident.

Sunday, November 15. We are on the move again. We left Gambut airfield at noon for a spot called Gazola, which was to be our stop for the night. On our way we had a chance to pass through Tobruk, the spot which changed hands many times between the Germans and the British.

It is hard to describe, but all I can say is Tobruk was in ruins. There were still many dead along the road. Many graves from previous fights were in evidence.

The airfield at Tobruk was a mess. The bombings by our boys and others did an outstanding job. The place was littered with wrecked aircraft which the Germans must have hated to lose.

We put up for the night at Gazola. The Germans left many bombs behind when they left this spot.

Monday, November 16. Out of Gazola at 8:00 am and joined a long convoy with the British. This was the first time we were with the British in a convoy. We were usually on our own and we liked it that way. They did not move the way we would have liked to. If the lead truck stopped, they would never seem to investigate. They would wait along the side of the road and make some tea.

They packed a lot of vehicles in this move, and we were packed tight with them which was not good convoy discipline. The convoy was held up for a long time and no one seemed to have reason why.

It was not until we started to roll again that we found the answer. The British officer, who was the convoy commander for this important move, was killed, along with three other officers riding with him, when they hit a mine. It was not a very nice sight to see the jeep and the four officers along the side of the road when we passed the spot.

They were digging graves for these officers, but the convoy was rolling again.

We arrived in Martuba behind schedule. It was raining cats and dogs, to use that expression. We were not used to rain as it had only rained a couple of times during our stay in Egypt. The rain never lasted more than a few minutes (except for one storm). We had to put the tents up in a sea of mud. During the night, water ran right through our tents.

For the first time we heard some of the experiences of the British armored car boys from around our area. These fellows, like all of the British troops I met, were dedicated soldiers.

Tuesday, November 17. Up early as usual but the rain is still with us. Boys are trying to fix up the tent area as it looks like rain will be with us for a while.

Had a pleasant experience this morning when I met my good friend Lieutenant Macklefactor, who commanded the Indian Gurkhas on the first field we were on in Egypt.

He was stationed nearby and came by to say hello. "Mac" was a British officer in the Reserves. I believe he had a tea plantation in India before the war started. I never saw him again. His outfit had heavy losses in the battle for Enfidaville, Tunisia.

We found the Jerries had again left lots of land mines in our area. The armored car boys went around selling pistols to our boys. They had plenty of German Lugers and Mausers. The Germans are bombing the road not far from our area. They also dropped bombs in our camp area during the night, but no hits. We spent a few hours in the slit trenches which we all had close by our tents.

Wednesday, November 18. Jerry around the area bombing again. We had many newspaper men with us today: Max Zineder of *Time* and *Life*; Whitehead and Kennedy of *AP News* and Aarons of *Yank* magazine.

Kennedy was Edward Kennedy of AP News *who broke the story of the end of the war in Europe the day before it was supposed to be released. General Eisenhower sent for him for this release.*

Many German ME-109 fighter planes on this field. The Germans did not have time to destroy them. The boys, in their spare time, are trying to get one to run.

Thursday, November 19. We moved to a better spot in this area and prepared to receive planes from the rear area. They are bogged down on the rear field due to lots of mud. For the first time we received some American food by the workhorse of World War II, a good old C-47. We had been on a small British ration since we arrived overseas; this American food was a real treat.

Friday, November 20. This was a banner day. Another C-47 arrived with more food and lots of mail.

When the mail arrived, it changed the morale of the unit 100%. We had not been receiving much mail and I had quite a scrap with one of the wheels at headquarters. He did not seem to realize how important it was to get mail. I let him know how I felt about the mail situation with some strong words. I told him he should get off his tail and do something about it. In fact, he was on the plane that brought in the mail.

Our rear party arrived late tonight, and we had a good hot meal for them. They brought with them two Italian soldiers. The soldiers surrendered to the water detail when they went to the water point a few days before they moved out of our last field.

I wanted to turn them in, but the CO said let them stay for a while. We will put them to work. This, I believe, was wrong but the CO was the boss. We used them

Captain Bob Barnum came back with bullet holes in his plane, although not this plane. This photo is from a later date. (57th Fighter Group website)

I can't emphasize enough the importance of the slit trench.

as kitchen patrol, and they seemed happy. They had been without food for a while before our detail brought them in.

The water detail had no arms with them when the Italian soldiers surrendered. You should see the slit trenches those Italian boys dug. They have great respect for bombs.

Saturday, November 21. Boys out this morning on a reconnaissance and they run into some action. Captain Robert Barnum comes home with a nice hole in the wing of his P-40.

After lunch I went to group headquarters to have Col. Frank Mears, the group commander, sign some flight certificates. We were sitting in his station wagon, which he used for an office, and out of nowhere came a German Ju-88 bomber. The German made a run across the middle of the 64th camp area.

I went looking for a hole to jump in. I couldn't find a single slit trench in the headquarters area. Mears was always yelling "Dig a slit trench." There wasn't one, I repeat, in his area. I just laid on my belly and said a few prayers.

The anti-aircraft (AA) guns did not open as we had a plane in the area being tested by Lieutenant Ottaway of Rome, New York. He had been shot up and this was his first day back and he was trying out his legs.

The Ju-88 came on course and dropped what I think were 1,000 pounders. Thank God he was a lousy pilot, or his navigator did not know his business. He missed the camp.

The makeshift tower we had tried to contact Lieutenant Ottaway, but he had his radio off. After our friend dropped his load and started to leave, the AA opened up and Ottaway turned on his radio. He received his instructions and chased the Ju but never did catch him.

Hilby officially took command on this date.

Sunday, November 22. Church services were held by Chaplain Louge in the officers mess tent. Another load of mail came in this afternoon. The men were happy.

Tuesday, November 24. We had been wondering what we would have to eat on our first Thanksgiving overseas. There had been rumors we would have turkey but that was asking too much.

Well, around noon a C-47 made its approach for a landing with a few P-40s as escorts. On board were turkeys for the gang. Colonel Mears and a few of the pilots escorted the transport from Cairo. We were given to understand that the turkeys were for some contractors working in the Suez. They were taken from them for our group.

Our pilots are out on patrol missions all day. There were rumors the Jerries were going to hit us around Thanksgiving Day for morale purposes.

Wednesday, November 25. Mears tried out a captured ME-109. A B-25 brought in another load of mail and even packages. This is the first time we have had packages since the El Alamein break through. A report came through intelligence that 12 Ju-88 bombers were on the way towards our field.

We put up quite a few planes to meet this thrust, but the report proved false. "No luck," to quote the boys returning from the mission.

The cooks are busy this afternoon preparing the turkeys for tomorrow.

Thursday, November 26, Thanksgiving Day. Chaplain Louge held church services and we had a real meal. This was the first fresh meat we have had since we left the States. We had an alert during the meal, but the boys took it in stride. We had a lot of alerts on this field.

We had the pleasure of the company of Leland Stowe, the famous correspondent, for this wonderful dinner.

He had just come in from Moscow. He said the fast trip to the Western Desert to have Thanksgiving dinner with a bunch of Yanks was worth it. Mr. Stowe was quite interested in the two Italian soldiers and filed a story with his newspaper.

Friday, November 27. More mail and we have a visitor, Captain Parkinson of No. 2 Squadron, South African Air Force. He was on his way back to his squadron, having escaped from the Germans. He told some good stories. Spent the night in my tent.

Sunday, November 29. A Party moves to new airfield at 9:00 am. Our field was bogged in with mud. No flying out of this field on account of mud.

Dining on a bunch of turkeys destined for some contractors this Thanksgiving in Martuba, Libya.

Beer was always hard to come by.

Monday, November 30. Lots of mail and no action.

Tuesday, December 1. Jerry overhead tonight dropping flares and bombs. I spent a good part of the night in the slit trench. Bombs land in rear of our camp.

Wednesday, December 2. Jerry around this morning with flares and bombs at 3:00 am. There were reports that a British Hurricane pilot shot down a Ju-88 over the field. We received a B-25 load of beer from Cairo today. This made us all happy as we have received very little beer.

Thursday, December 3. Camp a sea of mud today as we have had a lot of rain. I went to the British DID (Daily Issuing Depot). This is the spot we pick up our daily rations. They have not been very good; I was trying to see if they could give us better rations. I found they were doing the best they could. I had a talk with the group commander about making some contact

These are the articles Leland Stowe wrote about the 57th Fighter Group:

Two Lucky Italians Work and EAT with Americans
Globe Exclusive
By Leland Stowe
Special Cable to the *Boston Globe*
(Copyright 1942 by the *Boston Globe* and *Chicago Daily News*)

WITH THE MOST ADVANCED AMERICAN FIGHTER SQUADRONS IN CYRENAICA, Nov 27 (Delayed)—The two luckiest Italians in all North Africa are two deserters who were rounded up at an oasis near here by men of the American Black Scorpion squadron's ground crew and have been "inducted" into the outfit's staff on condition of good behavior.

As soon as they had one full meal of routine grub, the Italians decided that this was as close to earthly paradise as anything they had seen in the last five years of their lives and have been working like slaves to please everybody on the premises ever since.

Mess officer Capt. James Lynch, who hails from Boston, says: "Those workers work all the time. They sure hop around. Guess they're scared we might send them back to prison camp."

It looks like Bruno and Roberto may be with the Black Scorpions mess for the duration.

TURKEYS ACCORDED U.S. FLIERS' ESCORT FOR FEAST IN LIBYA
Colonel took No Chances in Preparing Thanksgiving for Yank Fighter Squadron
By Leland Stowe
Special Cable to *Buffalo Evening News* and *Chicago Daily News*

WITH ADVANCED U.S. FIGHTER SQUADRONS, Cyrenaica, Nov 26 (Delayed)—Only a hop, skip and jump from Tripolitania, hundreds of members of the American Air Force, in the rock-strewn wastelands of this section of Libya, celebrated Thanksgiving today with "operations as usual," but also with real roast turkey—and was it good!

It was well worth the fast trip from Moscow to the Western Desert to cut in on a Thanksgiving feast with a big crowd of fighting Yanks and likewise to help devour some very unique birds—the first turkeys I have ever heard of which were honored with fighter escort on their final lap to the oven and table.

More than 70 gobblers, totaling some 900 pounds in weight were flown up from Cairo two days ago, tagged for these forward squadrons, but a critical situation developed.

The gobblers were scheduled to be sent on by truck from a rear base several hundred miles back of here and Lieut. Col. Frank Mears discovered that it would take more than 30 hours to get them up by lorry.

"I wasn't going to take any chance on those birds getting spoiled. It would have been terrible for the boys' morale," the colonel said.

So, the colonel sent a bomber back to the edge of Egypt, accompanied by two fighters and the honorable gobblers came flying in, escorted by a fighter on either side. At the present moment, it is not turkeys, but your correspondent and hundreds of Yankee airmen who are stuffed.

In my existing condition, let me testify that Capt. James Lynch of Boston, mess officer of the Black Scorpions Squadron, and his cooking staff carried out their operation magnificently.

with the bomber outfit (Americans) on a nearby field about using one of their courier planes to bring in some American food from Cairo. We had heard they were bringing in American food for their group and our boys were complaining about the same old rations we were drawing from the British. I got nowhere with him. He thought the food was good enough. I did not agree with him but what can a captain do with a colonel?

Friday, December 4. Camp was still a sea of mud. Lots of rain during last night. I visited a small village called Giovani-Bert. A group of buildings in this small town were all painted with white and red crosses. The natives stated the Germans used this area for their headquarters.

Jerry was overhead again tonight about 11:30 with flares and bombs. The slit trenches were in use by all. Laying in the mud for quite a while was not the most ideal condition. We were very lucky the bombs fell over the hill in the rear of camp.

Saturday, December 5. Still raining. We were trying to get out of this camp, but the field is in poor condition and the planes cannot take off.

We were having lots of troubles with flat tires on all jeeps and trucks. The Jerries drop spikes in their raids. These spikes are three pronged and always have a sharp point sticking up. When they get in a tire, they really do a job on it.

This is the amount of food diverted from the contractors to the 57th Fighter Group for our Thanksgiving celebration, 1942:

345	Pounds of Turkey
30	Pounds of De-hydrated Potatoes
120	Pounds of Frozen Corn
45	Gallons of Coffee
12	Gallons of Gravy
15	Gallons Fruit Salad
800	Hot biscuits
5	Gallons of Jam
15	Pounds of fresh butter
24	Cans of Evaporated Milk
15	Pounds of sugar

We feed about 300 enlisted men and officers.

We were told that the turkeys we ate were assigned from the States for a construction company doing some work in the Suez Canal. Someone in Cairo Command had the food sent to the 57th Fighter Group instead.

I believe these spikes were supposed to be dropped on the airfield to blow plane tires on take-off or landing. Most of them were found in the camp area. No planes were bothered by these spikes.

Sunday, December 6. The rain is gone and the sun is out this morning. Part of B Party moves out. Planes get off late in afternoon for forward field called Belandau.

Tuesday, December 8. We all clear out of this field called Martuba. We were glad to leave. Between the rain, mud, spikes and bombs, this field will not be missed.

Spent the night on the road near a spot called De Martino. It was a cold, rainy night spent sleeping in the open.

Wednesday, December 9. Off at 7:30 this morning. We passed along the outskirts of Benghazi, the capital of Cyrenaica. By late afternoon we found a nice spot to put up for the night. It was near an airfield the British used.

We decided to move on to be away from any activity that might take place during the night. It was a good decision as the Jerries bombed the airfield heavily that night. We were in a good position to see a show of fireworks. The British expression would be "a bloody good show."

The little we saw of Benghazi had evidence of some fierce fighting and bombing. This town really took a pasting.

CHAPTER 10

Belandau, Libya

Thursday, December 10. Off this morning for Belandau. We arrived at 3:30 pm. We are back in the desert again. Another dustbowl. On the way to this field, we watched South African sappers clear some minefields. These fellows deserve all the credit you can give them for this dangerous job. The Germans were not stingy when it came to mines.

Being away from the planes for a few days, we had a lot of news to catch up on. The boys had been out on lots of missions. On one show they bagged five Jerries.

Captain George D. Mobbs of Little Rock, Arkansas, was shot up and in the hospital. There was lots of mail at this field for us. This always gives the boys a lift.

Some of our old friends are on this field: the South Africans of No. 2 Squadron. This is the squadron our boys worked with when they came down from Palestine to Egypt in September.

They had a monkey in the squadron as a mascot by the name of Jocko. He was a bright animal and was always into something. I remember him at one field when I was paying the boys, he kept trying to steal the bills from my car.

The commanding officer of the squadron told me of an experience he had had with Jocko one night in the club tent. He had been quite a pest on several occasions this night and the CO picked him up and tossed him out the door of the tent.

This Jocko did not like this and, a short time later, climbed up on the outside of the tent. He took position near the top opening, which was over the area where the boys were busy drinking, and took his revenge for being thrown out of the tent by pissing all over quite a few of the boys around the bar.

Captain George Mobbs was shot up and ended up in the hospital. (57th Fighter Group website)

Friday, December 11. For the first time since we came overseas, we had pancakes for breakfast this morning. Another good experience today, we received our November pay.

Saturday, December 12. We had been alerted that there were enemy planes in the air over us. We were closed down for flying today as the weather was bad with a very low ceiling.

We could hear the planes and watch the British anti-aircraft (AA) units which were on our field and had been on the alert all day. In the middle of the afternoon, we had quite a sight when a Ju-88 came out of the clouds and leveled off over our

---

Some reporting on the Black Scorpions and their exploits in the desert:

U.S. FLIERS IN LIBYA BAG 50 PLANES
Three Squadrons set up Desert Bases and take the Offensive
By the Associated Press
    At the most Advanced United Air Base in Libya, Dec 8 (Delayed)—Three United States fighter squadrons today celebrated their installation in this base behind the British front in the Libyan Desert by raising their collective total of enemy planes destroyed to 50.
    Fighter pilots of the Black Scorpions, Fighting Cock and Penguin Squadrons took the offensive in their first operational flight from this base and downed seven Messerschmitt 109s.
    This came shortly after Operations Officer, Major Harry A. French of Earl, Ark, with a jeep and truck convoy, completed a 350-mile trek across the desert and began clearing runways for the planes, with the front-line British Infantry men aiding.
    The planes came several hours after the jeeps and landed while men still were dynamiting rocks out of the runways.

Four Pilots Victorious
    Four pilots were credited with the first victories scored from the new base.
    Lieutenant Steven Merena of Anosnia, Conn, of the Black Scorpions, shot down two Messerschmitts, making his total victories three.
    Lieutenant George E. Mobbs, of Little Rock, Ark, also a Black Scorpion, got two before returning safely to base with dozens of holes in his plane.
    Lieutenant William Barnes, New York City, a Black Scorpion, got one.
    Lieutenant Arnold D Jaqua, South Bend, Ind, of the Fighting Cocks, downed two Messerschmitts in a dogfight over enemy territory.

Water Rationed
    Pilots flying fighter-bombers and fighters were rationed a quart of water a day, for drinking and washing and they slept in their flying outfits because their camp equipment had not caught up with the speedy advance party.
    Three trucks of this party drove through an enemy minefield and didn't know it until a British convoy behind lost three of its vehicles.
    Units of famed British regiments helped make runways.
    The Americans got their first dose of life in foxholes and slit trenches when enemy planes flew over to investigate the new base.

area with two British Spitfires right on its tail. All the AA guns on the field opened up. This really was the most exciting afternoon we had had for a long time.

A short time later, the Ju-88 tumbled through the clouds and crashed about two miles from our area. When we arrived at the scene, the plane was burning. Two Germans of the four-man crew burned up inside of the plane wreckage. There was nothing we could do as you could not get any firefighting equipment into the spot where the plane went down.

One dead member was outside the plane, and one had been taken to the nearby British hospital. He died shortly after arriving.

Sunday, December 13. Boys ran a shuttle service all day bombing the areas and roads of the retreating Jerries. Five-hundred-pound bombs were used all day. All boys back safe. The group destroyed four ME-109s. We received the first rumor today Italy will give up within a few months.

Monday, December 14. Very good this morning, clear skies and the boys are out again west of Agheila dropping 500 pounders on the retreating Jerries.

Tuesday, December 15. Boys out this morning escorting bombers. This is the first escort mission they have had in quite a few weeks. The bombers were dropping bombs on German trucks west of Agheila.

A British bomber landed on our field with a dead rear gunner. We buried him just off the runway.

Wednesday, December 16. Boys all off early this morning with 500 pounders for our retreating friends. Off again at 1:00 pm escorting bombers. In a repeat of yesterday, a South African bomber crew in an A-20 lands at the field with a dead bombardier. The medical boys bury him just off the runway.

What a surprise this afternoon. We received a shipment of bacon, pork, and ham. This is the first meat other than canned stuff we have had for some time. I believe it came in at Benghazi. We heard the port had been opened up for supplies and traffic.

Thursday, December 17. Boys spent most of the day out on patrol duty, little or no action reported. General Brereton paid a visit to the area. We had some good meals today due to the fact we received meat yesterday.

Friday, December 18. A quiet day other than a few patrols. We lost 600 gallons of gasoline in a fire near our main gasoline supply area.

Saturday–Sunday, December 19–20. Very quiet days. No flying so we had a chance for a few softball games. The U.S. Post Office in Cairo sent a member of their staff here to write money orders. He arrived today (Sunday). This was a very good service as the boys had no place to spend their money and it gave us a chance to send some money home.

Colonel Art Salisbury took over command of the 57th on December 23, 1942. (57th Fighter Group website)

Monday, December 21. No flying today. The sand blows and makes for a miserable feeling. It gets in your eyes, your nose, your clothes, and your food.

One of the British anti-aircraft officers spent some time with us this evening. I found these fellows very interesting. They have been in the desert for a few years. They have some real experiences to talk about.

We have a full moon this evening and we don't like it. These are the nights the Germans like to send a few bombers and spoil the evening.

We had no visitors and a good night's sleep.

Tuesday, December 22. Still no flying as the Germans were out of reach of our planes. New airstrips are being prepared up ahead. A C-47 arrives with some beer; first we have had for many days. The Black Scorpion softball team defeats the 57th Group team 12 to 7.

Wednesday, December 23. The sand blows like hell today. We had a meeting with all the officers and enlisted men in a big tent which we use for a hospital.

At the meeting, the group commander, who was the CO of the 64th Squadron before going overseas, Col. Frank Mears, made his farewell speech and turned the command of the 57th Fighter Group over to a real fighter pilot and squadron commander, Col. Art Salisbury.

We had another surprise this afternoon when a load of real American rations arrived, including candy and cigarettes. Nine enlisted men and officers go to Cairo on leave.

This letter was received from a British sergeant who commanded a 40-mm anti-aircraft gun in our camp area:

Dear Sir,

On behalf of the NCOs and men of this troop, I am penning a few lines to say how greatly appreciative we are of the kindness and generosity which has been extended to us in connection with larder supplies for Christmas.

Without your assistance and cooperation, the Festive Season would have been a most cheerless and joyless affair. But through your good offices, we look forward to a happy time.

To all the personnel in the Squadron, we send our best wishes for a Merry X-mas and the hope that X-mas 1943 will see us re-united with our dear ones.

Sincerely,
(Sgt) Norman L. G. Brown

We shared some of our rations and candy and cigarettes with some British anti-aircraft boys who manned the guns around our field. It sure made them happy.

Thursday, December 24. Still no flying. We looked for some turkey or chicken for our Christmas dinner, but it never arrived. Father Louge, the group chaplain, holds a midnight mass in the desert and it was well attended. He had us all singing Christmas carols.

Always on the move.

Friday, December 25, Christmas Day. Our first overseas. It was just another day, and we had some canned frankfurters instead of turkey or chicken. We had some rain this evening. We had a Christmas card a print shop in Alexandria made up for us.

Saturday, December 26. Still no flying. It rained hard this morning. We received, believe it or not, enough Birdseye frozen steaks this morning by C-47 to have steaks for supper. A real treat. This is the first steak we have had since we left the States.

Sunday, December 27. Our landing strip was in poor condition this morning, but the pilot of a C-47 made a good landing and produced a lot of mail for the gang.

The young men who fly these planes do an outstanding job during the push. They fly the mail, men, bombs, food, gasoline, or anything needed to win this crazy war. The C-47 pilots spent the night with us.

Monday, December 28. Up early this morning. The C-47 boys had to get back to their base for another important assignment. The field was really muddy, but the C-47 got off OK.

We were inspected by General Frank M. Andrews and his staff. I remember General Andrews asking me why there wasn't any meat on the menu we had pinned on the pole of the mess tent. I told him we had very little meat since we had been in the Western Desert. He told one of his staff to see that we had more meat.

This officer wrote it down in his little book, but the menus were the same for many months after the general's visit.

General Andrews was killed in Iceland on May 10, 1943, in a plane crash.

Tuesday–Wednesday, December 29–30. Lots of softball games on these two days. Lots of mail. We are glad as we are getting ready to move. When we are on the move, it takes a while for the mail to reach us at a new field.

Thursday, December 31. The last day of 1942. Drove out of Belindah. We have our lunch, which is usually C-rations, in a spot called Agedabia (try to find this place on a map), moved on and picked a spot outside Alageligh to camp.

This was a German stronghold for some time. It showed sign of lots of action. Before stopping, I remember seeing the arms, legs, and skull of a human. Someone had placed them in position along the road.

We found the area had been mined and we were lucky. Only one truck of the 66th Squadron hit a mine, which blew off its rear wheel.

It was damp and wet when we set up for the night.

After supper, we sat around and talked. We all thought it was a hell of a place to be in on the night before New Year's. We had saved a bottle of rye whiskey for a little celebration to welcome in the New Year.

In the group were: Capt. Gerald Krosnick of New Haven, Connecticut, our squadron surgeon; Capt. Henry Mack of St Petersburgh, Florida, the squadron supply officer; Capt. Carl Nelson of Los Angeles, California, the squadron intelligence officer; Major Gilbert T. Mullens of Pagosa, Colorado, pilot and flight commander; and Capt. Peter Mitchell of Nyssa, Oregon (population about twelve hundred in those days and Pete always took a kidding about this small town).

About 9:00 pm we decided to have our little celebration. Along with the whiskey, we had a can of issued juice, a mixture of orange and grapefruit juice. We made toasts and drank to the success of the campaign ahead. We all turned in within the next hour.

A card was made up by the author and presented to all the members of the Black Scorpion Squadron that passed over or under this Arch during the push from El Alamein to Cape Bone.

Marble Arch was on the coast road in Libya. It was on the line that separated Cyrenaica and Tripolitania.

Marble Arch marked the border between Tripolitania and Cyrenaica in Libya.

I'm handing out cards signifying we had passed under the Marble Arch in Libya.

We did not get much sleep as there was a lot of bombing and anti-aircraft fire not too far ahead of us. The sky was lit up like the Fourth of July back home.

This action lasted for a few hours. This closed out 1942 in a wide-open place in the Western Desert.

Friday, January 1, 1943. Here it is, a New Year's Day and we are on the move this morning. We crossed into Tripolitania. Entering this area, we left behind half of Libya, which was known as Cyrenaica. As we leave this part of Libya, we pass under a giant Marble Arch that stands 100 feet high.

We put up for the night in a spot they called Nufila. One of our trucks is missing from the convoy. All we can think is they took a wrong turn.

Father Louge, our Chaplain, conducted religious services at 6:00 pm.

Saturday, January 2. Up early. The convoy moved out at 7:45. Captains Henry Mack and Peter Mitchell start out on a hunt for our missing truck. The roads are very dusty, and the wind blows extra hard today. These roads were nothing more than a track through the desert selected by the British engineers and marked out with empty gas cans.

We moved the convoy over the dusty desert road, not making much time due to ruts and blowing sand. We put up for the night in the middle of nowhere at 5:00 pm.

We are not far from the so-called new field where we were supposed to set up. Mack and Mitchell return to the convoy without finding the truck. All I could think was they went too far forward and some Jerries captured them.

Sunday, January 3. This is my 37th birthday. No celebrations planned. The convoy moved out at 8:30 am. We only went a few miles before we received orders to standby for a move into a spot being prepared for us. We could not move if we had to as a real sandstorm was in progress.

We set up camp. It was hard to believe you could not drive a steel tent stake into the ground without it bending. We were in an area where the ground was hard. We lined the trucks and jeeps up and tied the tent ropes to the wheels. This was the only way we could get the tents up. We had to have cover as the sand was blowing so hard it cut your hands and face if you spent much time facing it.

We received a report from the rear field that Private Smith, one of the medical drivers, was killed when a plane on take-off ran into our ambulance. I believe this was our first death of an enlisted man since we left the States.

Monday, January 4. We were still standing by in the sandstorm, awaiting orders to move to the new landing ground. We were told it would be ready for us tomorrow if the sand lets up. The tents are taking a beating in this storm due to the fact we could not get them down close to the ground.

CHAPTER II

Harajet, Libya

Tuesday, January 5. Moved out to the new landing ground at 1:30 pm. It was called Harajet. The first order of business was to get the camp set up and then be ready to receive planes from the rear base in a few days.

Just after we laid out the camp, we had a raid of German ME-109s bombing and strafing the field.

There was no place to go. We laid on the ground and said our prayers. The good Lord must have been watching over the Black Scorpion boys. When the raid was over, we were all safe with the help of the terrific British anti-aircraft action. Despite the bombs dropped in the area, we were all safe.

Many of the British Royal Engineers working on the field were killed or wounded. This was our first real air raid, and the boys took it very well.

We spent the rest of the day digging slit trenches and setting up the tents. This was a lonely spot out in the Libyan desert.

Wednesday, January 6. We had our first breakfast at Harajet. Before we finished, Jerry was overhead with another air raid.

The planes came in so low that you could see the pilots in the cockpits. The slit trenches came in handy this morning.

Hot meals always boosted morale.

Spent a little time after the raid talking with the British anti-aircraft boys. They were in high spirits and seemed to enjoy the idea they were throwing up lots of steel at the Jerries.

We had another raid shortly after lunch. Another problem this afternoon is our water supply is getting low. The nearest water point is 400 miles away. We had been on the road for almost five days. There are no water points in the desert.

Later in the day, we received water by air. A big British transport plane brought us water in two-gallon cans. It was a long process pouring this water from the cans into our British-issued water bowsers. We had two of these bowsers, each with a capacity of 350 gallons.

It was a welcome sight to see the boys pouring this water. I remember seeing these gallon cans piled up at British depot not far from our first camp in Egypt. Little did I think we would be using them this far from our spot in Egypt.

We had no more problems with water as the planes made a regular run to us each day.

Thursday, January 7. Just as we finished breakfast this morning, the Jerries were back with their bombs and strafing. I was caught talking with our chaplain, Father Louge, when the raid started. Father started for a slit trench and so did I. We did not make it. A 100-lb bomb landed between us as we hit the ground. It was closer to Father Logue than me and I figured he got it.

But when the smoke cleared, I found him OK. His panel truck, which was also his chapel, received some damage, such as a hole in the gas tank and a blown-out tire.

Jerry paid us four visits today, strafing and bombing. Peter Mitchell, our armament officer, was caught during one of the raids just as he was changing his clothes. Pete landed in the slit trench in his birthday suit. I had just lathered up for a shave when they came over and had to move fast into the trench, lather and all. The steel helmets came in handy as we were in more danger from the falling fragments of the British anti-aircraft shells than from the German bombs and bullets.

We had a busy day. We had a British Spitfire pilot bail out of his plane after being shot up. He walked into our area and spent the night with us. We also had a South African pilot, who had been separated from his unit, spend the night with us.

Friday, January 8. This is the first day in three that we have not had a raid. We had a screen of British Spitfires over the area all day. This kept the Jerries away from us.

Some of the boys were a little jittery and Father Louge gave them a little talk. One of the squadrons in our group served one of their meals from a slit trench.

This afternoon, in the middle of this excitement, we received a lot of mail and our pay. We still flew the American flag in front of our orderly room, and we had a very important visitor drop his plane (a captured German Fieseler Storch) atop our side of the field: Sir Arthur Coningham who commanded the Desert Air Force. He thought he was dropping in at the group headquarters.

All the members of the 64th Fighter Squadron had similar experiences with diving into slit trenches as explained here. The exploits of the company censors are also covered.

Hub Censor, New Haven Surgeon Provide Laughs
By George Tucker

WITH AN AMERICAN FIGHTER GROUP IN THE LIBYAN DESERT, Jan 15 (Delayed)(AP)—Captain Gerald Crosnick, flight surgeon of New Haven, Conn., knows now that there is only a chalk-line difference between make-believe and reality.

REALLY HAPPENED
While dressing this morning, he stepped out of a tent and posed in a foxhole clad only in white underwear while a friend photographed him.

"I'll send this home just to show the folks how we drop everything when the Jerries come" Crosnick was saying.

Before he had time to get back in the tent to get his clothes, anti-aircraft guns opened up all over the desert and he had to leap back into a trench still wearing his white drawers.

The only difference this time was that he grabbed a steel helmet as he sailed past the door.

After the raid I walked into a big tent off to one side and found a familiar figure sleeping on a blanket in the sand, it was First Lieutenant William N. Pace of Guthrie, KY, who went through a harrowing experience with me off that Gold Coast when our plane ran into a storm and was blown 100 mile out to sea.

WARE MAN IN A NARROW ESCAPE
On that occasion, Pace, First Lieutenant Charles F. Hale of Ware, Mass,. and I were trying to get to Khartoum, and we spent more than four hours in a big ship which shuddered like a maple leaf and swung in blind circles trying to climb out of a storm. Visibility was zero.

We finally were caught in an icy down pull and fell 5,000 feet. We pulled out of it only 500 feet about the ocean and the forces of the pull-out was so great that you could feel the blood drain away from the head.

When it was over Pace let out a low whistle and said, "I hate to admit it, but I was worried. I never thought we'd get out of it."

Neither did I, but we did and here we were weeks later, thousands of miles away in the Western Desert. Pace is a fighter pilot and was the second man on the ground when the American group came in.

He said Hale had suffered appendicitis four nights previously but was in good condition.

Later we walked over to the tent where Captain Carl Nelson of Los Angeles and Captain James Lynch of Boston were busy censoring letters.

"It's a good thing I'm not sensitive," Lynch said. "The boys have started taking cracks at the censors (in letters) to their sweethearts. Listen to this: 'Sweetheart there used to be only two of us, but now there's a third party in our lives.'"

Then in brackets were the words, "Hello, Nosey."

Another lad had enclosed two Egyptian banknotes worth 45 cents in his letter and attached a note to them saying, "Put it back, Censor."

Air Vice-Marshal Coningham's captured German Fieseler Storch. (57th Fighter Group website)

He spent some time with a few of us and inquired as to how things were going. We told him how we were bothered by so many raids. He suggested some gazelle hunting. I offered to drive him to headquarters but he preferred to fly the mile across the landing field.

Saturday, January 9. We had a visit this morning from George Tucker of *AP News*. During his visit, we had a raid. He got quite a thrill by joining the boys in a slit trench and filed a story which was later in the *Boston Post*.

The folks back home were never told by me of any bombings; this gave them something to worry about.

I received a report our planes will be in tomorrow. We have been separated from the air echelon of the squadron since December 31. It will be good to have the pilots with us. I know they will be glad to be in the forward position so they can do some flying again.

Sunday, January 10. Church services were held with an orderly room used as the altar area. Our pilots came in this afternoon, and it was sort of a reunion as it was always quiet when we were separated from the planes and pilots.

Monday, January 11. Up early this morning and back on my old job to wake up the pilots for early missions. They flew five different missions today, which included three fighter sweeps over the retreating Jerries, one reconnaissance (we called them recce) and one interception mission. All in all, this was one of our busier days.

Captain Rocky Byrne of St. Louis, Missouri, had his plane shot up but made it back to the field OK. Lieutenant Bill Beck of Nashville, Tennessee, shot down an ME-109. Captain Jerry Brandon of Wayzata, Minnesota, landed in the desert out of gas and walked 10 miles before he was picked up.

Henry Mack and I took a trip this afternoon and had quite an experience. We had been told there was a water hole not too far from the camp. We were always looking for water. As we approached the area in question, we found a British air stores park, but no water.

On our way out of the area, we noticed a few new graves and decided to look the area over. Just as we left our jeep, a mine exploded. It was an anti-personnel mine which explodes at about four to five feet off the ground. This one must have been defective, as it went off about twenty-five feet in the air. We hit the ground quick and received only a good scare.

We quickly moved out of this area, which was supposed to have water, and returned to the camp.

The club was a busy place tonight with the boys telling various stories about their day in the air.

Tuesday, January 12. Jerry flew over this morning and dropped a few bombs in the camp area and in the plane parking area. No one was hurt but we lost a truck. A few planes were damaged. Jerry overhead this afternoon but dropped no bombs. The 8th Fighter Wing, where my buddy Major Frank Bechelder of my hometown of Medford was stationed, recorded the raids on our field as a blitz.

The wing also supplied this following information. On enemy airfields ahead of us, the following planes were reported: Bir Dufan, 88 German aircraft, including 20 Stukas, and 28 Italian; at Tauorga, 40 planes (Italian), and 25 at Crispi (Italian). In Tripoli, at Castel Benito airport, 120 Italian planes of which 60 are transports.

More information from the log of the 8th Fighter Wing. With the information about the aircraft ahead of us, the wing plans to send light bombers over Bir Dufan five times to take care of these 88 German aircraft. Tauorga, where there are 40 aircraft, they have decided to ground strafe twice.

The battle for Tripoli is in the making. The fall of this important stronghold is expected to happen in about a week after this push starts.

It was interesting to note in the log regarding a remark that General Montgomery had made to his officers. "After the fall of Tripoli, we may wait as long as two months for the next push and I will not be hurried by the powers that be."

Wednesday, January 13. We woke this morning with the sand blowing and a real storm. No planes could get off the ground. This, of course, gave the Jerries a break.

The traveling canteen made it to the field, and we were able to buy a few items.

Thursday, January 14. The storm is over and the boys were in the air this morning. Our boys had the pleasure of escorting the light bombers for a raid on Bir Dufan. From the reports of the boys and the log of the 8th Fighter Wing, they did a job on this enemy field.

The boys had a few fights with ME-109s and Macchi 202s. All returned safe except for a few holes in the planes.

They were also out on an interceptor patrol for a short time but were recalled. The afternoon mission was another bomber escort job. The mission was to attack motor transport (MT) in the Gheddia area. A few dogfights but no losses on either side. We had a few alerts in the area but the enemy never did show over the field.

Friday, January 15. The battle for Tripoli was on this morning. The boys were off this morning on protective patrols over the advancing New Zealanders. They also bombed motor transport on the Misrata–Tauoriga–Churgia road with good results.

P-40 out in the blue. The "blue" referred to the skies over the Western Desert. This is a P-40F powered by a Rolls-Royce Merlin. (57th Fighter Group website)

General Brereton landed at our field with an escort of four P-40s.

On the late afternoon show, we put up 12 aircraft. Eight planes failed to return. This put the squadron in a gloomy mood. We had never had this kind of a loss.

Before the night was over, we had all our boys back. The eight planes landed in various spots in the desert and the pilots all came in before the night was over. Some had a long walk. Others were picked up by the British front-line troops.

It was a happy night after a sad afternoon. There were lots of stories told by the boys as to how they landed their P-40s and made it back to the squadron.

One of the pilots, Lieutenant Abbot, had to make a belly landing on the field due to the fact he had been shot in the finger and could not let down his landing gear.

Saturday, January 16. Missions are on tap this morning. We had a bad accident when Lt. Richard Maloney of Kansas City, Missouri, and Lt. Raymond Palermo of Boston, Massachusetts, collided in midair on the way to the assigned target for this morning. Both planes burst into flames and only one parachute was seen to open. Later in the day, Maloney made it back to the squadron. He was picked up by a British truck. He was in good shape, but it looks like Palermo did not get out of his plane.

It was a busy day with many missions flown. The reports from the returning pilots were the Jerries were running.

Sunday, January 17. Although a Sunday, just another day in the desert with the boys on many missions with wing bombs.

They had many good targets of tanks and trucks along the road of retreat of the Jerries.

The enemy still had lots of aircraft on some forward bases. We received a report that Castel Benito Airfield had 194 planes. Al-Asabaa airfield had 73 aircraft. Mellaha Airfield had 74 aircraft. Finally, Bir el Ghanem had 21 aircraft.

You can be sure that these airfields will be given some attention during the night with a few bomber missions. Our A Party moves out this afternoon to Bir Dufan, also known as Darragh.

All reports coming in show the Jerries are moving out all along the front.

Monday, January 18. Boys were out all day dropping bombs on the retreating enemy. Lieutenant Robert A. Barnum of Lake City, Michigan, forced to land his plane in the desert, but he was picked up and returned to the squadron in good shape.

With the Jerries retreating, they have not sent any planes over us at night for a week or so. We had open-air movies in the desert tonight. All was peaceful until we were buzzed by a plane that came out of nowhere. We never did find out who he was.

Many of the boys received scratches and bruises when we made a mad dash for cover or foxholes. I received a bad gash on my wrist when I fell off the front of the jeep I sat on watching the movies.

Tuesday, January 19. Woke the boys up early this morning, but the missions were called off. This was a big day for all. A good old C-47 came in with a load of mail and packages.

Report received that A Party was set up on the forward base and was ready to receive planes.

Planes took off at 4:00 pm for the new field. They usually go out on a mission and return to the forward field, but the enemy targets were out of range for our fighter planes today.

The Eighth Army News *from Monday, January 18, 1943, reported on the advance on Tripoli the Black Scorpions supported, which forced them to regularly move bases as the Germans retreated.*

BEST SINCE ALAMEIN

Hurried enemy withdrawal into more difficult country and the speedy forward move by air transport of a fighter wing have enabled our desert air forces to make successful attacks on enemy concentrations such as have not been seen since Alamein.

On the night 16/17 January our light bombers attacked MT on the roads Zliten–Misurata Gioda while our medium bombers attacked the Homs and Castel Verde area, about thirty miles from Tripoli.

Yesterday's activity began when fighter-bomber formations strafed aircraft on Bir Dufan and MT in the neighborhood. Enemy tanks were also attacked.

By midday, however, the enemy had evacuated Bir Dufan and the air effort switched to enemy MT columns congested in defiles near Beni Ulid and northeast to the Tarhuna road.

Forced to evacuate his forward landing grounds, the enemy made only one offensive shot—in the Sedad area.

Last night and well into this morning our night fighters carried on non-stop attacks on the enemy and started no fewer that 40 fires amongst his MT on roads in the Tarhuna area.

LATE NEWS

A strong raid was made by our bombers on Castel Benito Airfield aerodrome last night. Light, medium, and heavy bombers took part. Full details are not yet to hand.

You do what you have to do to keep clean.

Wednesday, January 20. We moved to the new field to join up with A Party. This was a dusty ride across the desert. We moved though all kinds of minefields and blown-out roads as we headed towards the coast.

We have no prescribed area to put up for the night. What we do is pick some spot that is away from a village or airfield. We try to put up one hour before dark so we can feed the men and have the field ranges out before dark.

We found a post about twelve miles from Taraza. We were all pretty dirty from this wild ride over the desert road. We could not take a bath as we did not have much water. We limited men to a helmet full of water to take care of their shaving and bath.

CHAPTER 12

Bir Durfan, Libya

Thursday, January 21. Up early this morning. We broke our temporary camp and had breakfast. We were out on the road at 8:00 am. This was the dustiest of all the roads we had traveled so far. Lots of the desert roads were made up of a real hard surface. With the constant use of these roads by tanks, trucks, and jeeps, the surface was ground into two or three inches of dust. It is hard to take.

We pushed through this sea of dust and arrive at the new airfield at 3:00 pm. This was called Darragh, Libya. This was a busy field with all kinds of aircraft. They were ready to give Jerry the business in his retreat beyond Tripoli.

The Germans used these machines to destroy runways they abandoned.

Boys were out today, still pounding the retreating Germans. One report that came in was the Germans had plowed up the runways. The Germans carried this out many times when they left a field. Many times, the poor rear guard was left behind all alone with just a plow. He did not live long after the Germans moved out as he was a prime target for our boys on reconnaissance.

Friday, January 22. Our planes were in the air all day giving the retreating Germans a real pounding. Our area was a dust bowl. It is expected Tripoli will fall within the next 24 hours.

Saturday, January 23. Tripoli fell at 5:01 am this morning. General Brereton and Air Vice-Marshal Coningham arrived at our field. Captain Richard E. Ryan of Worcester, Massachusetts, Lt. William J. Mount of Kansas City, Missouri, and Lt. Gerald A. Brandon of Wayzata, Minnesota, are decorated with the Distinguished Flying Cross.

The big problem for the day was our water supply was running very low.

Sunday, January 24. Boys were off before dawn with a new type of mission. They were to work over some boats off the coast. All returned safe.

Monday, January 25. Boys have gone out in the desert to shoot some gazelle, a small and graceful animal with lots of speed. This animal is found in the desert and some of the boys claim they have clocked them from their jeeps running up to 45 miles per hour. The boys brought in a good lot. We planned to eat them tomorrow.

Tuesday, January 26. Boys were cutting up the gazelles. They were good eating. A rare thing happened today. A C-47 came in with some good American food.

Wednesday, January 27. This was a rough day for all. No flying. A real sandstorm in progress with plenty of rain, a thing which we don't often see. At least the rain held the sand down for a while.

A wrecked Italian Piaggio P.108 heavy bomber.

Thursday, January 28. For the next several days there was no flying due to sandstorms and the lack of targets. With the fall of Tripoli, we stand pat for a while.

With the lull in the war, we get a chance to roam around the countryside. We saw some wrecks of airplanes such as German Stukas, ME-109s, and transports.

This is the work of our boys and the fighter and bomber units assigned to the British Eighth Army.

Some of the brass came up with the idea our boys should have some infantry drill. This idea was not received too well but the drill went on for a few days. Then the idea seemed to fade away.

We had a chance to play some softball during this time.

Thursday, February 4. Our commanding officer, Major Buck Bilby of Skidmore, Missouri, along with the COs of the group and 65th and 66th Squadrons, takes off this morning for Tripoli for a meeting with Sir Winston Churchill. They took part in the celebration of the capture of Tripoli. The capture of this important port will be a great asset in the push to clear the Germans out of the rest of Africa.

When the port fell, the Germans blocked the harbor with ship and barges. The U.S. Navy played a big part in the reopening of the port.

Friday–Sunday, February 5–7. The sand was still blowing. We had a difficult job keeping the sand out of the engines of our planes, our trucks, and our jeeps. We lost a lot of tents from the storm. The pilots were in the club playing bridge with gas masks on. The food tastes sandy.

Monday, February 8. Took a trip into Tripoli and had a chance to watch the work around the docks. At night the dock was fully lit so the engineers could work round the clock to clean up the debris the Germans left behind.

While the 64th Fighter Squadron continued its air support for the troops, the Allied leaders met in Casablanca to discuss the course of the war. The Young Catholic Messenger, *on February 12, 1943, reported that, as British troops entered Tripoli, Churchill and President Roosevelt began to make plans regarding the invasion of Europe; clearing Axis forces from Africa made this possible. Several days earlier, on February 8, the* Tripoli Times *reminded its readers the Allied advance was still being heavily challenged in places.*

TUNISA FIGHTING FLARES UP
Enemy Attack Beaten off
Tripoli Times 2-8-1943
    In the Central sector, British and German forces southwest of Pont du Fahs are now much in the same positions as they were before the battle for Hill 648, southeast of Bu Arada. Before yielding the hill, British paratroops held out under deadly enemy mortar fire until they ran short of ammunition. Grenadier Guards and men of the French Foreign Legion also took part in the action.
    Morocco radio announces that Lt. General Fischer, commander of a German tank division in Tunisia, has been killed.
    Flying Fortress raids on the airfield at Gabes have been successful and in air combats 26 Axis planes were destroyed for the loss of 10 Allied planes.

I was quite interested in the British 3-inch and 40-mm guns around the perimeter of the harbor. One hundred forty in all. After dark we saw these guns in action as the Germans sent over some planes. In fact, it happened three times. With 140 guns blasting away, it was some show. Two German planes were shot down.

Tuesday, February 9. While I was still in Tripoli, I tried to make a deal with the local wine merchant. He has the wine in big vats but no containers. We found some old German gas cans, boiled them out and filled a few of them with the wine.

One of the most interesting sights was the changing of the guards at the castle by the Highland Division in their full dress of kilts and the bagpipe band.

At the breakthrough at El Alamein, the 51st Highland Division, Eighth Army, was on the line, as was their bagpipe band. The boys of the band put on their kilts and instruments and marched across this much talked about, written about, line as if they were on parade back home on a Sunday afternoon.

I met a few officers from the States at the Grand Hotel who were serving with the Royal Air Force.

Wednesday, February 10. Returned to the squadron from Tripoli this morning; on the way back, we stopped at a city called Homs, also known as Khoms. The population of this city was 40,000 in 1938 and from what we could see most of this population was absent. They, no doubt, moved out during the bitter battles waged during the past few years.

A city near Homs was a spot of interest to us. The city was Leptis Magna, which I had never heard of. It was once an important seaport in ancient Tripolis. Some research told me this city was settled by voyagers from Sicily in the 6th century BC. It became one of the three principal cities of the Tripolis under Carthaginian contract and was a major trading center with the African interior.

After the defeat of Carthage in 201 BC in the Second Punic War, Leptis came under the rule of Munidia and, after the Jugurthine War 111–105 BC, the town accepted the protection of Rome and made a colony by Trajan (Emperor, AD 99–117). Lucius Septimius Severus (Emperor, AD 193–211) was born here. He beautified the city and erected many public buildings.

Excavation of the ruins, which rank as the most important Roman relics in North Africa, was begun by the Italians in 1911. Among sites uncovered are the hippodrome, the forum, basilica, a palaestra (a wrestling school or gymnasia,) a theatre and an amphitheater.

We spent some time looking over the ruins and found many old Roman coins which Leptis Magna made for its own use. We found the ruins of the old showers and sulfur baths. We were told this spot was a playground for the Romans. Even with a silly war in progress, it was nice to take time out to visit. Many of the members of our squadron spent some hours going over this historic spot.

Thursday, February 11. This was the day we were supposed to move out of this dust bowl. But the dust and wind are in charge and the move is called off. The sand and wind blew all through the night. Usually, the wind dies down with the sunset but not today.

Friday, February 12. This morning, the wind, sand, and rain were in charge. The wind blew between 40–50 miles an hour. We lost lots of tents. The storm lasted until 7:00 pm and then we had the job of getting our tentage together so we would have a cover over us tonight.

Saturday, February 13. The storm was back again this morning. It blew like hell all day.

Sunday, February 14. The storm seems to be over, and the cleanup starts. The airplanes were full of sand. The crews worked right through until dark.

Monday, February 15. This was the first day we have had an airplane in the air in many days. This morning we put up a flight of 12 airplanes to try them. We knew the engines would have absorbed lots of sand with the wind blowing for so many days.

Even with all the work the crew chiefs and mechanics performed all day yesterday, we had eight failures out of the 12 planes that took off. Some of the pilots made belly landings and some were able to get their wheels down and make a normal landing. We were very fortunate none of the boys were hurt and the damage to the ships was slight.

There was still no combat flying.

This was a night that I will always remember. I took a pilot from one of the other fighter groups home, which was only a few miles from our area. On my way back to our squadron, I took a wrong turn and became lost.

I had a pretty good idea where I was, but it was a real dark night. I feared driving into a big gully not far from where I was; I decided to sit it out in the jeep for the night. When the dawn came up, after seven hours sitting alone, I made my move.

I smoked plenty of cigarettes during the night. I remembered back when we first came into Egypt and our patrol guards got lost. The desert was a very easy place to get lost in when you are away from the main roads and our camp was out in the blue, as the British call it.

I was glad to get back to the squadron, which was only six miles from where I spent the night. The gully was quite near where I parked my jeep. Seeing it in the morning made me feel good. If I went down in that hole, the jeep and I would be still there.

Tuesday, February 16. This was a big day for all. A C-47 came with a load of mail. Still no flying.

Wednesday–Friday, February 17–19. The sandstorms were with us for these days The boys were not very happy. No flying and loads of dust. We managed to get in some softball games during these days. We had some movies at night.

Monday, February 22. We received some good news today. A group of us could go to Cairo for rest leave. Before the day was over, this was changed. We were told that we would move out of this dust bowl tomorrow.

Tuesday, February 23. We moved out of this dust bowl called Darragh after 31 days of hell with the sand and the rain. We had 20 days of storms in this area. I can tell you the boys were happy when we pulled out at 9:30 am.

We had to leave the rear party and planes behind until we set up a new base.

We put up for the night in a cherry orchard 40 miles from Tripoli. The sand was deep, and we had quite a time pulling out stuck trucks and jeeps.

CHAPTER 13

Zuwara, Libya

Wednesday, February 24. We were up at dawn. We fed the men and drove off at 7:30 am for our new field. The boys enjoyed the trip once we got off the dust road and on to the coast road. We went through the center of Tripoli and stopped just outside for our C-ration lunch. It was nice to eat again without sand in our food.

We arrived at our new field at 3:00 pm. It was a small field called Zuwara. It was a pleasure to watch the boys set up a camp. They all act like they have been setting up camps for years. Had a good night's sleep tonight as the air was good. This camp was not too far from the Mediterranean Sea.

Thursday, February 25. The pilots had a morning and afternoon bombing mission. They all returned safe. Although, they were jumped by some ME-109s.

This was the first time the pilots have been in combat for many days. There is nothing worse than pilots laying around the squadron when there is no flying. These wonderful guys want to get out and fly and fight the enemy.

Saturday, February 27. The boys were out on morning and afternoon bomber missions dropping 500 pounders on the retreating Germans. Our rear party arrived, and we are all together again.

Monday, March 1. During the early evening, we were informed to be ready to receive a group of Spitfire pilots driven off a forward field.

These pilots started coming in about 6:00 pm. Some of them had two pilots in a cockpit built for one. They had one person sit on the lap of the other, not a very comfortable set up but it was a way to get away from a bad situation.

The Scorpion's Nest officers mess. (57th Fighter Group website)

Lieutenant Robert Overcash accidentally shot down an RAF Spitfire.

All of the Spitfires landed OK except for the last one which hit a ditch at the end of the runway. The two pilots were OK, but the plane needed new landing gear.

Talking with some of the boys, they told us how the Germans were on a high spot not far from their field and were dropping bombs all over their area. They were very happy to spend a few nights with us until the enemy were flushed out of their position near the Spitfire field.

We received our February pay today. It was in what was called invasion money.

Tuesday, March 2. A Party moves out this morning to set up a new base with the two other squadrons of the 57th Fighter Group.

Thursday, March 4. A Party is in Tunisia. The boys were out today on a bombing mission and were jumped by some '109s. All return safe but Capt. Alan H. Smith of Paw Paw, Michigan, had a 20-mm shell explode in the cockpit of his plane. Some shrapnel had to be removed from his legs. He made a nice landing despite his injury.

Lieutenant Robert J. Overcash shot down an ME-109.

Saturday, March 6. Boys were on standby this morning awaiting orders to take off. They did not get off the ground until 2:00 pm.

On the way home from the mission, a group of British Spitfires dived into the flight. Lieutenant Overcash of Carolina Beach, North Carolina, who shot down an ME-109 yesterday, shot down one of the Spitfires. The pilot bailed out and was OK. Overcash stated the Spit came straight at him. He figured it might be a captured Spit and he was not taking any chances.

The Spits should have known better. That night the CO of the Spit outfit visited the group and told group commander Col. Art Salisbury that Overcash made a lucky shot. The colonel failed to agree.

We had a briefing on the progress of the campaign and the coming battle which they expect to develop at the Mareth Line. It is expected the Germans will make a desperate stand at this important piece of real estate.

Sunday, March 7. Captain Gratwick, the group intelligence officer, spent a lot of time this morning with the pilots on what to do if they are shot down and become POWs (prisoners of war). This routine takes place each time we received new officers.

There had been reports some of the captured officers in our theater had been giving more information than they should have to the German intelligence officers during interrogation after capture.

Monday, March 8. General Auby Strickland, commander of the Tactical Air Force, arrived and presented Air Medals to a group of our pilots. No flying today.

Tuesday, March 9. Talks about moving were the rumors of the day. Some of the boys had their mail returned today from the censors. I remember Capt. Richard Ryan of Worcester, Massachusetts, remarking about a letter he had written his wife. He told her we had a cat in the squadron

General Strickland arrived to hand out medals to the men.

by the name of Zuwara and we usually named our animals after the landing grounds we were on. The letter made its way to Worcester without the censor's objection.

Colonel Art Salisbury told the officers tonight about his interesting visit with General Montgomery.

A party was held in the evening at the officers' club. We had a few officers from 57th Group Headquarters, namely Col. Art Salisbury, Lt Col. Jere Chase, Lt Col. Harry French, and Majors Howard Johnson and Morey Dyer, join us.

Another report of what we were up against in Tunisia:

THE BATTLEGROUND OF TUNISIA
Young Catholic Messenger Mar 5, 1943
During the past week, General Rommel's armored divisions launched a surprise attack against the southern end of the American line and pressed it back to the Algerian boundary. For the first time the Germans used their new 60-ton Mark VI tanks with armor seven inches thick.

The German and Italians hold the entire east coast of Tunisia. In the southeast, the German African [*sic*] Corps has reached the Mareth Line of fortifications and is holding it against the pursuing British Eighth Army.

Major "Buck" Bilby.

A good time was had by everybody. When the party broke up, the Ford station wagon assigned to Colonel Salisbury was missing. This proved to be very embarrassing to our commanding officer, Major Buck Bilby.

We arranged transportation for our guests. The next morning, we found the station wagon in our area motor pool. It had a few dents in the hood. Apparently, the station wagon was taken by someone who wanted a ride.

During the day, we came up with an idea who might have used the car. In the short time we were at Zuwara Landing Ground, one of our boys had struck up company with a young lady in the village. The investigation brought out that the car had been seen in the yard of this young lady's home during the evening of March 9.

This young man was questioned and stated he knew nothing about the car and had not been out to see the lady in the village.

We went to her village and had a talk with this young native of Zuwara. She admitted the boy in question had paid her a visit the night before.

Looking around the yard where the car was alleged to have been parked, we found, stuck in the tree, a piece of metal from the hood of the Ford. It was the V8 emblem. We removed this piece of what we thought was good evidence and returned to the squadron to examine the car. We found that the V8 emblem was missing and the piece that we removed from the tree fitted correctly in place.

We concluded, when the young man drove into the young lady's backyard, he made slight contact with the tree. The young man was called in again. He still stuck to the story he was not involved in this incident. When we told him the young lady had stated he was in her company, he admitted he was there but did not take the car.

He was told we had proof the car was there, and we produced the V8 piece of metal for the station wagon. He admitted then he was the guilty party.

When the investigation was completed, it was turned over to Colonel Salisbury to close off this affair. It was closed with a reprimand by the colonel.

CHAPTER 14

Ben Gardane, Tunisia

Wednesday, March 10. B Party enters Tunisia. B Party moved out of Zuwara Landing Ground to a spot called Ben Gardane. The road was a rough one, but we took it with a smile as we know that each mile brings us nearer to the end of this foolish war. We arrive at 5:30 pm and proceed to set up the area as the pilots will arrive first thing tomorrow morning.

Thursday, March 11. The rest of the squadron arrived at the new field ready for operations.

Friday, March 12. We had a few Jerries overhead today. They did not drop anything. I guess they were taking pictures. General Lewis A. Brereton arrived for the decoration of Lt. Alan Smith with the Silver Star.

Saturday, March 13. The boys were out on a fighter sweep this morning. They ran into quite a bit of anti-aircraft fire. Lieutenants Robert K. Douglas, of Fitchburg, Massachusetts, and Norman E. Jenkins fail to return. We received no report about what happened to these boys.

This would happen, especially when the boys would be busy with some enemy planes. In this case, they were on a low-level sweep. A pilot could be hit without the rest of the boys knowing about it when they are spread out all over the sky, especially when they are mixed in with some Jerries.

Major Archie Knight was found by the British after being reported missing.

In the case of Douglas, we heard later he was taken as POW and was in Stalag Luft III *in Germany. This was the camp where most of the Air Corps POWs were taken to.*

Major Archie Knight of group headquarters, who was on this mission, was also reported as missing in action. Later in the day, he was found on our side of the lines by a British patrol.

He was out on the end of a piece of land and the Germans were taking shots at him. The only way out for him was to swim. He swam and was none the worse for his experiences when he returned to the field the next morning.

Sunday, March 14. Boys were out this morning again on a fighter sweep. They all returned safe. Father Louge said mass in the big hospital-type tent the group has set up. We have been having a drive to have all the men and officers buy savings bonds. Today we wound up with everyone in the squadron buying a bond, or part of one. The officers were required to buy a full bond if they so desired, but the enlisted men could buy a part of a bond.

Monday, March 15. Our boys had no missions for today. Jerry was around most of the night dropping flares and then bombs. Other than losing sleep, we came through OK. Most of the bombs fell out of our area.

Tuesday, March 16. Boys had one fighter sweep today. All were back OK. One of the pilots had to crash land his P-40 due to engine failure on take-off. He walked away from the wreck.

Wednesday, March 17. Hell of a place to be on St. Patrick's Day but what can one do about it? The war goes on despite the Irish. Boys were out on a mission, but they had to return on account of clouds over target area.

Battle of the Mareth Line

The Desert Air Force rose to a supreme endeavour during the Battle of the Mareth Line.
WINSTON CHURCHILL

For the outline and strategy employed as explained in this narrative, I wish to thank Colonel Williams, intelligence officer of GSI, who I have quoted frequently and many times verbatim in this outline with his permission. Some of the material used here is from Intelligence Summary #467, March 28, 7:00 pm.

The actual attack on the main Mareth Line was prefaced by an attack in the east and north by three battalions of the 201st Guards Brigade—the Grenadiers, the Scots, and the Coldstream Guards—who attacked the horseshoe feature at E.5795 during the night of March 16/17, 1943.

The Coldstream Guards succeeded in gaining a foothold, but the other elements were not able to get on the horseshoe. The Scots advanced slightly north and to the east, protecting their flank and the Grenadier Guards moved into the wadi, but were not able to reach their objective so withdrew. Being unable to establish a bridgehead at this point, after particularly heavy fighting, the Guards Brigade withdrew to the main line east of the wadi.

While it was contemplated the main attack would come in the north of the Mareth Line, success, far beyond our expectation, in another sector changed our entire plan of strategy.

Free French coming up from Chad established screening patrols operating from the Lake Ksar Ghilane region, which prevented the presence of the New Zealand Division being discovered in this area. The New Zealanders were building a causeway, or bridgehead, across a wadi south of El Outid and up through a narrow front which the enemy apparently figured was protection enough for them.

A story that made the rounds during the Mareth Line battle was that the Indian Gurkhas, who were one of the outstanding organizations of the western desert forces, attacked a camp of Germans and found a tent with 3 Germans sleeping in it. They slit the throats of 2 and left the other one unharmed.

The disposition of German and Allied forces before the battle of the Mareth Line as the 57th Fighter Group left Libya and entered Tunisia.

While the feint attack was made in the north of the line, the New Zealanders, comprising the 5th and 6th New Zealand Divisions and the 8th Armored Brigade, moved swiftly up and over the causeway and advanced. They traveled approximately due north at 8:00 am, on March 21, and reached the point of Y.8804, a funnel of good going, but here they were held up. The Free French, then coming in the rear to plug up the pass, swung on the right flank and formed a screen from any opposition coming from the hills.

During the day of March 20, Bostons, Baltimores, and Mitchells made nine attacks, 18 aircraft in each operation, against dug-in and well-dispersed targets at the Mareth position. Considerable damage was believed to have been caused.

Aircraft of the 79th Fighter Group escorted bombers on three missions who bombed Mareth, Gabes West LG (landing ground) and enemy positions north of Mareth. The 57th Fighter Group made 61 sorties during the day, bombing and strafing Gabes West LG and positions at Z.1865 in front of the New Zealanders' positions.

On March 21, ten formations of Bostons, Baltimores, and Mitchells attacked enemy positions around and behind the Mareth Line. Enemy interference was slight. Fighter-bombers delivered their attacks on enemy tanks and dug-in, two Kittyhawks and Warhawks missing.

The 79th Group escorted bombers on the missions, attacking enemy positions at Z.4814, 4422, and 4818 (on the Medinine–Gabes road).

On the Mareth Line, the enemy had placed, from north to south, the *Young Fascisti*, the *Trieste*, and the 90th Light Divisions, the latter placed strategically on the main road from Mareth to Gabes, to spearhead an advance or to affect a retreat if necessary. To the south and behind the 90th Light were the *Spezia* and the *Pistoia* divisions. Northeast of these was the 15th Panzer Division. The 164th Light formed the right wing with two German armored divisions north of the Chotis. The enemy armor though, was spreadeagled and the 15th Armored Division was in the southeast facing the possible advance of the New Zealanders.

To the north, the American 1st Infantry Division and the 1st Armored Division were deployed along a line from Gafsa to Meknassy. The 1st Infantry engaged a position of the 10th Panzer and held him in this area.

Our advance through the Wadi Zigzaou in the north of the Mareth Line was rendered difficult because of heavy rains. Our tanks were bogged down and approximately thirty-nine of our MT (motor transport), which had successfully negotiated this wadi, were abandoned in water several feet deep. Our advance at this point was arrested. Meanwhile, it became evident the New Zealand column had caught the enemy flat-footed in their right and rear of the Mareth Line, indicated by the fact that this area had no mines.

After cleaning up the Italian garrison under General Mannerini, their first contact came with the 21st Armored Division which had been moved south to bar their progress. We hurriedly moved the armored units by a long circuitous route up in the west to reinforce the 8th Armored Brigade. To meet this threat, the enemy quickly brought over the 15th Armored Division to the west. General Mannerini's forces were by then eliminated and the 164th German Division and some of the *Specia* moved from the Mareth line to reinforce the 21st Armored Division. At this point, we decided to abandon the attempt to break through the Mareth Line and bend all our efforts to capitalizing on our already spectacular advance.

During the night of March 21/22, 51 Wellingtons and 10 Halifaxes, assisted by Albacores (flare dropping), dropped some 125 to 135 tons of bombs on a large concentration of enemy MT, tanks, and gun positions south of Matmata, the Gabes–Mareth Road on and near roads from Gabes to El Hamma, and from Bouchamma to Kettana.

Meanwhile, the 50th and 51st Divisions maintained continuous contact with the enemy, compelling them to hold a certain number of troops to maintain this line, and, in various raids, captured approximately 500 Italians.

On March 22, top clouds prevented operations by light bombers until late in the afternoon. Three attacks were then made to prevent the envelopment or counterattacks in the Mareth area. One Mitchell was lost by anti-aircraft fire in one of these raids.

Planes of the 79th Fighter Group escorted bombers on four missions. The first was forced to turn back because of clouds obscuring enemy positions on the Mareth–Gabes road at Z.5213. Those engaged, claimed one ME-109 destroyed, two ME-109s damaged, one Italian Macchi 202 damaged, and an ME-109 probable. A pilot crash landed in our lines, believed to be safe, and another crash landed at base. The 57th Group carried out 24 fighter-bomber sorties on the same target as above.

During the early days of this battle, and the entire week following, we enjoyed complete air superiority. The air forces from Northern Tunisia kept a up a continuous attack on all enemy LGs and egged them at every possible opportunity. Practically no enemy aircraft was seen south of Gabes.

During the night of March 22/23, the enemy counterattacked in force and we withdrew to a position east of the Wadi. The New Zealand advance was slowed a little at this point but, as of the morning of the 23rd, they had already captured approximately 1,500 prisoners of assorted types; recce reports indicated a major battle would soon take place on this front. Some 50-plus tanks were reported in the advance area.

The New Zealand column was receiving active support from fighter-bombers. Spitfires were strafing and bombing with splendid results in area Y.9010.

On the night of March 22/23, 35 Wellingtons and 10 Halifaxes, again assisted by Albacores, dropped 99 tons of bombs on MT between Mareth and Kettana, and gun positions.

During the day of March 23, fighter-bombers detailed to attack enemy dug-in positions and infantry in the Mareth area found a good target. Bostons, Baltimores, and Mitchells carried out 166 sorties against enemy positions and MT in the Zarat area with very good results. A Warhawk escort destroyed an ME-109. We suffered no losses during the day.

Planes of the 79th Fighter Group escorted bombers on 10 missions, bombing the area around Zarat and Mareth, and the road between Kareth and Gabes. Very few, if any, enemy aircraft were encountered.

At this point, the master blow was struck. The attack was simply conceived and depended on the complete maximum strength of the land and air forces combined, and the willingness to face casualties. Time was the essence of success. The enemy apparently made ready for a night assault. Suddenly, there was a barrage of 200 guns lasting one half hour. The enemy advancing from the general direction of El Hamma were already tired before the guns of the barrage were stilled. They were shattered with bombs of every description and strafed continuously for several hours without interruption.

Our forces' advance was uninterrupted by any mines and passed on in the moonlight.

The 15th and 21st Armored Divisions were busily occupied with our tanks; the 15th having moved to the rescue and took up a position in the left rear. The next day saw the breakthrough. The German 164th Light and 24th Armored Divisions had been severely damaged. By night fall, the 15th Armored Division had been steadily pushed back with losses.

Our attack had been so well conceived and executed that we caught the famous German armor spread out over four distinct areas. The principal battle took place in this funnel between the foothills. Both sides fought to maintain the line of communication. Our line ran from the south to north to reinforce the New Zealand Division.

Our thrust to the right toward Gabes endangered the German and Italian forces south of Gabes and the Mareth Line. The Germans had a fundamental problem; we couldn't be stopped. Recce planes brought back reports of a thinning out of the Mareth Line.

Meanwhile, our 50th and 51st Divisions were maintaining constant pressure against this line. The 4th Indian Division swung around to the south of the Mareth Line and deployed in order to feel out any minefields, clean up the enemy holding the pass at Hallouf, Touden, and Matmata, and, if possible, establish a shorter line of communication for our advance forces which moved north and northeast towards El Hamma.

During the night of March 23/24, 23 Wellingtons, three Halifaxes and several Albacores dropped some 57 tons of bombs on MT and gun positions between Mareth and Gabes.

On the day of March 24, five attacks were made by Bostons, Baltimores, and Mitchells near Zarat where important enemy armored forces were reported to be concentrated. Bombing was successful. Hurricanes, Spitfires, and Kittyhawks made heavy strafing attacks on the enemy, claiming very heavy damage on MT, tanks, armored cars, etc.

Aircraft of the 79th Fighter Group escorted bombers on six missions bombing the town of Zarat, and on a recce over the area Y.81-90 (southwest of El Hamma)

The 57th made 36 sorties on an armed recce southwest of El Hamma. Eight-plus enemy aircraft were seen taking off from Gabes West LG.

During the night of March 24/25, 149 Bostons, Baltimores, Mitchells, Wellingtons, Halifaxes, and Albacores dropped more than 156 tons of bombs southwest of El Hamma, on and near roads, in wadis, and on the El Hamma–Gabes Road. They attacked MT and enemy positions. It was the best targeting in this phase of operations.

On March 25, Baltimores, Spitfires, Kittyhawks, and Hurricanes attacked various targets, from Sfax on south. They destroyed many MT, tanks, equipment, and personnel. Pilots claimed four ME-109s, a Fieseler Storch, and an ME-210 destroyed or damaged. Five pilots force landed. All are safe.

The 79th Group made 22 sorties including a low-level attack on Sfax El Maou, strafing MT, personnel, and buildings. One pilot of the 85th Squadron is missing.

On the night of March 25/26, heavy, medium, and light bombers made a concentrated attack against enemy forces gathering in the El Hamma area. Good targets were found. About eight hundred eighty-five tons of bombs were dropped.

During the day, in conjunction with attack by our land forces, light bombers and fighter-bombers maintained an intensive effort against enemy concentrations south of El Hamma. Twenty-six squadrons in all bombed and strafed over a period of 2½ hours, causing a great deal of damage and confusion to the enemy. Three ME-109s were claimed damaged without loss to our aircraft. Thirteen pilots are not yet accounted for, as are two light bomber crews.

The 57th Group carried out 43 sorties, bombing and strafing enemy positions. One pilot of the 64th Squadron and two of the 66th were missing. The 79th Group flew 48 missions, bombing and strafing on the El Hamma Road and southwest of El Hamma. Three pilots of the 86th Squadron and one of the 87th are missing.

On March 27, the air attacks were shifted to the El Hamma LG. The 57th made 47 sorties bombing and strafing on the El Hamma LG. Two pilots are missing from these operations.

It became apparent at this point that the Mareth Line was untenable. Evidence that *PGR Afrika* (*Panzergrenadier* Regiment) had already been withdrawn and had proceeded north to Gabes, obviously to aid the already hard-pressed 10th Armored Division fighting the Americans in the Gafsa–Meknassy area. The air force battalions and some of the 90th Light Division had been hard-pressed south of El Hamma. Some of the *Spezia* had left and the *Pistoia* were being moved up. Reports from this area indicate well over twenty-two hundred prisoners had been taken, including 70 officers.

Constant pressure was met with less and less resistance. Soon the line cracked, and the retreat was on. The 4th Indian Division moved northwest and took large numbers of prisoners, mostly from the *Pistoia*. One enemy battery fired three rounds at no apparent target and surrendered.

The Mareth Line was now outflanked. By the morning of the 29th, forward troops of the 1st Armored Division occupied El Hamma and patrols approached Gabes from the west. Signals coming in report over six thousand prisoners, both German and Italian. A large number of guns and MT was also abandoned.

The 30th Corps now occupies the Mareth Line. The 52nd Highland Division passed on through Gabes. The 50th Division is engaged cleaning up the mines to the south of Mareth. The 4th Indian Division has moved north and northwest on a line along Beni Zelten to Matmata. The 7th Armored Division is making a southerly swing on a mopping-up process. The 1st Armored Division is now moving fast and at this point appears likely to cut off the retreat of the 16th Panzer Division, now engaged with the 1st American Division. The Free French, who have been reinforced at Chott El Fejad and are becoming very aggressive, are attempting to outflank them. They also are in position to engage any reinforcements coming up from the south.

In this battle, several facts stand out: the value of the gallant failure at the Mareth bridgehead, the American attacks giving our left swinging column a chance to advance uninterruptedly, the use of air power in a ground-strafing and tank-busting role in conjunction with land forces, and in sweeping the sky clear of enemy aircraft. Air superiority has a negative value only unless exploited to the hilt as in this battle.

It is noteworthy that we refused to waste time or energy on the Mareth Line. As a result, our policy to exploit success to the hilt in this battle was fully justified. Good gunnery, air photography, the careful and daring tactical reconnaissance in the air, and the reports by armored cars on the ground, all came together. The brave efforts of our sappers and infantry were never more noteworthy than on this occasion. Our tank crews showed themselves to be the masters of their machines and of their enemies.

As at El Agheila, motorized infantry formed the groups of outflanking columns, of which determination and skill are the essential qualifications. With the increasing move across of the enemy's reserves, our tanks were able to pass through and, in themselves, proved to be the best measure of success. The enemy's defense system had been fundamentally upset even before we moved the armored division around the deep flank. Above all, while the push at Wadi Kaiba Ouest alone remained but a partial victory, we did not surrender the initiative. The enemy made the fatal mistake of looking over his shoulder in attempting to stop up the gap at the Mareth Line and rush across in a last attempt to stem the tide at El Hamma.

Again, as at El Alamein, he threw all his reserves in, bit by bit, and in desperation committed himself, whereas we were spacing our forces to meet the requirements and held out our reserves to fill in any unexpected gap.

Again, as at El Alamein, the shadow of victory loomed up weeks before. A successful defensive battle on March 6 failed to interrupt our preparation. The enemy had committed his reserves three weeks before the battle even began. The 52 tanks lost before Medinine could have swung the tide of battle south of El Hamma.

CHAPTER 15

East Medinine, Tunisia

Thursday, March 18. This was the day the air battle was to start to close up the Mareth Line of battle. No flying today. The weather was in charge with high winds keeping all our planes on the ground.

Friday, March 19. A cold and rainy day kept the planes on the ground.

Saturday, March 20. Moved out of Ben Gardane at 9:15 am to a field called East Medinine only two hours away. We started to set up camp in a hurry as the planes would be starting at 5:00 pm and they arrived on time. The air was full of bombers all day. They were softening up for the push that would take place at 9:45 pm tonight. The push started on time. We could hear the artillery fire through the night. The Mareth Line was getting the works.

Sunday, March 21. Sunday morning and the P-40s were all loaded up with 500-lb bombs to be dropped around the defenses of the Mareth Line. All our boys returned safe.

Our rear party arrives. During these days we had to leave another party behind the rear party as we would have some planes that could not be moved due to the lack of repair parts. In some cases, planes that had been shot up would take more time to repair. The planes would be flown forward later.

Many times, we had planes grounded for want of a small oil filter. We would have to leave these planes with a crew at the rear base until we took a filter off one of the planes at the forward base and flew it back to attach to the grounded plane. This also meant sending pilots back to fly these planes forward.

We had a real thunder and lightning storm tonight. The tents could take the rain. Hats off to the British for these tents. They are terrific.

Monday, March 22. Raining this morning and the field was in no shape for flying. A very appropriate movie was held in the open tonight: *They Raid by Night*.

Tuesday, March 23. The sun was out this morning, but the field area is mucky. General Auby Strickland decorates a few of the pilots: Capt. Alan Smith received the Air

Medal; Capt. Dalton Hobbs of Little Rock, Arkansas, earned the Oak Leaf Cluster; and Capt. Ernest D. Hartman of Indianapolis, Indiana, received the Purple Heart.

Hartman was very lucky on the mission for which he earned the Purple Heart. A bullet went through the canopy of his P-40 and barely grazed him along the forehead. Another fraction of an inch and he would not be with us today.

Lieutenant William M. Ottaway of Rome, New York, also received the Purple Heart for bringing home his P-40 after a 20-mm shell exploded in the cockpit of his plane and filled one of his legs and foot with fragments.

Wednesday, March 24. Boys were out early this morning on a reconnaissance mission. All back safe. We were briefed the air battle would start on March 18. According to the Advanced Air Headquarters' Western Desert Daily Intelligence Summary, we have been pouring it on the Germans from all corners of the Western Desert.

The Germans have been hit with fighter-bombers all day and with bombers all day and all night. One wonders how much longer he can take this severe punishment. He is not putting up many planes to combat this attack. He has lost many of his planes on the ground with this constant attack since the Battle of El Alamein started back on October 23, 1942.

Tonight, the sky was still filled with bombers on their way to a target up front. Again, as we did many times before, we thanked God the bombers were ours.

Thursday, March 25. This was a real hot day. The sand blows again. Our planes were forced to remain on the ground. The pilots do not like this. They know there are some good targets out along the Mareth Line.

A number of German Ju-88 bombers were overhead tonight not far from our field, dropping flares. No bombs were dropped. It was assumed they were taking pictures.

Friday, March 26. We had a bad start this morning when Captains Wm S. Barnes, of New York City, and Lyman Middleditch of Highlands, New Jersey, had to belly land their P-40s after take-off. Both OK. In fact, they both took part in the big mission which took place today. We put every airplane that could fly in the air. That was true with all the air outfits in the area.

The plan for the Mareth Line, as I understood it from the planners, was they decided not to hit the forward part of the line head on. They went around the end of the line and took the Jerries by surprise.

Our boys, along with the rest of the air units of the Desert Air Force, came in from the south and dropped their eggs on the defenders of the Mareth Line. In doing so, some of the New Zealand troops had some of our bombs dropped on them. It was found out that they had proceeded much further than anticipated and our boys, dropping 500 pounders from 14,000 feet, did not know that some friendly troops were in this area. A few casualties occurred. This caused some friction between the

New Zealand and American troops when they met in the bar at Shepheard's Hotel later in Cairo.

It never became serious. Pilots have a way of straightening out affairs like this in short order.

When the day was over, we had one pilot missing, Captain Barnes, who had belly landed his P-40 early this morning and chose to find another ship. He joined in the mission, which became his last in the war in the desert. We found out later he was taken prisoner.

Our boys were assigned the area called El Hamma, a spot you probably could not find on a map, other than the maps we used for the battle of the important Mareth Line.

In a 2½-hour period today, 26 squadrons bombed and strafed the Mareth Line area with the British Spitfire squadrons providing the top cover to keep the Jerries from interfering with the assigned objectives.

CHAPTER 16

Soltone, Tunisia

Saturday, March 27. This was one of the days we were used to by this time. The wind blew and when the wind blows the sand starts to whirl. Everybody takes a beating. For the 64th Black Scorpion Squadron, the war will have to wait.

Sunday, March 28. The sand was still blowing this morning and operations were held up. This was a break for the Jerries. This gave him a chance to move out of the Mareth Line without being pounded from the air.

At our headquarters, when you read the reports, you wondered just how long he could take this punishment. It was felt he may move out of there under the cover of darkness tonight.

Monday, March 29. Good news. First thing this morning the Mareth Line was broken. Today our boys dropped 250 pounders on trucks. The returning pilots reported many destroyed and damaged trucks from their attack.

We had three missions assigned for the day. Two of them were accomplished. The third had to return due to nasty sandstorms in the target area.

The reports from the Advanced Air Headquarters, for the last 24 hours, revealed the roads and tracks across the desert were covered by retreating troops. Most of the targets for the day were motor transport. I know what the enemy must be going through as I saw many of the pictures from the cameras of our planes.

Over 300 German motor transports were destroyed or damaged in the last 24 hours. This was hurting him as his replacements are not getting through.

In a photograph taken of the Sfax El Maou Landing Ground,

Burned-out German vehicles by the side of the road.

General Eisenhower and his B-17 flew in to see the troops.

Birthday boy Lt. Pete Mitchell.

all the Germans had was 49 aircraft. Most of those were small aircraft except four Ju-88 bombers, 13 ME-210s and two ME-110s. I would say this would be the target for the bombers tonight.

With this small amount of aircraft, and little or no replacements, you can look ahead and say the war cannot last much longer in this part of the theater of operations.

Tuesday, March 30. General Eisenhower paid a short visit to the squadron. We received the European ribbons. These were distributed to the men and officers of the squadron. Even in this far away spot, we set aside an hour today to read and explain the Articles of War to the men.

Bombers were assigned the mission for today, so our boys had no missions.

Wednesday, March 31. Our boys had one mission today: take care of some motor transport tucked away in a wadi. All returned safe. General Eisenhower, who spent the night in the area, took off in his B-17 Flying Fortress.

The cooks went all out today and baked a cake for armament officer Lt. Peter Mitchell, who celebrated his birthday.

The air was again full of bombers going up towards Cape Bon in Tunisia. This was the spot we were all driving for. Cape Bon was the end of the road for the Jerries in this country.

Thursday, April 1. No missions today. The boys had some fun with April Fool's jokes. We received our March pay today. The post office in Cairo were most cooperative on payday. They had a clerk who would visit the squadrons and sell them money orders to send home. Out in this desert, there was nothing to buy; the boys appreciated this service.

Friday, April 2. Our boys were out this morning on what was called an armed-reconnaissance mission. In other words, if they found a target, bomb it. We put another mission out in the afternoon and ran into a few German ME-109 fighters. Captain Lyman Middleditch claimed the damage of one Jerry plane. In order to claim it as damaged, he must have seen some parts fall off. All boys return safe.

An evening in the club with the pilots after a mission like this makes for interesting conversation.

Saturday, April 3. The wind blows. The sand whirls around. No flying today. We received some good news from headquarters. The damaged ME-109 Middleditch claimed yesterday turned out to be destroyed. In other words, someone found this plane, thus making Middleditch the first ace in the 57th Fighter Group. This destroyed plane gave him a total of five destroyed Jerry planes.

Captain Lyman Middleditch failing to don proper military attire.

Lyman always complained about what a lousy plane the P-40 was. I asked him "How do you account for the German planes being shot down by the P-40's?" His answer was the American fighter pilot was a better pilot than the Jerries. That was the reason the pilots in the German planes did not do so well against the P-40s.

CHAPTER 17

Has Bub, Tunisia

Sunday, April 4. Here we go again. We're on the move. We left the landing ground called Soltone and moved to one called Has Bub near Medinine. This was not too much of a move. We set up before nightfall and the planes, those that can fly, joined us.

I saw a report from Advance Air Headquarters pertaining to the information extracted from a German prisoner taken after the March 26 attack by the air units of the Desert Air Force at El Hamma.

He stated the planes came in so low the German 88-mm guns couldn't be effective. He also claimed motor transport took a terrific beating from the air activity. The number of officers and enlisted personnel killed, or wounded, must have been very heavy from the reports of his interrogation.

Monday, April 5. B Party joined up with us. We were together again so we can start operating. Colonel Art Salisbury, and Group Captain Ted Underdown of the Royal Air Force gave a briefing of what is to come on what should be the last big push to get General Rommel and the *Afrika Korps* out of Africa.

In this area, I dug my tent in. I had a big slit trench and set the tent up over the hole. When we had a raid, I just fell out of bed and into the trench.

Tuesday, April 6. At 4:15 this morning we started to push the Germans out of Wadi Akarit. Our boys, along with all the fighters and bombers in the theater, worked today. The sky seemed to be full of aircraft on their way

Group Captain Underdown of the RAF (left) briefed us on the upcoming assault. "Buck" Bilby on the right. (57th Fighter Group website)

up front. As we said many times when we saw this show of strength, thank God they were our planes.

Wednesday, April 7. Jerry was driven out of the wadi. He was on the run again. Our boys and the bombers were working on the retreating troops. They were having a field day shooting up motor transport. The main road between Skhira and Sfax was loaded with trucks, many of them burning.

The lack of anti-aircraft fire or enemy air activity has made the job for our boys a little more pleasant, if you can call this type of work pleasant.

An action took place today that we had been looking forward to for many months. The 1st American Army, under the command of Dwight Eisenhower, and the British Eighth Army linked up.

We had trouble again with the sand fleas that dig right into your skin. The medical section had a lotion which gave us some relief by painting your whole body with a brush.

These fleas would get in your blankets and the only way you could get rid of them was to dunk the blankets in a tank of high-octane gasoline.

I wrote a friend of mine at home and told him how we did our cleaning. He wrote back and told me how tough it was to obtain gas. I don't think he liked the idea of us wasting gasoline. I told him I would gladly swap places with him.

Thursday, April 8. Reports this morning showed Jerry was running fast. Our boys and the bomber boys called this day "air shuttle day." They ran as many missions as they could. The targets for today were the same they have been for days, motor transport.

Each pilot's report was the same: lots of trucks burning.

We had a death in the squadron. When one of the missions returned this afternoon, Lieutenant Koele's plane developed engine trouble. He could not come in for a landing, so he bailed out. His chute made a normal opening and he drifted to earth.

The wind carried him away from the field and he landed on the edge of a wadi. A wadi is what we would call a ditch. Parts of the desert have many of them. When it rained, water flowed through them. In my nine months in the desert, I had not seen any water in them, some of them were deep and others were shallow.

When we arrived at the spot where Koele landed, we found him in the bottom of the wadi. He was dead from a broken neck. We felt when he hit the edge of the wadi, he must have lost his footing and fallen into it.

It was hard to believe when we saw him floating face down. We felt it would be a normal landing. All we had to do was to run out in a jeep and pick him up. A fine young man, like a lot of the boys of the Black Scorpion Squadron, had flown his last mission.

Further reports of the day revealed the Germans were retreating and leaving many Italians for the rear-guard action.

The frenetic flying by the Black Scorpions in early April 1943 was in support of the next big Allied advance, culminating in the Battle of Wadi Akarit. As the 65th Fighter Squadron shuttled back and forth to the front line, alongside Allied aircraft of all description, the ground forces that had been so successful outflanking the Mareth Line, continued their advance.

BATTLE OF WADI AKARIT
By Maj. McCall, Fifth U.S. Army

On the night of April 6, German dispositions facing Wadi Akarit are Dj. Roumana and Tebaga–Fatnassa ran from the sea inland. The *Young Fascisti*, 90th Light, *Spezia*, are to the right, mixed units of Italians and Germans. The 15th Pz [Panzer] Division held to the north in reserve. The 21st Pz Div was split, facing the Americans in the El Guettar–Maknassy areas.

The basic plan of attack was for the 201st Guards Brigade, on the right, during darkness, to advance and threaten an attack on the Wadi Akarit and the 90th Light, at daybreak, to dig in and open fire to keep the enemy's attention.

On the extreme left of the British Army, west of Tebaga–Fatnassa, the 1st Armored Division was to perform a similar mission, being prepared at any time to join the reserves of the British Army. However, this division was given sufficient freedom to permit it to create its own crossing if such were possible.

During the night, without artillery preparation, the 4th Indian Division was to attack silently and by 8:30 am, gain the high ground of Tebaga–Fatnassa. At 4:15 am, against the general ground of the Dj. Roumana, the 50th Division, on the left, the 51st Division, on the right, were to attack, covered by an artillery barrage of great violence. The mission of this was to seize the high ground of the east flank of Tebaga–Fatnassa and Dj. Roumana by 8:30 am, and to prepare crossings through the minefield for their own troops and widen them for the passage of reserves. All these troops were under command of the 30th Corps.

Upon the break-through, by the 50th and 51st Divisions, armored reserves, consisting of the New Zealand Division, probably the 1st Armored Division, were to follow through the gap, thrusting to the north, thereby attempting to cut off the enemy's withdrawal.

By 8:30 am, the 4th Indian Division had accomplished their mission and had reported about 1,500–2,000 prisoners. The Guards Brigade, on the right, performed its mission, the 51st had occupied its positions. The 50th Division had run into difficulty, anti-tank ditches on the reverse slope of the hill, but the plan seemed to be working according to schedule.

The New Zealand Division, escorted by two squadrons of tanks from the Armored Division, began to filter through.

During the day, the enemy's line was bent to the rear, but he resisted with great ferocity and counter-attacked violently, the Indian Division alone had three separate counterattacks during the day. All units maintained their positions.

(Continued)

During the night of April 6/7, the enemy withdrew to the north. Pursuit was organized by the New Zealand Division thrust, though still having trouble with the anti-tank ditches. The Guards Brigade followed along the coast. Contact was gained with American forces from the El Cuettar area by the 12th Lancers Brigade at approximately 4:00 pm on the 7th.

Considerable confused tank activity occurred during the afternoon; the enemy continued its efforts to break free of combat.

During the day of the 8th, advance continued to the north with personnel being taken. Among them, the Saharan Group, complete with leader, also General Mannerini. Another unit, approximately a battalion, was at one time reported forming to counterattack the British forces, and they requested air support. Within a quarter of an hour, the request was changed, reporting that the unit was simply reforming to surrender.

Many of the 8th and 9th Armored Brigade, and the New Zealanders, had reached the area approximately 25 miles west of Sfax.

Prisoners at that time totaled 9,600.

The prisoner count for the last 24 hours read 8,000. The next stand for Jerry will be in the Enfidaville area. There were reports of heavy guns emplaced in that area.

Friday, April 9. The first thing we did this morning was to conduct a burial service for Lieutenant Koele. He was wrapped in his parachute and a blanket and buried at a spot that we selected at the edge of the runway.

We didn't have a casket. He was buried like many of the fallen heroes of the battles of the Western Desert. We found an old building in this area and lined it up with a kilometer marking on the coast road. This made the grave easy to find by the detachment that would later remove the remains to a military cemetery.

A cross was made by our carpenters. The mound of dirt was covered with white painted stones.

One of Koele's dog tags was placed with the body. The other was tied to the cross. A small map was made of the burial area showing the building and the kilometer marking and any other landmarks in the near vicinity.

Jerry ran very fast today. We had no missions. We will have to move out of this spot. When Jerry runs too far, we could not reach him from this field.

I completed 15 years in the service today.

CHAPTER 18

Skhira, Tunisia

Saturday, April 10. The Germans were so far from our field this morning there were no missions on the schedule. We were on the move. B Party moves to a new landing ground tomorrow.

Sunday, April 11. B Party moved to a spot called Skhira, a small field outside Gabes. Squadron Leader Skalski, a Polish officer flying a Spitfire with the British spent the night with us. Skalski related his experience from the time Poland was overrun by the Germans up to this desert war where his Polish squadron fought. He had his squadron with him, and they fight the Germans with all they have.

They felt the Germans took everything their people had when they overran Poland early in this war in which we are still engaged. I have often thought of Skalski and what he is doing today with his country under the heel of the Communist regime.

During the day, or in the evening, we would censor the mail of the enlisted men.

I remember one boy wrote a letter to his mother. He told her about the bombing we had gone through. He did not think he would come through this war alive. This letter was sort of a goodbye note. We did not try to read the mail from start to finish but spent time looking for dates, times and places which were not to be written about. Only after you had looked for those things, would you get into the meat of a letter. In this case, I was sad, as no mother should be receiving this type of mail.

I called the young man into the orderly room the next day and had a talk with him.

Black Scorpions flight operations board.

He took the letter back and changed the gist of it to a more pleasant piece of mail his mother would enjoy.

Another case similar to this one was a boy writing to his brother, telling all about the bombing and how this would be his last letter as he knew that he was going to be killed. The young man changed the wording of the letter, and we sent the mail along.

We had another boy who was sort of a poet. He would write these poems. In many of his letters, he would give the officers the works. These letters went right along with our OK.

Although the Black Scorpion Squadron was on the move today and not flying, most of the hundreds of bombers and fighters were out harassing the retreating

Another publicity report from Eighth Army News, *on Monday April 12, 1943, detailing the events the 64th Fighter Squadron was part of, especially what the ground forces were doing. Of note is the interception of Axis aircraft flying between Italy and North Africa. The Black Scorpions would soon be involved in stopping these evacuation/resupply flights.*

SOUSSE OCCUPIED

Italians Up a Tree

Our armored cars entered Sousse early this morning.

The enemy has withdrawn towards the Enfidaville line, about 20 miles to the north, where the Italians have been digging in hurriedly for the past week.

On the western flank, Kairouan was left in flames by the retreating 10 Panzer Division and has been occupied by the British and Allied troops who launched an offensive from the Fondouk area to coincide with Eighth Army's drive from the south.

In the air, a number of armed reconnaissances were carried out yesterday by our fighters.

On the previous evening, light bombers made a last-light attack on the landing ground at Enfidaville and enemy MT concentrated in the area. A number of fires were started.

During the night medium bombers attacked Menzel Temine South landing ground, setting fire to dispersed aircraft.

AXIS AIR TOLL

Keeping up their attacks on the Axis supply-line to North Africa, our Lightnings destroyed 21 more enemy planes off the coast of Tunisia on Saturday.

This brings the total of Axis supply planes and flights shot down between Italy and Africa in the past week to 79.

Meanwhile, our aircraft based on Malta attacked an enemy convoy off the Tunisian coast and raided enemy airfields on Lampedusa Island which lies about 70 miles off the coast east of Mahdi.

Other aircraft attacked Naples for the third time in a week.

Photographs taken since Friday's raid by Flying Fortresses on the Italian naval base at La Maddalena, in the northeast corner of Sardinia, show that the *Trieste*, one of the two 10,000-ton cruisers hit, has now sunk …

enemy. The heavy bombers now worked over Sicily airfields and coastal areas with some nice fat bombs.

An intelligence report from the Advanced Air Headquarters of the Western Desert stated many jetties were found constructed along the coast of Tunisia. These piers were probably going to be used for small boats to bring in supplies and to evacuate troops, which they must, as the British Eighth Army and the U.S. First Army and their supporting air forces are working them over from all sides.

More reports that we captured about a thousand prisoners yesterday. Along with these prisoners were 10 truckloads of loot from this general area. Another prize was two ME-109s in their packing crates.

Monday, April 12. We saw our Polish friends off this morning after we gave them a good breakfast. How can we lose a war with the spirit these men have helping us?

Our rear party was with us again. We were ready to operate this afternoon, but no missions were assigned.

Lots of mail and packages today. I want to say that we have been getting A-1 service from the mail department during this push across the Western Desert of Africa. I must repeat that mail and packages were the greatest morale builder for all the troops.

We heard many bombers during the night. No doubt they dropped bombs on the Jerries' night movements. The Germans were having trouble trying to move during the day with the air filled with fighters and bombers.

The town of Sousse was taken at first light this morning. Many prisoners were taken. According to the *Eighth Army News*, since March 20, twenty thousand prisoners had been taken. The western flank, Kairouan, was left in flames by the retreating German 10th Panzer Division.

In a telegram from General de Gaulle to General Eisenhower, he stated that the Battles of Tunisia were but a prelude to the liberation of France. He further sent his good wishes to "Ike" for the success of the Tunisian fighting.

Notes from the commanding general of the British forces at a new meeting:

You are here at a big moment. That moment was a perfect ending for a perfect squeeze which drove Rommel farther North into the steadily shrinking bridgehead.

German motor transport began evacuating Kairouan on Wednesday night. But on Saturday afternoon, the British forces striking towards Kairouan found between forty and fifty German tanks still withdrawing from the town. They were the remnants of the Tenth and Twenty First Panzer divisions.

The British knocked out eighteen of these German tanks. These tanks were the escort of the retreating German column. The British attacked three columns and over 26 trucks were blasted, and twenty anti-tank guns were captured. Between 500 and 600 prisoners were taken.

Some of the pilots taking a break at the beach.

This was largely a British show, but the Americans are following it up today. The Eighth Army was only a few miles south of Kairouan when the First American Army had beaten General Montgomery's spearhead into the 'Holy City'.

Tuesday, April 13. Our boys had a new type of mission today. They were out protecting the British convoys moving up. This type of protection in the daytime allows the convoys to make good time and bring their troops and supplies up to a fast-moving front.

We were not far from the coast. The boys got a chance to get in some swimming today.

CHAPTER 19

El Djem, Tunisia

Wednesday, April 14. Here we go again. A Party moved out to El Djem Landing Ground. On the way, a British truck with a load of detonators hit a mine and held the convoy up for some time.

Two British soldiers were burnt to a crisp. No one could get near the truck. We were lucky our whole convoy was not enveloped in the flames that spread to a few other trucks in the convoy ahead of us.

Along this convoy route to our new landing ground, a few mines go off. The retreating Germans were famous for their mine laying in the retreat from El Alamein.

The historic city of El Djem.

We found if you stayed on the road and did not hit the verges of the road, you were safe.

To prove that, we lost no trucks or jeeps to mines in our longest trek since last October across this miserable land.

This field and tent area left a lot to be desired. It was a small field and the planes had to be parked among the tents. This was not good, when you also had armored trucks, jeeps, and big gasoline trucks parked in the living area too.

Our tent area was put up in between the many wadis, the most we had seen so far. These wadis could be used for slit trenches if they were needed.

We were all set up in a short time. We were like gypsies from this many moves. Our planes will be in tomorrow morning.

About ¼ mile from the landing ground was the El Djem coliseum. El Djem is similar to the one in Rome. From the stories we picked up from the natives, the Romans held many parties in this spot. Many Christians were fed to the lions in this arena.

I did not like this field as it was on the main coast road. With the coliseum so close, it would give Jerry a good target for bombing especially at night. With his knowledge of this field, we were the target for him.

This report from headquarters shows what the other members of the Air Corps were doing and what the Luftwaffe *was not doing. This is from the* Eighth Army News, *Wednesday, April 14, 1943.*

ENEMY SCREEN CONTACTED
Armored Cars Take Sub Crew

Our forward patrols were in contact this morning with a thin screen of enemy tanks, armored cars and guns a few thousand yards in front of his main line of resistance from Enfidaville to the hills.

A feature of yesterday's news was a report from our armored cars on the coast that they had captured the crew of an Italian submarine, including the captain.

The burnt-out hulk of a second "Tiger" heavy tank has been found in the wake of our advance.

On the western side of the hills the enemy has evacuated the Ousseltia Valley, and no Axis troops are reported south of the 70 Northing Grid.

Luftwaffe Lies Low
On the other hand, the Luftwaffe was not in evidence yesterday on the Eighth Army's front, where our fighters carried out offensive patrols in the forward areas without encountering enemy machines.

During the night April 12/13 our attacks on the enemy's landing-grounds continued. St. Marie du Zit landing-ground was again the target for our light bombers, which started fires and caused a very large explosion. Korba South and Temine Main, on the Nabul peninsula, were also attacked by medium bombers.

Across the road, only a few hundred yards away, was a medium bomber outfit, which you could say was an added attraction for the enemy.

Although we were setting up a new field, the war goes on and on. The fighters and bombers continued their constant hammering of the retreating Germans.

Thursday, April 15. The planes left Skhira and landed shortly thereafter at the new base, El Djem. The rear party moved shortly after the planes left. You never had to worry about the rear party getting out of their field once the planes left. They did not want to miss out on any of the action at the forward base. They also knew they would be needed at the forward area.

In most cases, we had to leave crews behind to take care of some repairs to a shot-up plane or a plane grounded for parts.

It did not take the boys long to get set up when they arrived at El Djem, they were real artists of breaking and setting up camps. This was the 17th field we used since leaving the States 10 months ago.

This countryside was a real change from the desert. We were seeing some green countryside. The boys were not happy with the tent area as they had very little room with all the planes and trucks parked among the tents. There was not much we could do as we had no space to spread out. We make the best of it hoping we will not stay in this area too long.

Friday, April 16. Since our boys did not have any missions today, many of them took a chance to look over the ancient arena which was built many hundreds of years ago. In fact, I could not find the date it was built. It seated 5,000 and the natives told us each of the spectators had an excellent view of the activities, described previously, that took place.

Although our boys had a day off, the air was full of bombers and fighters giving the retreating enemy a real pasting.

Late this afternoon, we had the pleasure of having Cardinal Spellman, Military Vicar of the Catholic Church, arrive at our field in a B-25 medium bomber. The cardinal said mass. Before he left, Cardinal Spellman had a meeting with all the troops and shook hands with most of them. His assistant took the names of many of the troops and stated he would write the folks back home about his visit with the fighter group. He carried out his promise. We heard from our families about the letter that Cardinal Spellman wrote to our folks. I still have the letter he wrote to Mrs. Lynch.

The city of Kairouan was only a few miles from the field. It was called the "City of History." It has a famous mosque, called the Great Mosque. The story goes that seven visits to the Great Mosque is equal to one visit to Mecca.

During a visit to this famous temple, we were escorted by a guide. Of course, you took your shoes off before entering the building. After the tour, he took us out of the building by the rear door. We could not figure this out until we wound

Cardinal Spellman, military vicar of the Catholic Church.

up in the local rug mart and then the Arabs started their salesmanship, trying to sell famous Kairouan rugs to the boys. Not many rugs were sold to our outfit. I understand they sold many rugs to the soldiers during their stay in this area.

Saturday, April 17. A busy day at the field with lots of P-51s and P-39s landing for repairs or for gas. Most of the missions were sweeps over Cape Bon as there have been rumors the Germans would start to move out some troops by air.

Our boys, and the boys of the other squadrons, had no action to report. We lost a plane on the ground from a short circuit. The plane burned up before we could get a foam wagon to it.

CHAPTER 20

Palm Sunday Massacre

Sunday, April 18, Palm Sunday. This was one of the greatest days for the 57th Fighter Group, its squadrons, and a British Spitfire squadron from No. 244 Wing, Royal Air Force.

We had mass early this morning. It seemed to be just another day of patrolling over Cape Bon. Our boys went out early and returned without a contact. All squadrons, American and British, had a timetable for this day for the patrol over the Cape.

Our next allotted time was at 5:15 pm. Three squadrons took off for the Cape. A Spitfire squadron joined us and acted as top cover. Top cover means this squadron flies over the three squadrons on patrol and prevents the enemy from coming down on top of them.

The participants of the Palm Sunday Massacre.

Shortly before the time our boys needed to return home, someone spotted a fleet of enemy aircraft forming up below them, just over Cape Bon. Here was the official entry in the intelligence log of the Advance Air Headquarters of the Western Desert.

> Day 18 Apr With the object of intercepting enemy transport traffic between Sicily and Tunisia, strong Fighter Formations were maintained over the Cape Bon Peninsula for long periods. During the day, in late afternoon 3 Squadrons of Warhawks (P-40) and a Squadron of Spitfires encountered about 100 Ju 52s flying North-East at sea level covered by a strong fighter escort. The Warhawks engaged and claimed 58 Ju 52s, 14 Me109s and 2 ME-110s destroyed, 1 ME-109 probably destroyed and 19 Ju 52s, 9 ME-109s and 1 ME-110 damaged. The majority of the Ju 52s destroyed are "Flamers" and believed to have been carrying personnel. 6 pilots failed to return.

The first indication our boys had a good show this afternoon was when they arrived over our field at El Djem, a few of the planes pulled out of formation and came down low, buzzed us and slow rolled over the headquarters operations tent.

We knew something was up and we beat the trail to the operations tent of the Black Scorpion Squadron. The stories that came from the boys were fantastic. They were almost ready to come home when they spotted the big formation. Down they went and in 15 minutes these boys made history.

Captain Rocky Byrne of St. Louis, Missouri, claimed three '109s, Capt. Alan Smith claimed one ME-109 (little did we know that this would be Smith's last mission). Captains George Mobbs, of Little Rock, Arkansas, and Art Exon, of Estherville, Iowa, each claimed an ME-109.

After a most hectic debriefing by our operations and intelligence officers, the boys made their way to their tents. We had quite a night at the club and the stories continued throughout the evening.

The bar was a busy spot. The boys really had something to celebrate. They had been on many missions since we started the push behind the British Eighth Army, six months before when we pulled up the tent pins at Landing Ground 174 near the Alexandria–Cairo Road, in back of the El Alamein Line.

Many of the boys on this mission had flown a lot of missions but never ran into much of the enemy. Many stories have been written about this historic mission. *Yank* magazine called it one of the greatest aerial engagements in history. The *Stars and Stripes* newspaper, Middle East edition, called it the "Greatest Air Battle since the Battle of Britain."

This was the first time that the War Department allowed a newspaper permission to identify the 57th Fighter Group as fighting in the Middle East.

The boys paid high praise to the British Spitfire squadron that gave them the superb top cover. Without this support, our boys claimed, we would have had many losses. These top British pilots engaged the enemy and allowed our boys to perform the greatest kill in this Middle East war against Rommel and his *Africa Korps*.

Here are the scores claimed, as listed in the *Stars and Stripes* newspaper, Middle East Edition, April 23, 1942:

64th Fighter Squadron

	DESTROYED	PROBABLE	DAMAGED
Lt. Allan H. Smith, Pawpaw, Mich	1 ME-109 ½ Ju 52		1 ME-109
Capt. George D. Mobbs, Wooster, Ark	1 ME-109		1 ME-109
Lt. Arthur E. Exon, Esterville, Iowa	1 ME-109		1 ME-109
Lt. Edward C. Fletcher, Cranston, RI	1 ME-109		1 ME-109
Capt. Richard E. Ryan, Worcester, Mass		1 ME-109	
Lt. Robert J. Byrne Pyrne St. Louis, MO	3 ME-109		

65th Fighter Squadron

	DESTROYED	PROBABLE	DAMAGED
Lt. Albert C. Froning, La Porte City, Iowa	2 Ju 52		1 ME-109
Capt. Roy E. Whittaker, Knoxville, Tenn	3 Ju 42		1 ME-109
Lt. Harry H. Stanford, Munising, Mich	3 Ju 52		
Lt. Edward R. Weaver, Lock Haven, PA	2 Ju 52		1 Ju 52
Lt. Walter H. Reed, Shelington, PA	1 Ju 52		
Lt. Huntzinger	1 ME-109		1 Ju 52
Major Gordon F. Thomas, Barbaroo, Wis	1 ME-109		1 ME-109
Lt. Walter M. Swartz, Mt. Airy, PA	1 ME-109		1 ME-109
Lt. Francis S. Mande, Mentemore, NM	1 Ju 52		1 Ju 52

66th Fighter Squadron

	DESTROYED	PROBABLE	DAMAGED
Lt. William E. Campbell, Blissfield, Mich	3 Ju 52 1 ME-109		
Lt. John J. Gilbertson, Memphis, Tenn	1 ME-109		1 ME-109
FO William F. Livesey, Madison, NJ	3½ Ju 52		2 Ju 52
Lt. John J. Stefanik, Chicopee, Mass	3 Ju 52		1 Ju 52
Lt. Charles C. Leaf, S. Orange, NJ	2 Ju 52		1 ME-109
Lt. Robert Looney, Rochester, NY	1 Ju 52		3 Ju 52
Captain James G. Curl, Columbus, Ohio	2 Ju 52 1 ME-109		
Lt. James W. Santry, Kosse, Texas	2 Ju 52		1 ME-109 2 Ju 52
Capt. George W. Long, Lexington, MO	2 Ju 52		
Lt. Arthur B. Cleveland, Springville, Ohio	4 Ju 52		

314th Fighter Squadron

	DESTROYED	PROBABLE	DAMAGED
Lt. Col William W. Long, Lexington, Kans	2 Ju 52		
Lt. McArthur Robert Powers, Inwood, NY	4 Ju 52 1 ME-109		
Lt. Richard E. Duffey, Walled Lake, Mich	5 Ju 52		1 ME-109
Lt. Marvin D. Warnke	2 Ju 52		
Lt. Vernon K. Yehle, Enid, Okla	1 Ju 52		
Lt. Roy L. Huser, Lincoln, Ill	1 Ju 52 1 ME-109		2 Ju 52
Lt. Frank K. Everest, Fairmount, WVa	2 Ju 52		1 Ju 52
Lt. James S. Whiting	3 Ju 52		1 Ju 52
Lt. Howard L. Stout	3 Ju 52		3 Ju 52
Total	57 Ju 52 16 ME-109	1 ME-109	16 Ju 52 10 ME-109

There have been stories written about the Palm Sunday Massacre; you will find something about this show in most of the history books and encyclopedias. No one can really talk about this show in its true spectrum but the boys that were flying in the Warhawks over the Gulf of Tunis and Cape Bon.

I could never figure out why the Germans, on a bright sunny afternoon, would put up as many airplanes as they did, knowing the Allies had planes over their area all day.

It would be interesting to talk to the commander that ordered such a move. We know they were desperate for supplies, especially motor parts, and they were evacuating troops as they had no place to go but into the Bay of Tunis.

The 57th Fighter Group had articles written about us after the Palm Sunday battle. In this article in Yank *July 16, 1943, by Sergeant Burgess Scott, they interviewed our commanding officer, Col. Art Salisbury:*

"Kids" of Army Air Force

Cairo—On sunny Palm Sunday over the Straits of Sicily, the youngsters of the U.S. Army Air Forces' 57th Fighter Group shot down 74 German and Italian sky transports and pursuit planes in one of the greatest aerial engagements in history. But still the pilots and the ground crews in this veteran African outfit are not satisfied.

"Give us some Mustangs and we'll really show you something," they tell you when you try to hand them compliments.

The big battle over the Straits of Sicily was a fitting climax to the 57th's campaign in Africa. All the way from Alamein to Tunis, they ran interference for Montgomery's British Eighth Army, destroying enemy planes and landing fields, strafing Axis motor convoys and assuming the role of fighter-bombers to pound Rommel's concentrations on land and transports at sea.

In North Africa, the four squadrons in the outfit rolled up this impressive final score: 152 planes destroyed, 18 enemy planes probably destroyed, 77 enemy planes damaged and approximately 12 enemy freighters and naval craft destroyed or damaged.

The kids in the 57th—it's difficult to find one over 24 and the commanding officer, Col. Arthur Salisbury of Sedaliea, MO, is only 26—likes to point out that this record was made with P-40s, ships that could not take general initiative over the wieldier (German) ME-109s and had to battle whenever they went into the air.

Then how did the fighter pilots in the 57th operate so successfully under this handicap?

Well, they explain, up to a certain altitude, the P-40s had an advantage over the German pursuit ships, and the 57th pilots learned to trick the Nazi into fighting them at that height. When the ME-109s came down and engaged them at their level, the '40s were able to turn inside the enemy thrust using aviation's equivalent of the boxer's left hook. With that maneuver, the 57th downed most of its victims.

"But we could down a hell of a lot more if we could fight them at any altitude," a pilot adds. "That's why we're praying that we can get these ships replaced with Mustangs."

Monday, April 19. They still talked about the big show yesterday, but the boys all knew there were more missions today. They were anxious to get going this morning.

We had an old radio in the officers' club and we listened for the news this morning. Of course, the Italian station which we listened to said nothing about the big show of yesterday.

We heard our friend "Axis Sally" calling the 57th Fighter Group a bunch of murderers and we would be dealt with. I remember a broadcast she did, reported a unit sailing out of Bizerte. She named the unit and said she would play a number

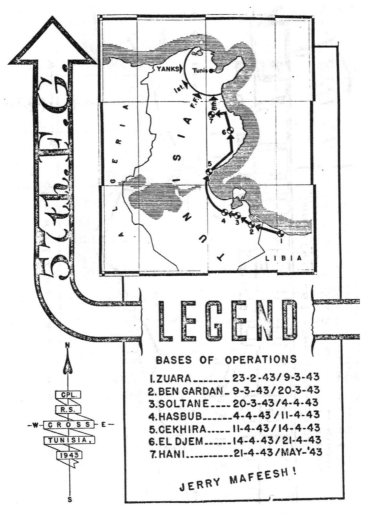

A handy guide to our stops along the way as the 57th Fighter group rapidly moved from Libya through Tunis. Jerry Mafeesh indeed.

Lieutenant Bill Beck was MIA after landing in the ocean.

for them, *How Deep is the Ocean*, stating that she hoped they would get to their destination.

Fighter sweeps over Cape Bon were the missions for all day. The results were nil. On a late afternoon mission, Lieutenants Jerry Brandon and Bill Beck failed to return. Later in the afternoon, Brandon was returned to the squadron by a British unit. He had belly landed in a salt flat, having run out of gas while trying to help Beck, who landed in the ocean; Brandon dropped him a dinghy then had to leave on account of his fuel problem.

Beck was never found, and we felt he must have drowned. Bill Beck was the youngest pilot in the Black Scorpion Squadron and a real good guy. It was tough to see a young man like Bill leave us.

Shortly after 10 o'clock all the boys had gone to bed, and I closed the club for the night. On the way to my tent, I heard the familiar sound of a German Ju-88. You could identify them as their motors were unsynchronized. After hearing them for many nights during the last eight months during our trek across the sand of the Western Desert, you paid little attention to them.

An hour later, a couple of them were right over our field. The siren sounded which meant leave your bunk and head into the slit trench.

The slit trenches at this field did not have to be dug. The area had wadis through the whole camp. That saved us from some digging.

Captain Alan Smith, whom I referred to a short time ago, and I landed in the same wadi. I kidded him about his lack of clothes. All he had on was a t-shirt.

Within a few minutes, our German friends dropped flares that lit the camp up like Broadway. A short time later, they dropped bombs and canisters filled with three-pronged spikes that were supposed to take care of your tires on planes or vehicles. These spikes would normally be exploded out of the canisters about ten to twelve feet in the air to spread them over a great area of a landing strip or the motor area.

One of these canisters landed in the middle of the camp. There seemed to be a chemical in it that burned brightly. A group of our boys came out of their slit trench and tried to put it out.

With the planes still in the area dropping bombs, I used some rough language to get them back to their slit trench.

A short time later, Jerry dropped a bomb in our camp. We were lucky no one was killed. Two of our crew chiefs, Master Sergeants Buck Rivers and Philip Fox along with Sergeants Roy and Gaetano Tropea, and Corp. Norman Zeisloft, received severe shrapnel wounds. They were taken to the squadron medical tent after being given first aid by our medical boys. Fox, I believe, received the most severe wounds as a piece of shrapnel lodged in the muscle of one of his legs.

These two Ju-88s, there may have been more, really worked the area over. They crossed over the road and dropped some bombs in the middle of the camp of some bomber crews. They had several planes burning like hell.

During the raid I saw a young man get in a 2,200-gallon gas truck and drive it to the end of the camp area. Some may say "What were you doing with a gas truck in your camp area?" Well, we also had our planes

Captain Alan Smith was killed during a bombing raid on our camp.

in the camp area. This was the most crowded area in all the fields we were on since leaving Alexandria months ago.

The raid lasted about one hour. We evacuated our wounded to a British hospital down the road. In the headquarters area, our friends had dropped some canisters loaded with little booby traps. When the men started back to their tents, one boy was killed and a few wounded. These traps exploded out of their canisters like the spikes. They would not explode unless someone kicked them.

I got to bed about one o'clock. At 2:00 am, I heard another plane diving on the camp. I did not have time to get out of bed when a bomb exploded in the rear of my tent. This plane kept on going.

This bomb killed Capt. Alan Smith of Paw Paw, Michigan. A piece of shrapnel went through his heart. Another real pilot had flown his last mission.

Most of the bombs dropped had whistles on them. This did not make you feel very good as you lay in the slit trench. You felt one of them had your name on it.

Tuesday, April 20. We had a lot of cleaning up to do this morning. The burial of Lieutenant Smith received top priority. We selected a spot along the side of the road near a kilometer mark. The boys dug a grave and Alan was wrapped in a blanket. The chaplain conducted services.

This was the third or fourth boy we had buried. I always wondered whether they would be found and placed in a proper cemetery.

Sometime later, a U.S. Army nurse and relative of Smith visited the squadron and told us of visiting Alan's grave in an American cemetery near Tunis.

We found that a piece of shrapnel went through the side of one of our gas tanks and out the top. Had this tank been made of steel, I may not have been able to tell this story as it was close to my tent.

CHAPTER 21

El Hania, Tunisia

We moved out of El Djem airfield and into a field called El Hania. It was not too far away but we could disperse our camp.

This field, which would be our home for a while, covered a lot of ground. This was how we set it up. Our operations tents, the heart of any fighter squadron was on what we called "the line," very close to the runway. Our mess tent was one mile from the operations tent. Our tents for living quarters were spread out about fifty or sixty feet apart. This gave us the best dispersal we ever had.

The first order of business was everybody dug a slit trench close to their tent. The experiences at El Djem would not be forgotten for a while. Everybody wanted protection. A good slit trench was always an asset to any man when the siren sounded.

By five o'clock, most of the planes and personnel were at this new field. During this first night at El Hania there was lots of enemy air activity, but they did not drop any eggs on us. We were only about twenty miles from the front at this spot. We expected some air activity.

We did our housekeeping today and the balance of our planes did not arrive until late afternoon, so we had no missions. The British, South Africans, and the American 79th Fighter Group were busy and destroyed 20 to 30 aircraft. We all had a good night's sleep in our 18th airfield since leaving Palestine eight months ago.

Wednesday, April 21. We were up early this morning. The boys were still fixing up their slit trenches. We had no missions today. The boys had a chance to do some visiting in this strange land. We received a report that No. 7 Wing, South African Air Force, destroyed 40 Jerries over Cape Bon.

The battle for Enfidaville was on today. We were briefed by the British liaison officers about this important mission. They felt this area was the key to the end of the war in Tunisia. The Indian Gurkhas were given the task of taking this important area.

The briefing officer informed us they expected to have about a thousand casualties before taking Enfidaville. From an unofficial source, we heard the casualties were about seven hundred, but they took the important area assigned to them.

Thursday, April 22. As usual, when we set up in a new area, we liked to look around. This morning, a few of us took off for Sousse. This was a town to which we sent many missions. The bombers had also worked it over as the Germans had used it.

This was the same as the rest of the towns we had visited along our trek from Alexandria. The bombers and the fighters had done their work well. The buildings, or what were once buildings, showed the marks of war. We took pictures of the ruins.

Here is an official account from headquarters, not to be confused with the Eighth Army News *report about the Palm Sunday air battle and the events that surrounded it.*

ADVANCED AIR HQ WESTERN DESERT APRIL 20/43

The capture of Enfidaville by the Eighth Army on April 20th marks the beginning of the last phase of the Tunisian campaign. General Montgomery's troops have now thrust their way along the coast to a point a mile north of Enfidaville. The fortified village of Takrouna was occupied on April 21st after a fierce struggle in which the bayonet, hand grenades, and machine guns play a more important part than tanks or artillery. West of Enfidaville elements of the Eighth Army were pushed off the top of Djebel Garci but continued to hold the southern slopes. About 500 prisoners, mostly German, have so far been captured in this area. The importance the enemy attached to the high ground around Takrouna is indicated by his readiness to throw in one counterattack after another regardless of casualties.

After waiting for the German reserves to be committed against the Eighth Army, the First Army launched their attack on the whole front between Bou Arad and Medjez El Bab. Crich el Oued and Goubellat have been captured and the enemy has been cleared from the plain which lies southeast of Goubellat itself. Further to the north American troops have advanced on the road leading from Sedjenane to Mateur, and on the coast plain the French troops have reached a point 12 miles east of Cap Serrat.

While there is no evidence yet that the enemy are planning a large-scale evacuation the steady pressure along the entire 110 mi. front offers a startling parallel to the contraction of the walls of the prison in Edgar Allen Poe's story "The Pit and the Pendulum."

Throughout the week the ground attack has been supplemented by a tremendous air offensive. On Sunday, April 18th, a devastating raid on Ju 52s over Cape Bon accounted for 57 Ju 52s and 10 ME-109s damaged. On Thursday, April 22nd, another German air convoy was annihilated consisting of 31 Me 323s six engine transports together with 9 ME-109s, 1 Me 202, and one Caproni Reggiane 2001.

The Me 323, originally known as the Merseburg Glider, can carry a load of 22,000 lbs. While it is possible that these giant transports, together with the Ju 52s have been attempting to evacuate key personnel, their chief purpose has been one of reinforcement rather than evacuation. As the tempo of the battle rises the German need for fuel becomes daily more urgent. The fact that these aircraft caught fire so readily indicated that they were being used to transport oil and gas.

We also visited Kairouan and the mosque which is said to be 1,200 years old. The guide, who was a sharp Arab, gave us a good tour but at the end of the tour he took us down a dirty alley which the local inhabitants used as a latrine. The flies would almost drive you out of your mind.

We ended up in a first-class rug store. The guide who spoke English to us, would talk to the rug merchant in Arabic. We always felt they were plotting to give us the business. We listened and saw some beautiful rugs, but we were not in the market to buy rugs. The problem of getting them home came up.

The Great Mosque of Kairouan in Tunisia.

Back to the field later in the afternoon, we watched the boys take off on an offensive patrol mission to the Cape Bon area. All planes returned safely and reported no results.

One of the other squadrons ran into a few enemy aircraft and shot one of them down.

Although there was very little fighter action, the sky was filled with bombers, with fighter escorts from many of the fields in this area, on their way to plaster the retreating Germans.

Friday, April 23. We had some visitors this morning: George Tucker and George Palmer, American news correspondents. They spent the day talking to the pilots and enlisted men seeking out stories for their respective papers.

Our pilots had no missions today, but the sky was again filled with bombers and fighters on their way to the enemy area which gets smaller by the day. General Eisenhower pushed from one side and General Montgomery from the other; the Germans had their back to the sea.

Saturday, April 24. Ed Kennedy, the *AP News* correspondent, dropped in this morning. Our boys had a noon-time mission as top cover for the 65th Squadron, who were out with a load of 500-lb bombs for an enemy position. No enemy aircraft were sighted, and the bombs fell in the assigned area.

The following three editions of Eighth Army News *highlight the tremendous fighting and maneuvering occurring in Tunisia in late April 1943.*

No. 272 SATURDAY, 24 APRIL, 1943
FIRST ARMY ADVANCES

Important Hill Taken
Good progress was made yesterday by the First Army in their offensive on the 30-mile front East of the line Bou Arada-Medjez el Bab

In the Southern sector we reached a point about eight miles West of Pont du Fahs.

North of the Sebkhet el Kourzia our tanks engaged armor of the 10th Panzer Division and claim to have knocked out several enemy machines.

The plain of Goubellat is now reported clear.

Further North, our troops have advanced some eight miles East of Medjez el Bab and the important height of Heidous dominating the road to Tebourba, is now in our hands.

The total of enemy tanks claimed to have been knocked out by the First Army in the abortive "spoiling attack" by the Hermann Goering [*sic*] and the 10th Panzer Division on the night 20/21 April has now risen to 33, including three Mk VI "Tigers."

Lull on Our Front
On the Eighth Army's front there was little change yesterday. The enemy has been strengthening his outpost in front of the razor-back ridge beyond Takrouna.

A successful attack was made by our light bombers on his gun positions behind this area, despite the good cover given by the olive trees.

On our Western flank a slight thinning-out by the enemy was noticed.

According to prisoners taken from the Italian Centauro Armoured Division West of Gebel Garce this formation has few, if any, tanks left and is being used mainly as infantry.

No. 273 SUNDAY, 25 APRIL, 1943
FIERCE FIGHTING IN CENTRE

Enemy Reserves committed
Fierce Fighting raged all yesterday on the First Army's front east of the Goubellat plain.

The enemy is putting up a most determined defense in favorable country, knowing full well that a breakthrough here would let our armor into the plain of Tunis and shatter his whole North African bridgehead.

Although no spectacular advances were claimed yesterday by our forces, steady progress has been made and the Germans have suffered severe casualties in men and tanks.

The fact that motor-cycle reconnaissance battalions and engineer units have been identified in the lines fighting as infantry indicates that he is committing his reserves.

21st Panzer Division, recently on Eighth Army's front, has now hurried over to support 10th Panzer Division and 501 Heavy Battalion

Their shrunken ranks were slimmed yet further yesterday by considerable losses on top of Thursday's sacrifice of some 16 machines, including four heavies. By 09.00hrs this morning a further eight tanks had been claimed by us.

(Continued)

North of Medjez el Eba a struggle is going on for Longstop Hill, the feature East of Heidous which overlooks the road to Tebourba.

More Germans Taken
In this sector some 350 German prisoners have been taken in recent fighting.

At the Northern end of the Tunisian front our American Allies have made progress toward Mateur but no details are yet available.

On the Eighth Army's front we improved our positions last night in the coast sector North of Enfidaville, taking about 50 prisoners.

Yesterday fighter-bombers again attacked enemy positions North-West of the town, but the close nature of the country made it impossible to observe results.

Meanwhile, our fighters carried out sweeps over the coast and over enemy landing-grounds without meeting any opposition.

Good Work by Our Subs
British submarines are keeping up their attacks on the Axis supply lines to Tunisia and in the latest engagements have sunk or damaged ten more enemy supply ships.

Several times our submarines have even shelled war factories close to the shore on the Italian mainland.

One boat opened fire on a factory from 3,000 yards and then, after ten rounds, closed in to only 1,000 yards. From this range our gunners were able to put their shots through the window so that the shells burst inside the buildings.

After a few rounds the factory blew up, debris flying 300 feet into the air.

The submarine then went on to shell an ammunition dump, where fierce fires were started.

When she finally withdrew, the munitions factory, which had been humming with activity before her raid, was silent but for the crackle of flames and the crash of falling masonry.

No. 274 MONDAY, 26 APRIL, 1943

CENTRAL STRUGGLE CONTINUES
Enemy loses more Tanks
Heavy fighting continued yesterday on the 30-mile central sector between Medjez el Bab and Pont du Fahs.

Though no major advance has yet been made we are steadily eating away the enemy's forces, in particular his armor.

Yesterday a further 17 tanks, including five "Tigers" were destroyed. This brings the total claimed by First Army since 21st April up to 65.

The enemy has, of course, inflicted casualties on us in the process.

In particular, his tank destroying aircraft—the Henschel 129 which fires a 30mm cannon through the airscrew [sic]—were much in evidence the day before yesterday and caused losses among our tanks.

Further North "Longstop Hill," the important feature East of Heidous overlooking the road to Tebourba, is now in our hands after fierce fighting.

In the hilly country between the First and Eighth Armies our French Allies are pressing forward some 15 miles South of Pont du Fahs.

On the Eighth Army's front we have consolidated the positions we captured on the night 24/25 April in the coastal sector about five North of Enfidaville.

(Continued)

Otherwise, activity on land has been confined to patrols and artillery exchanges.

In the air, however, our light bombers yesterday made many sorties against enemy positions North-West of Enfidaville. Fires were started and our land troops report that the bombing was accurate.

Escorted fighter-bombers also attacked enemy shipping in the Cape Bon area and claim near misses on three vessels.

Late in the afternoon light bombers attacked Soliman South landing-ground and caused a number of fires.

During the day our fighters destroyed an ME-110 and a MC.202. We lost four machines, but the pilots of two are safe.

Easter Hope Call to Europe

"The final phase of the war is approaching," declared Dr. Benes, President of Czechoslovakia, in an Easter message to the Czech people from London last night.

"Expect decisive military operations very soon," he assured them, "and be prepared for them. Go on resisting the Germans stubbornly and steadily."

"The Axis satellites are already preparing to desert Germany. Finland has sent messages several times to the allies saying she is ready to stop fighting."

"Romania, who has gambled everything she had, will probably be the first to collapse. And the recent changes in the Italian Government were made because Mussolini discovered a plot to get Italy out of the hands of the Germans at the first opportunity."

From the report I looked over, there were fighters and bombers in the air from 5:00 am to 6:00 pm. With this much pounding, I don't see how the Germans can hold out much longer.

Sunday, April 25. Woke the boys up early this morning and they were off on an early morning sweep. The squadron dropped a load of bombs in the Cape Bon area. All returned without meeting any enemy action.

Boys were off again after lunch on a bomber escort mission. They ran into lots of enemy ME-109s. Captain Rocky Byrne of St Louis, Missouri, shot down two and Capt. Robert Overcash of Carolina Beach, North Carolina, also claimed two. Although there was lots of action on this mission, all bombers and fighters returned to base safe.

This was a big day for the Air Force. They flew 736 sorties for the fighters and 174 bomber sorties. The total losses on our side were 11 planes. Two of our pilots were reported safe. Our boys destroyed six enemy aircraft in the air and damaged eight.

With all this activity today, the scheduled volleyball game with the 66th Squadron was played after supper. Another important factor for this day was many of the pilots received promotions. We usually do not receive much information about Army activities but today I saw a report that showed the enemy had lost, in the battle for Goubellat, between 60 and 70 tanks.

With all this day action, the night action went on as always. The Royal Air Force (RAF) had planes in the air all night long. The Navy patrols the shore to make sure that none of the enemy is going to leave Northern Tunisia by air.

Monday, April 26. For the squadron, this was a quiet day. Our boys went on a fighter sweep over the Cape Bon area. Nothing to report only that they came home safe.

In a bombing operation over Cape Bon, 20 ME-109s rose to challenge the mission. Five were shot down and one was damaged. A Mitchell bomber was seen losing altitude and looked like it was going towards enemy territory. In the Tunisian area,

---

Since the 57th Fighter Group was attached to the Eighth Army, General Montgomery was our senior commanding officer. This message was delivered to us and read to our group.

Personal Message from the Army Commander
(To be read out to all troops)

1. On 20th March, before we began the Battle of Mareth, I told you that the Eighth Army would do three things.

2. On 8th April, I told you that all these things had been done except the final one of securing Tunis—or whatever area the enemy chooses for his last stand. We are now getting on with this last task.

3. We have joined up with the Allied Forces in Northern Tunisia and we no longer operate as an independent Army. The operations are coordinated by Army Group Headquarters, and it is very necessary that the Allied thrust all along the front be kept up; the enemy has not sufficient resources to meet all our thrusts, and that will be his undoing.

4. I call on every commander and every soldier to give of his best and to keep up the pressure. No one must relax for a moment. Keep the tempo of the operation at a high level. The enemy is caught in a trap and will resist desperately. But bit by bit, and part by part, we will fight him to a standstill and will "eat the guts" out of him. It may be difficult, but we will do it.

5. When we have done our duty, and the task is finished, then we can relax. And you will all well deserve it.

6. And so to every officer and I say:
   FORWARD TO BATTLE!
   DO NOT RELAX!
   KEEP UP THE PRESSURE!

7. And in God's good time we will finish the third and final task.

8. Good luck to each one of you. You can rest assured that I am watching over the battle carefully and together we will finish the job.

B. L. MONTGOMERY
GENERAL, EIGHTH ARMY

28.4.43
TUNISIA

the bombers flew 108 sorties, and the fighters flew 546 sorties. We lost three Spitfires. The enemy lost seven with 10 damaged.

Wednesday, April 28. Boys were out on three missions today looking for boats off the shores of Tunisia. It was reported one of the squadrons dropped a 500-lb bomb on a British destroyer and the bomb bounced all around the deck of the ship but failed to explode. A few days later, the crew was invited ashore to the squadron mess for a little celebration. Everybody was happy the bomb was a dud.

In the daily journal of the 8th Fighter Wing for this date, I am going to report what Brig. Gen. A. C. Strickland stated, "The Germans will be lucky if they have left a single aircraft that is capable of being operated when the final phase of the battle to squeeze the Axis out of Africa begins."

He further stated, "If the Germans attempt an evacuation, the slaughter by the Allied Air Forces will be the most terrific thing you ever imagined. And when I say Allied, I mean just that. We are all operating as a single force, and the only way that you can tell the difference between the Americans and the British is by their uniforms. There are definite signs," he continued, "that the morale of the remaining air crews (German) in Tunisia has been so badly shaken now that they often evade combat. At other times, when it is possible to engage them, they are shot down like ducks."

In the Bay of Tunis this morning, a British squadron had the mission of seeking out some enemy landing craft. They ran into the landing craft, escorted by two naval vessels, heading for Tunis.

They strafed all craft. From the explosions that followed, we can assume they were trying to land petrol, what we call gasoline.

The landing craft were destroyed and one of the naval vessels was beached. The top cover for this mission had a job to do as the enemy sent up some ME-109s, ME-110s, and MC.202s. Ten enemy aircraft were shot out of the sky. One Spitfire pilot was forced to land on our side of the lines.

Apparently, the Germans were getting desperate as all missions that flew today reported barges or landing craft heading for the Bay of Tunis. From the RAF reports, their boys had some good hunting, shooting up targets in the Bay of Tunis area.

Thursday, April 29. Boys were out in the Bay of Tunis shooting up boats and landing craft in the morning and afternoon. The boys ran into eight ME-109s, but the Jerries ran away. Hospital ship sighted on the Bay of Tunis. One hundred thirty-seven bomber sorties and 499 fighter sorties on this date.

On their return from their mission over the Bay of Tunis, our boys stated, after a strafing run, a motor vessel was in flames.

The plan for the day was to go to the Bay of Tunis, drop bombs, come back, and strafe the boats. One thing a pilot likes to do is come in low and buzz with all his guns blazing.

Many of the boys on these missions will complete their tour of duty in this theater as they have made their quota.

The Western Desert daily intelligence report showed planes in the air all day working, mostly in the Gulf of Tunis area. With all these missions, only a token resistance from the enemy was recorded. When they did attack our mission, they were driven away or shot down. With this lack of interference, it leads one to believe they just don't have the planes to put up.

Friday, April 30. Our boys were out again on sweeps over the Gulf of Tunis. They dropped bombs and then returned to strafe. A message was sent down, via our 8th Fighter Wing, from the British air officer commanding, Air Vice-Marshal Broadhurst, which said "Please convey to all units under your command my heartiest congratulations on your magnificent bombing today. Such efforts will do much towards hastening the end of the Germans in Tunisia."

The score for the day was:

Destroyed:	2 destroyers, 1 Siebel Ferry, 1 1,500-ton ship, 1 corvette, 1 E-boat, 1 F-boat.
Probables:	2
Damaged:	10

One can see from this report the amount of boat traffic in the Tunis Gulf area. This report only covers the American missions. The Germans were trying to get supplies in and, no doubt, thinking of getting some of their troops out.

If their intelligence worked and gave them the true picture, they could have saved a lot of lives.

To conclude this report, I must submit news of a tragic incident. Shortly after breakfast, this morning, one of our cooks was cleaning our field ranges. He committed the unpardonable sin of pouring gasoline into a range next to another burning for a test after cleaning.

The gasoline slopped over and caused an explosion. The nearest fire engine was on the flight line over a mile away. By the time the fire engine

The aftermath when our cooking grills caught fire and burned down the mess tents.

arrived, we had lost the enlisted mess, officers mess, the kitchen, storage tents, and the officers' club attached to the mess.

In all, we lost six tents. In the officers' club, we lost a lot of the pilot's briefcases and billfolds. The pilots were out on a mission when the fire started. There was quite a bit of money in the billfolds because the pilots had been paid the day before.

A pilot never carries his billfold on a combat mission, though he would have what we called invasion currency with him, usually for the country he might have to bail out over in the event he was shot down or crash landed.

We lost a record player and a wonderful collection of records sent to the boys from home. We also lost a piano a wonderful woman in Cairo had recently donated.

We had one pilot who was an outstanding boogie-woogie piano player. A few more of the boys spent quite a bit of time at the ivory keys.

In this edition of Eighth Army News, *there is confirmation of the work the 57th Fighter Group did against the enemy at sea. To be clear, the 57th was operating with the RAF*

No. 279 SATURDAY, 1 MAY, 1943

AXIS SUPPLIES HIT

RAF Get Six Ships
The outstanding feature of yesterday's fighting was an offensive by our fighter-bombers against the enemy's vital sea communications.

As a result of this we claim to have sunk one destroyer, a Siebel ferry, an E-boat, and a 120-ft launch.

We also damaged another destroyer and left a second E-boat and medium size motor vessel in flames.

Confirmation of these results was later obtained from our fighters, which reported seeing five vessels burning around Cape Bon.

At the same time jetties at Kelibia and Sid Daoud, on Cape Bon peninsula, were bombed with good effect.

Unusually strong formations of enemy fighters tried to interfere with our attacks, but their efforts cost them seven planes destroyed and a dozen damaged. Two of our fighters were shot down.

On land there was little change to report yesterday. There was some local activity north of the Sebkret el Kourzia but the dominating feature of the Gebel Bou Kournine is still in enemy hands.

Twelve Tanks Destroyed
In the Central sector bitter but indecisive fighting continued. We claim to have destroyed at least 12 enemy tanks in this area between 29/30 April.

In the extreme north more progress has been made in the coastal sector, where it seems possible the enemy will soon withdraw to the 10-mile bottleneck between the sea and the Garaet Aohkel, about 12 miles west of Bizerta.

On the Eighth Army's front there is nothing new to report.

The young man who caused the incident was very lucky he only received minor burns. He also received a lower rank than he had prior to the fire.

Saturday, May 1. The first order of business this morning was to get the mess and club back in operation. We were able to draw some new tents and ranges immediately after the fire. Rations were picked up from the various units in the area in enough quantity to get us by until we draw some new rations from the local DID (Daily Issuing Depot).

A British unit was not too far from our field. We drew from them what they thought we should have for a few days. With my good adjutant, Henry Mack, and a good-sized truck, we started out early to look for some furniture for the mess and club. The Germans were not too far from our area a few days before the fire. We headed for a village we thought would be deserted.

We were fortunate in the first village and found tables and chairs. Before the morning was over, we had been through several small villages and had a truck load of merchandise required to set up a new mess and club.

We even found an electric Frigidaire from a German aid station near Enfidaville. We had quite a scare when we came out of the aid station and found it had been booby trapped.

While all this scrounging was going on, we had proof that we were not far from the front as the gunfire was in full swing. We returned to our field in good shape and had the mess and the club almost back to normal for a good supper.

Our boys were out on missions at 7:20 this morning with a good load of bombs. In fact, the boys flew the limit of the planes with one bomb under the belly and one on each wing. With three 500-lb pound bombs, this gives them a 1,500-lb load of destruction.

The target this morning was a jetty in the Gulf of Tunis area. This area received special attention from all the fighter-bombers in the Desert Air Force. The results of this mission were a freighter and destroyer hit along with many large explosions around the jetty.

The boys were out again at 3:55 pm on an escort for a squadron bombing some barges in the same area they had visited in the early morning mission.

According to the Western Desert daily intelligence report, no enemy aircraft had been seen during today's operations by the fighter-bombers. Some enemy aircraft were seen by some patrol planes, but they failed to come within actionable distance. A bomber escorted by the enemy was shot down.

The report stated they hoped some high-ranking enemy official may have embarked on a Sicily to Tunis run once too often. Two hundred seventy-four fighter sorties were flown today.

Sunday, May 2. This was one of the hottest days we have had for a long time. The wind blew a real gale. Our boys had no missions. They spent most of the time putting the finishing touches on the mess and club.

Monday, May 3. The air was full of bombers this morning. Our boys took off at 11:00 am with 500 pounders on board for an attack on enemy shipping. They had to return as the weather closed in over the target area. They were later assigned to patrol over some British destroyers which were now appearing in force to make sure no enemy ship gets in or out of the shores of Tunisia.

Tuesday, May 4. As usual, this morning, lots of bombers were in the air. Our boys had a couple of missions today. One was cover for the British destroyers returning from their night patrol duty of the Cape Bon area. The second mission was a milk run to look over the enemy boats and barges. They had been working over these for many days.

All home safe with no enemy sighted.

Wednesday, May 5. Our assignment for this morning was to fly up to Kelibia at 7:40 with 500 pounders and bomb the warehouses and jetty. The reports showed they had several direct hits. No interference from the enemy.

They went back to the same spot again at 11:30 am to drop some more 500 pounders. They went out again at 3:45 pm after the same target. One must conclude those warehouses were important.

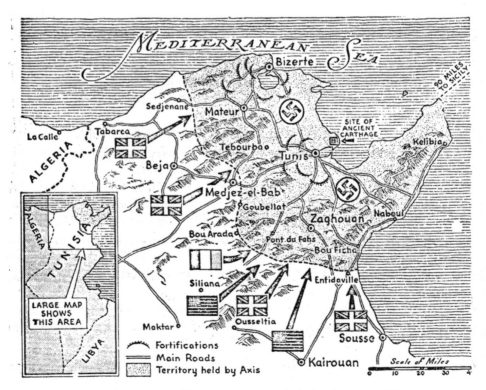

Here are the positions of the various groups right before the Battle of Tunis.

In looking over the intelligence report, you would say the boys of the Desert Air Force had a busy day. They started at 4:55 am. The last mission came back at 7:25 pm. It looks like every unit of the force was out. The fighters flew 389 sorties and the fighter-bombers flew 389. The bomb line moved so fast it was going to be hard to find targets on the ground our troops had not captured.

Some of the pilots had no flying duties today. They went out with a truck and came back with some good furniture.

I had a chance to look at the prisoner of war (POW) statements in the intelligence report. One stated a hospital ship bringing wounded from Tunisia returned with munitions and supplies. Some POWs told how they sabotaged their airplanes when they were ordered to fly from Sfax when it was imminent it would fall. They would take off but crash land not far from their field and were captured.

Thursday, May 6. Our boys were out at 5:35 am for a mission over the Cape Bon area. They were bombed up, with guns full of ammunition, for any target they could find. They came back with their bombs on. No targets. No enemy.

At 7:30, their mission was to escort 17 Mitchell bombers to a target in the Cape Bon area. All bombers and fighters returned safely.

This was another one of those days with the sky full of fighters and bombers. Looking over the reports, you could see every unit gave a slap at the retreating enemy.

I did not receive the total sorties of the day, but I am sure this will be one of the highest of the campaign.

Our British liaison officer, who was stationed with our group headquarters, reported the Eighth Army advance party passed into the City of Tunis.

For a change, this evening we were entertained by a roving group of entertainers called the "Yacht Club Boys." We have had little or no entertainment during our trek across the desert sands of Egypt, Libya, and Tunisia. We had some old movies about a dozen times during the past nine months. The boys did not seem to mind the lack of entertainment during the trek as most everybody went to bed early.

We were not near towns or cities to draw the troops. Another thing was they had to be up early in the morning. By early, I mean early. While going across this vast wasteland, the workday started many mornings shortly after 3:00 as we had the dawn mission. The planes, in most cases, were loaded with bombs and gassed before we went to bed. There were many times, though, the armament had to be changed on the ships before take-off. In many cases, armaments were changed an hour before the plane moved up to the take-off point.

At this point I want to say the Black Scorpion Squadron had the most dedicated group of enlisted men I have ever worked with. They had the highest *esprit de corps* of any unit I have ever had.

We have had little or no rain since we left Libya but, tonight, we had the works. We really had to nail down the tents as we had a real blow, and our area was on the top of a slope. We got through the night without losing any of our equipment.

I have found the sortie report: fighters, 437 sorties; fighter-bombers, 196 sorties. The light and medium bombers put up 197 sorties. Quite a day. As I have said many times, thank God they are our planes.

Friday, May 7. The field was a real mud pie this morning after the terrific rain last night. The good news this morning is the Germans and Italians have been driven out of Tunis and Bizerte. With the fall of these two important pieces of territory, a great number of soldiers of the enemy are trapped. It was good news to hear they trapped so many. I do not have the official count.

This news means the war was over for them. It also means less troops attacking our troops. Our boys had a mission at 1:00 pm in the Gulf of Tunis. After the mission returned, the report was a lot of near misses and a destroyed E-boat.

They were out again at 4:50 pm with 500 pounders for any shipping they could find. They patrolled the gulf area but no targets. They came home with the bombs on.

In looking over the reports of the day, this is the same pattern we have had for days. The sky is full of planes on their way to destroy the men and equipment of the enemy. The report shows the bombers were out at night. They dropped their loads of bombs on the retreating enemy.

One bomber found a good target in the La Goulette area, barges loaded with troops. They were set on fire and destroyed.

This was another big day for the fighters and fighter-bombers with 685 sorties against a retreating enemy. Also, the Army reported 13,000 German prisoners taken in the last two days.

We had a lot of extra work along the flight line with P-38s landing for gas. These boys had been working over a few islands off the coast of Cape Bon. They have been doing some skip bombing. I remember one pilot stating he dropped a bomb right in a hangar. Some of our boys visited this island later and did not agree with this young man. They found the hangar intact.

Here I am with two of the locals.

We had beer on ice tonight. During our trek across the desert, we have had beer from time to time, but no ice. Some of the boys must have found an ice plant in one of the captured towns. The British would never worry about ice as they drank their beer warm. Many times, I heard the expression, when they would see British soldiers drinking warm beer, "Pour it back in the horse."

On this field, a lot of clothing was reported missing. With the boys away from their tents most of the day, it was easy for the locals to sneak into the area and help themselves. Our tent area was spread out for about three or four miles on this field with a few villages not far from us. This gave us something else to worry about as far as thefts of shoes and shirts.

We had a meeting. I remembered when we first moved into this area, I had a visit from one of the Arab chiefs from a nearby village. He had been educated in the States. He offered his help if we ever needed it.

I sent Sgt Charles Bischara of Sanford, Maine, to see the chief and had him report about the many missing shoes and shirts. I told the sergeant to tell the chief we would give his village until sundown to come up with the missing equipment or we would drop some 500 pounders on the village.

This was all a bluff, but it paid off. The next day we received from the chief much more equipment than we had lost. We had quite a chat. I thanked him for his courtesy.

In another squadron on our field, a local was found in the tent area with a load of stolen GI (general issue) clothing. When he failed to halt, he was shot. From what I remember about this incident, he died and was unclaimed by his people. He was buried on the airfield.

Saturday, May 8. All during the night we heard the bombers on their way to enemy targets. The fighters were busy patrolling over Cap Bon and ran into some German Ju-88s. Our boys had a mission at 1:00 pm on some shipping in the coast area. The bombs exploded on the deck of a motor vessel. Many of the bombs were recorded as near misses.

British Spitfires started working over the island of Pantelleria off the coast of Tunisia. The Germans had a landing ground there with a few planes still able to operate. From the reports, it looks like the Germans are retreating to the Cape Bon area. There was no place to go except the water and that is being taken care of day and night by fighters, bombers, and destroyers off the coast.

Sunday, May 9. The first order of business for this day was to escort some bombers over Pantelleria. A total of 126 Bostons, Mitchells, and Baltimores plastered the landing ground. Fire and smoke were seen for miles and the smoke from one fire rose to the height of 4,000 feet.

No enemy aircraft was seen. Fighter missions ran from 4:55 am to 6:20 pm. Our boys had their first mission at 7:40 to take care of some shipping, which they did very well. On their way back to the field, they strafed some motor transport.

It must be nice to be driving along in a truck and have a group of fighters pouring six .50-caliber machine guns from each plane into you. Not many lived to tell about it.

They had another mission at 11:40 am but no results. On this mission, our boys were top cover for the other three squadrons on the mission. They were out again at 1:00 pm with Spitfires for top cover but, again, no results. The enemy, in the area assigned to them, were in hiding or had moved out.

Another stunning day for the Allied forces in Africa.

No. 288 MONDAY, 10 MAY, 1943

Prisoners Flock In
German Generals Taken
Eight German Generals are among the 50,000 Axis prisoners who have now fallen into our hands.

They include G.O.C. of *Panzerarmee 5*, General von Vaerst: the commanders of *Manteurffel* and 334 Division, Generals Buelowius and Edar: and the commander of the famous 15th Panzer Division, Major-General Borowitz.

The leader of these "desert rats" of the *Afrika Korps* surrendered appropriately to a unit of the 7th Armored Division—which may take some of the sting from so humiliating an end to a gallant and distinguished record.

15th Panzer Division, it may be recalled, arrived in Africa in the spring of 1941 and played a leading part in all the battles of the Western Desert.

It was the tanks of this division which got nearest to the Nile during Rommel's abortive attack at the beginning of September last.

Survivors Fight On
But although the major part of the Axis army of Africa is now "mafeesh" the survivors are still fighting back grimly in the 40-mile strip from Enfidaville and Saouaf to the Cape Bon "bottleneck."

They are estimated at about 30,000 men with some 50 tanks of 10 and 21 Panzer Divisions. Among the infantry are the remnants of the veteran German 90 Light Division and also of the 164 Divisions, who arrived in Africa last summer to take part in what was to have been Rommel's final advance to the Nile.

In the north, however, our forces have broken through Hammam Lif and are thrusting towards Soliman and Grombaia, thus threatening the enemy's last line of retreat.

Resistance Strong
Nevertheless, north and south of Zaghouan resistance is still strong and our French allies have been unable to make further progress against the enemy's positions in the hills.

On the Eighth Army's front no withdrawal has yet taken place and a local attack last night by our troops in the coast sector made no progress in face of strong opposition from 90 Light Division.

Sicilian Port Blasted
Palermo was the target yesterday for the heaviest raid ever in the Mediterranean war zone.

Four hundred American aircraft took part in the attack on this Sicilian port.

They dropped five times the weight of bombs previously dropped on a single target in a single raid throughout the North African campaign.

The attack was concentrated on a single square mile of docks and buildings and great damage was done. An hour after the raid photographs could not be taken owing to the vast pall of smoke which hung over the dock area.

The report for this day was a long one. It seemed all outfits of the Desert Air Force had their turn in the air. The bombers who started out this day were again busy this afternoon.

An interesting note in the report was an Army unit captured an airfield and found 14 ME-109s and two Ju-88s, all dummies. The British used this trick back in the days when we were near El Alamein. They had a field set up with lots of dummy anti-aircraft guns. With all the activity this day, hardly any enemy aircraft rose to challenge this onslaught of air power.

To close off this day's activity, I read in the report that the number of German prisoners taken for today was about thirty thousand.

Monday, May 10. During the early hours after midnight, the bombers gave the island of Pantelleria the works. Many fires were seen. It was thought they hit a fuel dump.

Our boys were off at 6:00 am with Spitfires and a squadron of South Africans as their top cover. This mission was without results. They were off again on a worthless mission at 12:55 pm.

The end is coming for the enemy in Tunisia. In the last four days it was estimated that about sixty thousand Germans and Italians have been captured. The report states that leaves 60,000 to be killed or captured.

When you drove along the road you saw the prisoners by the thousands heading for the POW cages. Some of them were in trucks and others walked along the road. Others tried to bum a ride. It's a strange sight.

In this area, most of the troops were Eighth Army soldiers. From what they have been through with the Germans, I doubt many would stop to give any rides to the surrendering members of the now defeated *Afrika Korps*.

From the intelligence report, it looked like the Desert Air Force had every plane in the air sometime during the last 24 hours, pounding away at any target they could find. Looking at the operations map in our own ops tent, this mess is about over.

The following message was received from General Eisenhower:

> No words of mine could possibly express the depth of my appreciation and gratitude to you and all ranks of the 18 Army Group and to the Allied Air and Naval forces in this theatre for your recent brilliant successes.
>
> Every citizen of each of the United Nations would like to send you similar messages.
>
> I know that these victories are merely spurring you on to utilize every last atom of strength to destroy the enemy speedily and completely.
>
> Best wishes and good luck to you and every man in your magnificent command.

News like this in the Eighth Army News *was the reason the 64th Fighter Squadron ran out of targets.*

No. 289 TUESDAY, 11 MAY, 1943
ENEMY SURROUNDED

Hammamet, Bou Ficha Fall
Tanks of the First Army advancing from Tunis reached Hammamet early this morning, thus closing the circle around the bulk of the surviving Axis forces, who are now in the southern pocket.

Subsequently Bou Ficha, only 12 miles northeast of Enfidaville, was occupied.

Meanwhile, our French allies have launched an attack under cover of a heavy artillery barrage upon the formidable Gebel Garci feature six miles west of Takrouna.

The remains of the Army of Africa, estimated at less than 30,000 men and a few tanks, are thus imprisoned in a rough quadrilateral about 30 miles long and 20 broad, the southern side being represented by the Eighth Army's front north and west of Enfidaville.

No supplies can reach them, and it is only a matter of time before lack of food and ammunition forces them to surrender although scattered parties could probably carry-on guerrilla warfare in the hills for some time.

This Eighth Army News *report indicates we won't be in Africa much longer, but the war is still far from over for the 64th.*

No. 290 WEDNESDAY, 12 MAY 1943

THE END IS NEAR

More Divisions Surrender
The enemy's last armored divisions, 10th and 21st Panzers, have surrendered.

Tens of thousands more prisoners have been taken and the total since 6th May is now nearly 120,000.

Most of the 10th Panzer Division capitulated yesterday afternoon after stern fighting with our 1st Armored Division in the area south of the Creteville–Grombalia road.

The remainder surrendered this morning after scuttling most of their surviving tanks.

In addition, the remnants of 3 Recce Unit, which played a distinguished part in the desert war, have laid down their arms.

21st Panzer Surrenders
In the Zaghouan area 21st Panzer accepted terms of surrender from the French 19 Corps after fierce infantry fighting that raged all yesterday morning.

It was this division—under the title of 5th Light—which was the first German formation to reach Africa to reinforce the shattered Italians in February 1941.

It took a leading part in Rommel's subsequent counter-offensive which drove our depleted forces back to the Egyptian frontier two months later. With the surrender of their comrades to the north the last remnants of the Axis army—the survivors of the German 90th and 164th Light Divisions and the Italian *Pistoia, Trieste,* and Young

(Continued)

Fascists, totaling less than 20,000 men—were confined this morning in a mountainous "coffin" about 20 miles long by 10 miles deep opposite the Eighth Army front.

Forlorn Hope
Nevertheless, the G.O.C. of 90th Lights, Major General Graf von Sponek, yesterday afternoon replied to Lt. General Freyberg's invitation to surrender with a refusal.

Proof that this was no mere gesture was given by the stern resistance made to the French attack on the Gebel Garci, which failed to progress in face of fierce machine-gun and mortar fire from the well-placed enemy positions in this rugged country to the east, however, ground was gained, and some German prisoners were brought in.

In the Cape Bon Peninsula, our mobile forces have completed the circuit of the coastline, joining hands at Kelibia. Some 10,000 of the enemy who had been waiting more or less hopelessly to be taken off by air or submarine were rounded up.

Churchill in U.S.A.
Mr. Churchill is now in Washington for important discussions with President Roosevelt.

The prime minister arrived yesterday afternoon and was met by the president, who drove with him to the White House, where he will stay during his visit.

Mr. Churchill was accompanied by high-ranking British military and naval officers.

It is more than three months since the prime minister and President Roosevelt met at the Casablanca conference following which Mr. Churchill said: "We have now completed our plan of action. This plan is going to be carried out within the next nine months, during which time we will make efforts to meet again."

The present talks are not expected to be confined to the war against Germany but will also cover the struggle against Japan.

Tuesday, May 11. Took a trip over to Constantine through the Kasserine Pass where the American First Army had some tough fighting during the past few months. The area showed signs of the tremendous battles fought there.

We needed rings for our jeeps and GMC 2½-ton trucks. The British didn't have any parts. This gave us a chance to see this part of the country.

We could not obtain the rings at the American depot. The American officer in charge of the depot brushed us off as if we were poison. He stated it was not in his books to take care of some Americans assigned to the British Eighth Army.

A kindly officer, who seemed to be ashamed of the conduct of the officer in charge, followed us from the depot. He stated, if we came back later, he would take care of our needs.

After lunch we returned to the depot and met with this young man. We found

64th Squadron enlisted men.

out that he had no rings. Instead, we left there with our truck filled with complete engines for our jeeps and 2½-ton trucks.

Back at the squadron area, the flying was still in full swing, but targets were hard to find. The reports showed the only ground fighting going on was in the Zaghouan–Bou Ficha road area and the German 90th Light Infantry was fighting its last battle.

Our boys went out on a mission at 12:45 pm loaded with 500 pounders and 40 pounders. They bombed a 25-truck convoy. All the other fighter and bomber groups filled the sky with planes. Some of these boys might be flying their last mission. A rumor went around that some of the boys of the 57th were going home very soon.

The reports showed the Germans, although almost done as far as Africa was concerned, were putting up some heavy anti-aircraft fire. Most of our targets for the day were motor transport on the road heading for nowhere. It must be a terrifying experience for the troops in these trucks to be driving along and to have a load of 500-pound bombs dropped on or near you. I am sure the number of casualties during these last days of Africa for the enemy reached tremendous numbers.

Wednesday, May 12. We had no missions. There were few enemy targets. Some of the other units were assigned a few missions in one area where the last of the Germans held out. A few missions were confined to patrols over His Majesty's ships off the shores of Cape Bon.

From the Army side, there was still some ground fighting on the Zaghouan–Bou Ficha line this morning. Before noon, the Eighth Army units attacking from the northeast took 12,000 prisoners including General von Arnim, commanding general of the Axis forces in Africa.

The French, coming in from the west, picked up 22,000 prisoners in the last 48 hours. Negotiations for surrender took place during the afternoon between General Messe, commanding general of the First Italian Army, and General Montgomery. By nightfall, all resistance had ceased.

To use the last remark of the intelligence officer of the Advance Headquarters in the Western Desert, "The Campaign in North Africa is over, and it was ended in a resounding disaster for the German Army."

The headline in the *Tripoli Times*, North Africa's first English daily, read: "Final African Defeat, Our booty now is 150,000 Axis Prisoners, Van Arnim Captured, 1,200 Guns + 250 Tanks and Thousands of Vehicles."

The headline continued with "the War in Africa has ended." The dramatic finale was written when the British 6th Armored Division joined up with the Eighth Army and the German commander-in-chief of the Axis Forces, General von Arnim, was taken prisoner together with 11 other generals.

The 150,000 prisoners taken means the smashing of 11 German divisions and 26 Italian divisions; 110,000 of the prisoners were German.

Cease-fire in Africa

Reporting on the end of the *war in Africa emphasized the vital role air power had played.*

CEASE FIRE
By *Tripoli Times* War Correspondent Richard Elley

Enfidaville, Thursday, May 14, 1943

At 9.15 this morning came the final <<Cease Fire>> order to Eighth Army units. It marked not only the end of the North African campaign but the end of the pathetic attempt by the enemy remnant to hold the last stretch of the North African coasts, a stretch—seven or eight miles between Bou Ficha and Enfidaville—flat and marshy, dominated by hills in which the enemy troops were almost surrounded. Across it runs the coast road and to the seawards there is a biggish lake.

Air power, employed in close concert with the Army, has proved itself for all time in a strategy which has carried the Allied forces from victory to victory. The *Tripoli Times* published this article as a tribute to the men of the Western Desert Air Force—to the flying crews and the ground personnel who, for three years, have played an epic part in the winning the Battle for Africa.

DESERT AIR FORCE

A sheik's grave, an old port, a delightful bathing beach and a seldom used aerodrome— that is Maaten Bagush.

Here, three years ago, was formed a mixed group of squadrons whose task was to assist in the defense of Egypt and to seek out and destroy whosoever might attempt to cross the Western Desert and invade the Nile delta. This was the nuclei of what was to become the most acclaimed Air Command in the world—Desert Air Force.

Tedder's Command

Today the Desert Air Force is part of the North African Tactical Air Force. This with the strategic and Coastal forces, forms the North African Air Force—an important part of Sir Arthur Tedder's Mediterranean Air Command.

Air Chief Marshal Sir Arthur Tedder made possible Coningham's plans for an air victory in the desert. With a staff of specialists, the intricate details of supplies and maintenance were thrashed out. The desert air weapons came from far and wide. Equipment flown over the Congo swamps, trained pilots from the Union of South Africa. Tedder coordinated the elements; Canal-based bombers, R.A.F. and Naval Coastal aircraft, Malta squadrons—which were vital if the Desert Air Force was to succeed in its three important tasks.

Never has the Desert Air Force rendered greater service to the army than during those weeks when the Army of the Nile withdrew for nearly six hundred miles. Not once during that long journey was the vulnerable coast road attacked. Our squadrons remained at Gambut and operated against the most advanced enemy Landing-Grounds with such ferocity that our ground troops were able to withdraw unmolested. Our fighters fought from Gambut until the enemy tanks were within ten miles and they flew to another base. In the withdrawal from Gazala to Alamein less than two per cent of the R.A.F. equipment was lost.

The Daily Mail *article below gives some idea of what the boys were seeing, and some of the frustration they felt, when they flew their missions against the rapidly shrinking enemy forces in Tunisia.*

CAPE BON-FIRE
By Paul Bewsher of the *Daily Mail*
With the Western Desert Air Force, Thursday

"Nobody told them the war is over. That's the trouble. We know it, but they don't know it."

A young pilot summed up the situation aptly with these few words as he reported the strange scene in the last pocket of enemy resistance north of Enfidaville.

He had just been flying round to see what was happening in the swiftly changing situation.

He gave me a vivid picture of the last fighting hours of the trapped remnants of the once vaunted *Afrika Korps*.

"There were columns of transports driving up and down the roads in both directions", he said, "but they didn't seem to realize that wherever they went they were just driving into the bag. I suppose they didn't understand the situation and were trying to find some way out."

Other pilots described how the whole area was covered with fires and explosions as the cornered army blew up dumps and stores.

HUGE FIRES

"Great pillars of dust and smoke and debris were shooting up into the air and billowing out into mushroom heads." they said. "Black oily columns of smoke were curling up all over the place from dozens of fires."

"Just by the coast an ammunition dump was blazing, and continual explosions were flashing out amidst the flames. But way down in the south our guns were still busily shelling their lines which they were still holding in the hills."

"The whole of the sunlit fingers of the Cape Bon Peninsula pointing out into the blue Mediterranean was smoking as if it were dotted with volcanoes."

"A Cape Bon-Fire," remarked another pilot.

That same night the pilots, together with all men, of a South African squadron were watching the film "Desert Victory," recalling many events which they had studied in the air at the time and faithfully reported.

For them, at this swift ending of the whole campaign, it had a very special significance.

As they walked back to their tents there was still the heavy thump and rumbling of guns from the Enfidaville front where the trapped remnants of an overwhelmed army were putting up a hopeless and useless resistance in the mountains—for no reason at all.

As that pilot put it, "Nobody told them the war is over. That's the trouble."

CHAPTER 22

Causeway Field, Tunisia

Thursday, May 13. The first order of business this morning was that all the boys went out on scrounge detail. By nightfall, it seemed every officer and enlisted man had a German or Italian motorcycle, truck, or automobile. The boys had a few days of this and, of course, we had some accidents with the motorcycles. Headquarters issued orders that most of the vehicles were to be turned in within the next 24 hours.

This did not appeal to the boys as they felt they should be able to drive all over the countryside with the new toys they had acquired. As far as they were concerned, the war was over for them.

This was not true as the invasion of Sicily was the next order of business. There were many rumors around that the squadron would go home now the war had ended in Africa. This was not true. The work was all laid out for the squadron and the group to play an important part in the coming invasion. The only ones to go home were nine of the original pilots who came over with the squadron almost eleven months ago. They had flown their quota of missions and had done an outstanding job. One of the pilots came back later to command the squadron; he was Major Robert A. Barnum of Lake City, Michigan.

We had a gang of new officers come in as replacements. Of course, there was training for these boys as the training they received in the States did not have the complete picture as to the methods of flying in combat.

We had some boys who would give them the firsthand story. They had been through many combat missions. They made a superior teacher for a newcomer arriving on the sands of Cape Bon, Tunisia.

Major Robert Barnum helping with his plane.

The training started at once. Some of the boys flew patrol missions off the coast of Tunisia. The training program for the new pilots continued during two moves of the squadron around the Cape Bon area. One field was called Cape Bon and the other, a short distance away, was called Causeway.

A percentage of the enlisted men and officers were given leave in Tunis. Some were lucky enough to go to Cairo and Alexandria, Egypt.

This Causeway field was the bottom of a dried-up lakebed and made a good runway. It had a hard-packed soil and made for good take-offs and landings. This field was close to the water and made for daily swimming and bathing.

The Mediterranean Sea at this spot was pretty hot. You had to get up early in the morning to get your dip in.

We were lucky that a small village not far from the field had a sulfur bath. Many of us arrived early each morning for our bath rather than go in the Mediterranean Sea.

It was hard to get used to this inactivity as far as the war was concerned. We had been on the go since we left Landing Ground 174 in Egypt on November 16, 1942. It has been a long and trying trek. At least, when we moved out of this desert terrain, we should be free of the dust and terrific heat.

We were going to miss the thievery of the locals who prowled the desert, for the most part looking for something to steal. We know we will not have to move at the same pace we had during the days of chasing the Germans and Italians. I am sure we can look forward to better rations and supplies. We know part of the squadron will move to Tripoli and then on to Malta for the invasion of Sicily.

As we went into a new phase of the war for the Black Scorpion Squadron, I will leave out the day-by-day activity as we were in a standby status waiting for headquarters to give us the info on the coming events to complete this campaign that will take many more months to complete.

The important part of the coming days was to give rest and recreation to the enlisted men and officers who have been under pressure for the past 10 months. Many of us had the opportunity to travel around this strange land which we had read about and studied in school. During the days ahead, there was not much to do. I will put in writing a few highlights that took place. Tunis seemed to attract many people, even this writer.

During the first part of our trek across the sands of the Western Desert, we were out of touch with the world for news. We had no radios and had to get our news of the war from what the pilots did, with an occasional news clipping from the British.

We obtained a couple of radios from the British. The first broadcast of the day was from the British Broadcasting Corporation. This news you could depend on as they told the truth. We enjoyed this news, and it was free of commercials.

The next news we would tune in for was the fascist broadcast from Rome. These were far from the truth as far as the war in the desert. They covered up the bad news to the home folks. Many times, they would talk about an orderly retreat from a spot that we had taken many days before. I remember one village they talked about and reported about their troops in this particular town. We had been in that town for several days.

The news was followed by a commentator who called himself Mr. Impertanix. It seemed his job was to pick on some prominent person. One day he took Winston Churchill over the coals and one morning it was Eleanor Roosevelt, the wife of our President Franklin D. Roosevelt. One morning it was the mayor of New York, LaGuardia. He gave him the same treatment as the rest but closed off with the remark that the mayor had one good attribute, he was an Italian.

Later, when we were in Florence, Italy, I found out this fellow had a noble background and did these broadcasts for a lark. Lark or not, he was in prison for his fascist activities during the war.

I remember one incident that took place while we were spending a few days in an assigned hotel. I had let one of the pilots have my jeep. This young man came to my room to report the jeep had been stolen. He had just lost a vehicle that cost $1,400.00, and he was responsible for it.

I told him he was in trouble and when he went back to our base, he had better have my jeep or be prepared to stand a court-martial for the loss of the $1,400.00. He knew what I meant, as many times we saw reports of courts-martial with soldiers being assessed similar amounts for the loss of vehicles.

All officers and men were warned in advance about vehicles being stolen. It became a vicious circle, this stealing of cars. We even had a report some Navy people had stolen a jeep, disassembled it, and taken it on board a submarine. There were also claims the Navy took some jeeps and put them on board their ships.

About an hour after he lost my jeep, the pilot came back to my room and reported he had a jeep. I found out he roamed around Tunis looking for my jeep. During the search, he found a jeep parked outside a hotel with the engine running and no one in it.

He jumped at the opportunity to have a jeep and save $1,400.00. So, he took off and hid the jeep somewhere in Tunis. I found out later it had British markings on it.

When I returned to our field, I found my assigned jeep in its proper place with a new coat of paint and the correct numbers. The Black Scorpion insignia was painted in the proper place.

I did not ask any more questions about it as we had the correct number in the motor pool.

It was good to be out of a tent for a few days. The rooms were in good shape but no lights or water. When the Germans evacuated a city, town, or village, it was standard operating procedure for them to see facilities were disrupted. This condition was usually overcome in a few days once the engineers went to work.

Back at the field, the boys were out on patrol daily just in case the Germans decided to pay the tip of Cape Bon a visit. They were not too far away on Sicily.

This patrol activity gave the new pilots an opportunity to work out with some of the senior pilots of the Black Scorpion Squadron. They were the best teachers any new young pilot could find.

Most of these new young men wanted action at once. You had to hold the reins on these young stallions, keep them in line. It was good for the squadron, and good for the young pilots, we had the time to give them proper training. During the push across the Western Desert, we did not always have so much time to train the new boys when they reported as replacements.

PART II

The Italian Campaign: Malta to the Po Valley

CHAPTER 23

Malta

During the next month, the squadron moved to the island of Malta to await the invasion of Sicily, except for a few members of the rear party who stayed behind to take care of planes that needed parts. This was a normal operation. We were always short of some part which grounded a plane.

Although, we went across the Western Desert with a high rate of serviceability. The crew chiefs, along with all the other men who kept the planes flying, took pride in keeping the planes ready for action. They would forget about the number of hours it would take. Many times, they were on the line until late, working under the lights of a jeep or truck.

The Germans, in their retreat across the Western Desert, sacked the wells that could have been used by the Eighth Army. They salted some, blew up others, or filled them with oil.

The Germans had a 5-gallon can that we called a "Jerry can." It was used for water and gas. In their retreat from El Alamein, all the way to Cape Bon, they left thousands of these cans. Little did they know that the British Eighth Army made good use of them. These cans had a much better outlet than the cans we had.

I know the supply problems for the Eighth Army were gigantic ones. The people that carried out this mission did an outstanding job. The Black Scorpion Squadron can vouch for same. Although we moved fast, many times off the beaten track in the long trek from El Alamein to Cape Bon, we never wanted for food, ammunition, or petrol.

The Germans were famous for planting mines. The Germans and Italians laid 500,000 mines and we can vouch for that. We were briefed on the importance of the rules of transiting areas marked with mines. Not a single member of the Black Scorpion Squadron died or was injured from German mines or our own.

At one spot, we witnessed German dead laying in a mined area.

I am not sure how many people know the amount of American equipment used in the victory of the Western Desert by the British and Americans: trucks; Sherman and Grant tanks; Boston and Baltimore (as the British called them) medium bombers, and B-24s and B-25s; and the C-47 transport all played a part. One British writer stated victory would have been impossible without American equipment.

On an airfield called Daba, the enemy left over 200 German and Italian planes behind during their retreat. On one airfield in Tunisia, many planes were found in their original crates, never opened.

SCORPIONS' FAREWELL TO THE WESTERN DESERT

Bleak and barren and windy
A waste land as ancients could tell
Blasted with cold in the winter.
In summer heat hotter than hell,
No place for a white man's dwelling
And the wandering tribes of the Arabs
Went further in search of a home.

But the fates had decided before us,
That the battles of life should be here
And this land should be hallowed and sacred
to the men who never knew fear,
Twas here that they won and lost battles,
Though many are forgotten by name,
As a group they will live on forever
And others shall hear of their fame.

When peace comes once more to the weary,
And the homeless and starving are free,
Perhaps some will come as to Mecca
This desert and vastness to see.
As they stand on this ridge and see outward
The azure and pearly hues
will answer the question you wondered,
Why was it they called it the blue.

Let's hope they can see as a vision
the tanks as the gave what they had.
And the guns as they pounded the trenches
With a sound like heavens gone mad.
May they think of the soldier they're charging
And the planes droning high overhead
And when they come to the group of white crosses,
Just ponder a time, by the dead.

And here feel the thought of the dying
wondering why all it should be
And remember their valor and glory
Are what gave all a chance to be free.

CHAPTER 24

Scordia, Sicily

Monday, July 19. The squadron's A Party arrived in Pachino, Sicily. This is a small town on the east coast of Sicily, about one hundred fifty miles across the water from Cape Bon in Africa, our last base during the push to drive Hitler out of Africa.

The route the advance party took to get there was from Cape Bon to Tripoli to Malta and then over to this new base which belonged, at one time, to Benito Mussolini and his partner, Adolf Hitler.

The first thing, as we mentioned many times, A Party did was set the base up for the planes to operate. This was always done quickly. The planes came in late and prepared for their first mission tomorrow.

Tuesday, July 20. All squadrons flew their first mission from the island of Sicily. A large group of the boys of the squadron were from Italian parents. This was an asset in the dealings with the natives.

Being with the rear party, I did not have all the information of the action that took place while we were still in Africa except the squadron flew the maximum number of missions daily.

I received a report that the group commander, Col. Art Salisbury, was shot up on a mission over Italy and had to bail out over Sicily. He was uninjured. B Party is in a staging area in Tripoli. We loaded the trucks and supplies and left Tripoli Harbor for the port of Syracuse, Sicily.

It took us a day and a half to reach the shores of Sicily. We proceeded towards the harbor entrance, but the ship turned around and went back out to sea.

Colonel Art Salisbury, CO of the 57th Fighter Group, and his P-40 showing each of the logos of the group's squadrons. (57th Fighter Group website, Carl Lovick Collection)

I had many talks with the ship's captain during our trip. Being the commander of the troops on this short voyage, I headed to the bridge to inquire the reason for not putting into Syracuse.

He was very calm and said the enemy had been around during the night. Mines had been found by some of the destroyers escorting us.

Port Augusta was to be our new port of entrance and was about twenty-five miles to the west of Syracuse. We went ashore and proceeded to a field called Scordia.

A Party had moved to this spot the day before we arrived. It was good to be together again as the squadron had been separated for about fifty days.

We had quite a reunion that evening at the new base. The base was hacked out of a piece of farmland at the foot of Mt. Etna.

One of the great morale builders for any unit was to have lots of mail and packages. These awaited us as the mail for the past two weeks had been sent to the advance unit. The boys were always in a happy mood when they heard from home.

Sunday, August 15. It was quiet. Rumors were that in a few days all the enemy will be out of Sicily. A group of the boys went to Lentini, a few miles from our base. We witnessed a group of happy townspeople listening to the Lentini Town Band in their first concert in many years.

Under Fascist rule, there were no concerts, no record players or listening to the radio except to the Fascist-controlled stations. All the radios we saw were built so that only those stations could be tuned in.

It was a happy sight to see so many people laughing and dancing to the music of their own town band. I had a talk with the bandmaster and arranged for him to bring his band to the base later in the month.

Monday, August 16. During our stay in the Alexandria, Egypt, area, we purchased beer from a local merchant. We had to pay him 40 cents a can for American beer that was made in good old Brooklyn, New York. This bothered us, but what could we do? He used to say, "Take it or leave it." With the sand of the desert and the heat, the beer was a welcome relief once the day's work was complete.

After leaving Egypt, we were told by the British we were entitled to a tax rebate on the beer. I filed the proper papers with our headquarters in Cairo, but never did receive an answer.

The Sicilian town of Lentini.

I made up my mind, if there was to be a rebate, I would work on this project without the aid of what we called the "Cairo Commanders."

With a new set of properly prepared papers, I went to the controller-general's office in Alexandria. I was given the run around by these slick Arabs, but I stayed on him and insisted he honor my claim, or I would proceed to Cairo and ask for a hearing with King Farouk.

Several hours later, he seemed to give in. To bring this incident to a happy close, I left the controller's office with a check for $1,200.00.

I proceeded to the Barclays Bank, where I had done business while stationed in Egypt, and cashed the check. I was afraid these slippery characters might cancel or stop payment on the check.

One of our sergeants, who could speak Italian as well as he spoke English, came to me and informed me a merchant in a village almost on the top of Mt. Etna had stored away a good stock of beer, wine, and champagne.

With the $1,200.00 in hand and no beer issue in sight, it sounded like we should make a proper investigation for this vital product. After a long session with this merchant, we came to an agreement. We would buy his stock, which included about two thousand four hundred bottles of Munich beer plus a good supply of champagne and a few bottles of wine, for $1,600.00. I remember one wine that was 1870 vintage.

When this transaction was completed, we dispatched trucks to the garage where the precious cargo was stored. On August 20, we were scheduled to have a 24-hour relief from flying so we set this day apart to have a good celebration. Every enlisted man and officer received 12 quart bottles of beer. The champagne was distributed in what was a fair amount to the officers and enlisted men.

Tuesday, August 17. The Germans and Italians have left the soil of Sicily. It took 36 days to capture all the island. The next move will be an invasion of Italy to push the enemy out of this part of the world.

With the enemy out of the island, the men were off on trips to various parts of Sicily. There were many places of interest to see.

One trip we took was to the town of Catania, not that far from our field. This spot had been hard hit and many of the modern buildings were in ruins. We were able to obtain some furniture from a few of the buildings that were split apart.

Friday, August 20. This was the day set apart for a celebration. The beer and champagne were dispatched. By the end of the day, we had some very happy officers and enlisted men.

Friday, August 27. The air was full of planes. Our boys were out in full strength. This is the kind of action that proceeds a big push or invasion. With Italy the next spot to be taken care of, we should be hearing the news about the invasion any time now.

Lieutenant Maurice Raskin prepping a cow for the evening meal.

Final arrangements were made with the bandmaster of the Lentini Town Band to give a concert at our airfield.

Tuesday, August 31. Lentini Town Band came to the field in the late afternoon to give a concert. We also had a stage show given by local girls. One of the girls in the show was a relative of one of the sergeants of our squadron. It was a real change, with the music and entertainment.

This evening we were briefed about the push in Italy with landings at Salerno.

Wednesday, September 1. The U.S. Red Cross girls are in the area today with their doughnuts and coffee. It is nice to have doughnuts. It has been a long time since any of us have had doughnuts.

We had a pilot from Steven's Point, Wisconsin, by the name of Lt. Maurice Raskin. He apparently had been in the meat business and was anxious to find an animal for the mess. In his afternoon off, he took a tour of the countryside. He came home with a cow which he cut up like a real meat cutter. We enjoyed fresh meat for the first time since we left the States.

CHAPTER 25

Salerno, Italy

Friday, September 3. Our troops landed at Salerno this morning. A barrage was laid down that started at 4:30 am. Our boys were out on a bomber escort mission. They were jumped by some German ME-109s. After the action was over, all our boys returned home safe. Lieutenant Paul L. Carl of Seneca, Pennsylvania, recorded shooting down an ME-109.

For September 4–7, our boys were on bomber escort missions over the area of the new invasion. During these days we were not bothered by the enemy planes. All returned safely.

Sunday, September 5. We had a peaceful day Sunday. No missions.

Monday, September 6. Payday. This was always a happy occasion. There were many rumors around about the Italians giving up and how some of their air force have flown their planes to some of our fields. It was reported the Italians have had it as far as the Fascist regime is concerned.

Tuesday, September 7. The sky was again full of bombers on their way to an enemy target. Our boys had a bomber squadron to escort. Reports came in that the push was going well in the Salerno area. A new push is in the wind. We will be briefed tomorrow on the plan.

Wednesday, September 8. Our group commander, Col. Art Salisbury, had a meeting

Lieutenant Paul Carl and his P-40. (57th Fighter Group website)

with all the squadrons and told us the new push will take place in the Naples area tomorrow.

Italy gave up at 5:30 pm. They will now be on the side of the Allies.

Thursday, September 9. At 4:00 this morning, a push started to capture Naples. Our boys were out this morning and afternoon strafing the enemy who tried to hold up the troops entering Naples.

The evening report on the day's actions was very good. We were told the latest action was proceeding according to headquarters' plans.

Friday, September 10. The progress on the front is going well. Our boys are not needed today. The talk is to move to a new base near Messina.

Sunday, September 12. We moved A Party out of Scordia to a field called Milazzo. The only thing wrong with this move was, when we arrived, there was no room on the field. We stood by for further orders.

We set up outside the field area and waited. During the day we were able to buy some live chickens from the local people for delivery in a couple of days.

Tuesday, September 14. We still stood outside the airfield at Milazzo awaiting orders. Our planes were working from the rear base on a very important target in Italy. They will land at this airbase we set up for operations. The reason for landing here was because they will not have enough gas to get home otherwise.

Some of our boys assisted the drivers of the large gas trucks. The trucks pulled between the P-40s and fueled them so they can return to our rear base. This operation took about one hour, and the pilots were off OK.

The chickens we purchased a few days ago arrived. Our cooks preceded to kill them and get them ready for a meal tomorrow.

CHAPTER 26

Messina, Sicily

Wednesday, September 15. We received orders to move to Messina for a later movement to Italy which made us very happy. The field at Milazzo was very dusty. As each plane took off, they threw up clouds of dust. It was like being back in the Western Desert.

We also had a problem of a couple hundred pounds of chickens in the pots for a noon meal. When we arrived at Messina, we were told we were on a five-minute standby, so we decided to feed the men with C-rations instead of the chickens.

We laid around this town, that had been hit very hard by bombs and artillery, until about 5:00 pm. Then we were told we would not move to Italy until tomorrow.

The streets were full of long lines of convoys waiting their turn to be loaded on the ferries. The ferries did the best they could under a lot of pressure in a business they were not used to.

We parked for the night in a tenement district area with people living close by. We set up our kitchens right on the street. We also set up our cots with the mosquito bars attached as this was going to be our home for the evening.

Little did I ever think that I would be sleeping on the sidewalk of a street in Messina, Sicily.

When the chickens started to cook, we had a problem with the natives who lived close to the area where we had set up our home for the night. We found many hungry people were nearby. They were looking for someone to feed them. With only enough food for our own men, we had to place a guard around the block we had taken over for the night.

We had quite a problem with the natives milling around the area where we set up. They did not seem to understand we only had enough food for our own troops. The boys who could speak Italian really earned their pay as they explained, very well, we would like to feed them but the amount of food we had was just enough for our own men. Reluctantly, they moved behind the lines we had established.

We served our men. The natives stayed outside the line. It made you feel guilty eating your supper while hungry people stared at you.

We got through the meal and prepared for a night on the streets of Messina. We went to bed late that night and had to be ready to move early the next morning.

Thursday, September 16. Everybody was up at 5:30 am. We had the same problem this morning with the hungry natives, but the breakfast meal was served without incident.

We packed up and proceeded to the ferry area but there were long lines. We had to be patient and wait our turn. The ferries had seen better days. We finally loaded and pushed off for Italy.

CHAPTER 27

Rocco Bernardo, Italy

It was a beautiful sight to see the mountains of southern Italy. Our destination was Reggio Calabria, a one-hour ride from the docks of Messina. We crossed the Messina Straits, a spot we had heard about some time back when one of our squadron commanders (Major Glade Bilby of Skidmore, Missouri) spent the night in a dinghy here after bailing out on a mission. He was rescued in good condition by a PT Boat.

Major Bilby was killed in an airplane accident in the States while training new pilots in 1960.

We landed at Reggio Calabria at 10:00 am. We moved our convoy away from the docks and found an airfield where we could reassemble our convoy for our destination, which was to be a spot called Rocco Bernardo.

While we waited for all the vehicles to arrive, we found a nice beach. This gave all of us a chance to relax after a few hectic days since we left our last home base of Scordia.

We had our lunch in this nice area and moved on till about 4:30 pm. The move was very slow as the roads had been mined and we had to use caution. We had not traveled mined roads since back in the Western Desert. We always have great respect for them. As usual, the engineers did an outstanding job clearing the mines.

The progress of the convoy was also slowed by the roads

The convoy moves out again to our next airfield.

being cluttered with Italian soldiers on their way home. For most of them, they were done. They were a sad looking lot. Many had poor uniforms and equipment which had seen better days.

I guess they were glad someone else was doing the fighting now. We only made about fifty miles this day. We set up camp in a grove for the night.

Friday, September 17. We were up at 6:00 am, served breakfast, and moved out of the area by 7:00 am. The movement was slow this morning as the heavy equipment from some of the outfits in the long convoy had trouble getting around some old houses built too close to the road.

In one spot, we were held up for five hours until the bulldozers were brought up to push the house out of the way.

Marker of the grave of Lieutenant Kowalski killed in a crash with an RAF Hurricane.

Group Captain Walter D. Butler was the RAF pilot killed when Kowalski's plane hit him on the runway.

Some of the people in this little town did not like the idea but the war had to move on. This convoy was a very important part of this latest push.

We arrived at our destination, a spot called Rocco Bernardo. It does not show on many maps. I believe it was an estate of some rich Italian farmer. Getting up early gave us the jump on the other squadrons as we were the first to arrive. This gave us the choice of some buildings on this estate.

For the first time since we came overseas, we had some buildings to set up our headquarters in. We even found some wine and champagne in the closet.

Saturday, September 18. Pilots flew in this morning. They were happy with the setup of this new station as they had been used to living in the tents for so long. They could not believe it. Some of them even had rooms for themselves. Shortly after they arrived, there was a call for a mission. We had our first casualty in a long time.

Lieutenant Eugene E. Kowalski of Calumet City, Illinois, was killed when his plane ran into a British Hurricane fighter waiting on the edge of the runway for clearance to take off. The Hurricane pilot was also killed.

We held services for both brave pilots and buried both just off the runway this evening.

Sunday, September 19. Father Louge conducted a church service in the area where Group HQ had set up.

Our boys found an abandoned freight car full of flares used by the Italians. They had a real Fourth of July celebration.

Included in the freight car was a large quantity of children's shoes. We almost had a mob scene when we distributed the shoes to the children of this area. By the looks of some of them, they hadn't had shoes for some time.

Some of us took a trip a few miles from our field to see Jack Benny and company put on a show in a big field near the 79th Fighter Group. The 79th was a unit made up of many of the boys who were with us before we formed the 57th Fighter Group. It was sort of a reunion to see them again.

Monday, September 20. Father Louge said mass in the small chapel on this farm, now used as an American airfield, for Lieutenant Kowalski. He made the supreme sacrifice a few days ago. All the pilots of the squadron attended this service and later went out on another mission.

The enemy is moving out so fast we will have to move from this field as the P-40s do not have the range to go much further than they have been going on the last few missions. They reported very little enemy air action but lots of anti-aircraft artillery. The boys were still shooting up the flares.

Tuesday, September 21. Boys had an early morning mission, but it's a milk run. No action and no enemy for them to shoot up. We will move out of this field tomorrow to a spot south of Taranto.

CHAPTER 28

Gioia Tauro, Italy

Wednesday, September 22. We moved out with the advance party at 1:00 pm and the move went slowly due to the long lines of trucks and equipment on the road. We did not reach our destination and put up for the night just off the road.

Thursday, September 23. Up early this morning and off to the area assigned to the group. When we arrived in the spot that was supposed to be our airfield, we found it was only a wooded area. There were no engineers around to prepare it for our planes to take off. Apparently, someone along the way forgot to tell us they did not plan to use this area.

It was nice enough for a camping site. We were close to the water, so we all had a little vacation bathing at the seaside.

Friday, September 24. Still waiting for orders to move out. We felt, with the Germans running fast, we could never operate out of this spot. The most important thing that happened today was we received lots of rations. In view of the fact we were in a combat area, all of the candy, cigars, and cigarettes were free. They were welcomed by all. We distributed them according to the strength of the advance party.

Later in the day, we received a radio message saying we had received the rations for the whole squadron by mistake. I found it very difficult to go to the men and take back some of the rations they had been issued.

I decided to let the matter stand and would discuss it when we got together again as one unit. We received a message in the late afternoon that we would move out of this area early tomorrow morning to a field not too far from where we were.

Saturday, September 25. Up early and off to a spot called Gioia at 7:00 am. It only took a couple of hours to reach a base recently used by the Italian Air Force.

The field was in good shape, and we had lots of barracks to live in. They were in very good condition and fairly clean.

One thing about this spot, there were lots of grapes and nuts in the area. We, of course, ate them with ease. The pilots flew in this afternoon. They were happy with the field and the housing conditions. Some of them had a house to live in for the first time since they left the States.

Sunday, September 26. This was Sunday. It is usually just another day, but we had early church services and no missions today. Lots of the boys went to look over the surrounding countryside.

The town of Gioia was small but had a few spots with lots of good wine and champagne. Everybody had lots of money. We have had no place to spend it since we left Tunis. We found a nice Italian restaurant. It was good to taste something different from the GI menu.

Monday, September 27. Boys were out on an early morning mission but had to return due to the fact they ran into some bad weather. They were given the rest of the day off. They all took off and went to Taranto and Bari and had quite a time for themselves.

When they arrived back after their day in the big cities, they all seemed to be driving cars and motorcycles.

The boys told a lot of amusing stories about how the vehicles were obtained.

Later, in northern Italy, there was an investigation about all these so-called "captured" cars.

CHAPTER 29

Foggia, Italy

Thursday, September 30. We are on the move again this morning. Targets were hard to find with the limited range of the P-40. It took us about five hours to reach a spot in the Foggia area called Foggia No. 8.

The field was not quite ready for full operations, but the British engineers were extending the runway. It should be ready tomorrow. Our ships were expected to come in and start operating again.

It was very difficult to keep the pilots happy when there was no flying. That has been the problem since moving into Italy.

This should be a good field. The tents will be in a grove, which we are not used to. We had a building for the enlisted men and officers' club. A club is an important

Foggia, Italy.

part of the running of a squadron, especially when the pilots have lots of time on their hands. We tried to have a bar with enough beverages to satisfy the thirst of all, a record player, and a radio in working condition.

Later in the day, we had a report the field would not be ready until Saturday, October 2.

Saturday, October 2. Boys flew in this morning. They remained in their planes long enough to be gassed up and then they were off on a mission. They were a happy lot as always when they have a plane and a mission to perform.

The missions were mostly shooting up retreating trucks and tanks along the road. There were not many good targets during these days.

We had a very important young man land at our field this afternoon, Major Lance Wade. He was an American serving with the Royal Air Force and is a real ace. On this date, Wade shot down two ME-109s. This brings his total to 25.

We had a happy evening as the last of the rear party came in. We are all together again. We should not be moving too far from this field as there are mountains ahead and the Germans are expected to make a stand just beyond the Foggia area.

In this area, the engineers, both British and American, prepared about thirty-three airfields for fighters and bombers. It was expected that 1,000-plane sorties will start from this area very soon to bring devastation to the Germans in Italy and Germany.

In this attack, B-17 and B-24 heavy bombers will drop their loads of bombs on targets that will bring this crazy war to an end.

During the next few days, we were out of action as far as getting airplanes off the ground. The field was a sea of mud. Operations were held up until the sun shone again.

Wednesday, October 6. The field dried out some. The boys were off on a mission but bad weather over the assigned target area forced them to return to the field. We had a few crack ups, but no one was hurt.

Thursday, October 7. We were on the move again this morning, but remained in the Foggia area. A nice sight on this field when we arrived were many

The boys found lots of souvenirs.

German Ju-88s wrecked from some bombing missions and others from crashed landings.

It makes no difference what caused them to be there. The fact they are no longer flying was a welcome sight.

Many of the enlisted men and officers selected souvenirs from the wrecks of these planes. There was also a great pile of enemy bombs of all kinds piled up on one end of this big field. This was one of the prime bases of the Italians, and the Germans during their occupation. The base looked like it may have been used long before the war started.

Friday, October 8. The rear party arrived; we were together again as one squadron. The rain came down like cats and dogs.

During our operations in the Western Desert, we never worried too much about bad weather. This kind of weather was a new pitch for us when you tried to plan a mission. It makes it very difficult, especially when enemy targets are few and far between,

Later this afternoon, the rain let up. The boys were off on a mission. All returned safe.

Saturday, October 9. We were not far from a fishing village called Manfredonia. I paid this small place a visit in the hopes of buying some fish for a squadron meal. I was unsuccessful as I found out this town was poor. They hardly had enough food, including the fish they caught, for themselves. They depended greatly on the catch. Catching fish slowed down due to the war conditions.

Today we received our September pay. As always, we played lots of card games this evening.

The Foggia area, I would say, was bombed as much as any place I have seen so far. Many civilians were killed in the town when the Allies bombed it back during the push up the coast.

The reason so many civilians were killed during the air raids was the Germans would not allow them to leave the town. Before the bombings, we dropped pamphlets warning the civilian population to leave.

I talked with a few men who worked for us. They told us how cruel the Germans were to them. We know, when we arrived, many bodies were still in the ruins of this community. The stench in parts of the town was evidence bodies were under the rubble. The town officials worked to clear it out.

I talked with many of the men who worked for us at the field. They were bitter about the Germans for not allowing the townsfolk to leave after the pamphlets were dropped by our Air Force. They had ample warning of bombings coming to their town.

These men who worked at the airfield were Italian civilians. The service group in charge of this area hired them by the day and sent them to various units. They were glad for this chance to earn some money. There was nothing for them to do in Foggia. Their jobs had been wiped out by the war.

I was surprised they did not resent Americans being in their town and running it. They seemed very happy the Germans had left. They were looking for a better way of life than they had for the past years under the Fascist regime.

Sunday, October 10. Church services were held this morning. The weather was still poor. We decided to take a trip to see the countryside. That was the order of the day for everyone except the security guards.

Monday, October 11. Took off this morning for the Naples and Salerno area. One of the reasons for going on this trip was to see if we could obtain some information about one of our pilots, Lt. Steven Merena, of Ilion, New York. He had been shot down in this area on a mission before we came to Italy. We had some information he had been held in the small town of Nocera.

We found many prisoners had been held in this area, but they were all taken away a short time after capture. I believe Lieutenant Merena wound up in one of the prison camps for airmen in Germany.

We had an opportunity to see the effects of the bombing in Salerno and Naples. These towns were really given the business by the artillery and bombing raids.

We stayed overnight in the Naples area. There were a couple of towns we wanted to visit as they were mentioned in our information about Merena. We put up for the night with the 31st Fighter Group.

Tuesday, October 12. We visited the towns of Cava and Argni in our further search for information about Lieutenant Merena. Our search was in vain. We left after a visit to Major C. E. Cain, the American representative who helped to bring this town back to normal after many days of bitter fighting.

He promised to search for further information from the civilians. Someone had an idea that this young officer was still being held in the town. We did not believe this, but we wanted to run it down as long as we were in the vicinity.

This evening we had our first chance to see what Mt. Vesuvius looks likes at night from where we stayed in Sorrento. She was flaming. This did not happen very often.

Wednesday–Thursday, October 13–14. Spent some time looking over the city of Naples. The ruins were proof of what bombings will do to a city. Most of the hotels were burned out. The city was like a ghost town except for the military.

We found only one restaurant and that was sort of a black-market deal. We had been on C-rations since we left the squadron. We were glad to have a nice meal with even some real Italian wine.

We headed back to the squadron and Foggia in a cold, driving rain. This was not the best way to travel when you have an open jeep for transportation. The only blessing was we had some heavy winter flying clothes.

They had bad weather at the squadron. They had done little or no flying for a few days.

Friday, October 15. Boys did a lot of flying for the first time in a week. The mission today was to find trains. They did. At the debriefing, which I always tried to attend, it was something to hear how they busted up the targets of the day.

They had a very successful day. They blew up many locomotives. This was what they liked to see: engines blown up that will never run again to pull cars with supplies for the enemy.

Late this afternoon, a large shipment of mail arrived. As I have mentioned many times, this perks the boys up. "Mail, the greatest of all morale builders."

Mail did not always bring good news. Many times, some of the boys were recipients of bad news from home, such as wives not being faithful, or the girlfriend getting tired of waiting for him to return.

I remember one officer receiving the so-called "Dear John" letter. He remarked, "She just sent me a Kay Woodie pipe for a gift."

One boy's wife had a child. He had been gone for over 2½ years. There were many days when these boys would come into the orderly room with their problems after a mail delivery. I would try to do my best to console them. There was always the wonderful Father Louge to talk to. Many boys went to him; he seemed to be able to put them at ease.

One boy had me lock up a lot of letters in the safe until he went home. He claimed the letters were evidence he would use in a divorce suit after he returned to the States. I sealed the envelope and placed it in our squadron safe.

This young man paid me a visit at my place of business in Boston, Massachusetts, after the war. He informed me he went back to his wife and children. He showed me a picture of the family and pointed out one of the children in the picture. He stated he was not the father of that one, but everything was forgotten, and he was happy.

Saturday–Tuesday, October 16–19. No action, just hanging around waiting for some good weather. Spent some time trying to make arrangements for one of the local printers to make up some Christmas cards as it looked like we would spend our second Christmas overseas.

Wednesday, October 20. Boys off this morning on another train-searching mission. They found one long train and strafed it from one end to the other. One of the cars must have had high explosives as, when Lt. Maurice Raskin of Stevens Point, Wisconsin, made his pass to strafe, it blew up and sent fragments high in the air.

Raskin did not return from the mission. We believed he was in the middle of this large explosion. Some of the other planes received slight damage but they returned to base OK.

Thursday–Friday, October 21–22. No action for two days as the weather holds up the missions again. A few missions were scheduled but they never got off the ground.

Each day, the B-17s and B-24s form up over the Foggia area. They drop their loads in northern Italy, Austria, and Germany. On some of the missions for the bombers, they bomb their assigned targets in Germany and continue on to England. They spend the night at an American or English base and leave there the next day, doing a bombing run on their return to their base here in the Foggia area.

The most wonderful thing is we are not being bothered by any enemy aircraft. It looks like they have run out of planes. Once in a while, they send over a reconnaissance aircraft to take some pictures. They usually fly at great heights and all you can see are the vapor trails.

We didn't have a plane that could fly high enough to reach this ship but the rumor around was the British were working on a Spitfire to take care of future missions like this.

Saturday, October 23. This morning we received a call to take care of a batch of P-38s and their pilots. They were going on a very important mission with the bombers tomorrow morning. We had to feed these men and service their ships and put them up for the night. This put us to work in order to find room for them to sleep.

I never did find out what kind of mission they were going on but, adding things up from past experiences, I would say that the bombers wanted lots of protection for a mission. The enemy area probably had some fighters that would challenge them when they approached their assigned target. The P-38 was a great plane for escort work.

Sunday, October 24. We were all up early this morning. The sky was full of bombers and fighter-escort planes. It was a beautiful sight to see them form up for this big mission over enemy territory.

The fighters did not return to our base until late in the afternoon. The sky was full of bombers; it took some time to bring them all down.

As they approached the field, the bombers with dead or wounded, or in trouble from enemy flak, would send out a series of red flares. They were given priority on landing.

CHAPTER 30

Amendola, Italy

October 25–December 31

Monday, October 25. We were on the move again this morning. Only a few miles but we took it in stride. We had a big field and they wanted to use this for another bomber group. The long runway was ideal for their take-off.

The field we moved to was only a few miles away. It was newly made for our group. We do not have buildings other than an old house, which we will make over for a mess hall for the officers. We will draw a Nissen hut for the enlisted mess. Everybody will be in tents again.

This field was called Amendola. We were sandwiched in between a couple of bomber fields. I could see the bombers and our squadron would have to take off in turns.

Before we moved out, the P-38 pilots and their planes took off. They told us about their mission over Germany, classified as a milk run without any enemy planes bothering them.

The pilots were not happy with the runway of this new field, but we have been on all types of fields since we left East Boston 16 months ago. With all the rain we have had, a newly made field would be kind of muddy until they really finished it. We were told the metal strips would be laid as quickly as possible.

Tuesday–Thursday, October 26–28. Took a trip to the Bari area and picked up the Christmas cards for the squadron. We were not receiving enough cigarettes, so I visited the dock area of the port of Bari. I went on board a few American freighters that were unloading supplies and was able to pick up several cases of American cigarettes. Enough to give each man four packs.

Had a meal on one of the ships. I must say, they eat well.

October 20–November 10. The weather was bad. It got colder every day and sleeping in a tent on a hill left a lot to be desired. The boys had a few missions but nothing alarming happened. They strafed a few bridges.

There were lots of bridge games in the club during these dull days. There were a few good poker parties with lots of money on the tables. Some of the young pilots had no place to put their money; at least that is the way it looked when they started

Plenty of card games were played in our officers' club.

betting. Lots of times I saw thousands of dollars change hands.

Thursday, November 11. One year ago today we lost our first squadron commander, Major Clermont Wheeler, when he was shot down near El Alamein. Reports indicated he was a prisoner in Germany.

It looked like the boys were going to fly their last P-40 missions pretty soon. A group of pilots left today to be checked out in P-47s. That was good news. The P-40 had such a short range, and its top speed left a lot to be desired.

Friday, November 12. The weather was still bad, but the day was brightened by lots of mail.

Saturday–Thursday, November 13–18. During these days we had no operations other than to check out some new pilots. They came overseas trained in P-40s. They had to be given some training primarily in what the terrain was like in this strange country. They, of course, will have to be checked out in the P-47s when we receive them shortly. We hope.

The weather during these days gets colder and colder. Some of the boys who have finished their missions are getting ready to go home.

One of my missions was to see that we had liquor for the clubs. This meant a little travel around the countryside. We bought whatever we could. The pilots would like to drink in the evening. The prices we had to pay was irksome. There was a shortage of this product. The merchants figured all Americans were millionaires and this made the product costly.

The town of Manfredonia was about fifteen miles away. They had a theater. We did get to see a few shows, some bad and some good. I am talking about USO (United Service Organizations) shows.

The night before a pilot goes home, it is customary for them to buy the drinks at the club. This happened when Captains Maloney, Cencak, and Volker left for home.

With the cold weather bothering me, I decided to see if we could get under cover. The only spot in the area was a barn full of straw and horse manure. I thought about this spot for days and talked with my tent mates who also suffered from this cold weather. We figured we were going to be in this area for quite a while.

We hired some Italian laborers to clean the mess out. Then we found some cement blocks and had the laborers lay them on the floor. We had a cement factory that had been bombed out close by. We had them build a fireplace. We picked up a door and window from some bombed out buildings in Foggia. We were in good shape.

There were six of us to live in this room which we called "Horseshit Haven." It cost us about five dollars apiece for the laborers. They only received about $1.00 a day so we had a home for a very cheap price.

In the fireplace we used wood from Mussolini's private estate in the forest not far from our field. How we found the wood is interesting. A pilot flew a mission one day and saw all this wood piled up in this reserve that later proved to be a good rest area for the men. There were enough lodges at the estate to take about twenty men for leave and some hunting.

When the boys would return from leave, they would bring back a supply

I built a room out of some stables to get out of the tents and the cold.

of this well-seasoned timber which I believe was cut up for spokes of wagon wheels. It made for good fireplace wood. Little did Benito Mussolini know he would keep some American officers, all the way from Boston, warm.

When the wood ran out, we built an oil burner with a 55-gallon gas drum, some copper tubing, a steel plate, and a smokestack from a discarded piece of pipe.

Friday–Wednesday, November 19–24. These were dull days with bad weather over the target area. For a couple of these days, the mail poured in.

We had a P-38 forced down with a bad engine at the field. We fixed his plane after he spent the night with us.

On the 22nd, the boys had a mission and busted up a few trains. The 23rd, rain again and the field was a sea of mud.

Art Salisbury had dinner with us this evening. There are rumors we will lose him as our group commander. He will go to England and form a fighter group in preparation for the invasion we hope will take place next summer. Colonel Salisbury did not talk at this time.

Thursday, November 25. This was a busy day for the pilots and those connected with keeping the planes flying. The boys were out on three different missions. That was a lot of work for all. On days like this it takes everybody to put his shoulder to the wheel.

I believe this was the date that President Roosevelt, Stalin and Churchill met in Africa. We hoped they settled the course of this crazy war.

Talked with one of the pilots from the 65th Squadron. He told me I had been promoted to major in October. This was good news, but I had no orders giving me the right to change from bars to leaves.

Friday, November 26. This was a big day for the squadron. They broke the sortie record for the group, which they had held for some time. Our record was 47 sorties in one day. Today they made 54. A sortie is one plane on one mission. So, today, we had 54 planes fly one mission each. That was a lot of effort. They all came back safe.

A little more excitement around the field this afternoon. Jerry was overhead taking pictures. A couple of weeks ago there was a rumor the British Spitfire outfit on the field next to us was working on something to take care of this reconnaissance plane if he returned. We were told they were ready for him if he came back.

The Spitfire took off to try to shoot down this enemy plane before he returned to his outfit with pictures of this area where there were thousands of planes. Our base would make an excellent target if the enemy could put up some planes to bomb them.

We could observe this Jerry with his vapor trail all over the sky. We could not see the Spitfire, but we were told that he was up there, and he made it. The Jerry plane came tumbling down and crashed along the coast not far from our field. The pilot bailed out and was met by some British unit. That was the last mission he would fly for Mr. Hitler.

Lieutenants Frank and Novy. Frank was shot up over Yugoslavia and bailed out.

We found out the Spitfire had been stripped of all its armament and equipment except for its 20-mm cannons and radio. With this weight out of the plane, he could reach the height of the plane taking important pictures for the enemy. It was a nice sight to see the plane come down.

Saturday, November 27. The boys were off on an early mission this morning. All returned safe. Some of these missions escort C-47s towing gliders to Yugoslavia with supplies and equipment.

Sunday, November 28. Lieutenant Steve Turner of Lancaster, Massachusetts, failed to return from an escort mission this morning over Yugoslavia. At the debriefing after the boys came back from this mission, one of the boys was sure Steve bailed out. He was right. We later received a letter from his folks stating he was a prisoner.

Thursday, December 2. Boys were on an escort mission over Yugoslavia this morning. Lieutenant Louis Frank III of Louisville, Kentucky, had his plane shot up and he bailed out.

At the debriefing after the mission, it was reported he landed in the water. When last seen, he was in his dinghy, paddling towards an island off the coast. The spot he headed for was said to be friendly.

Sunday, December 5. We have our new P-47s. The boys are happy. The boys were going to try them out for a few days before they take them on a combat mission.

With the P-40s gone, we received orders to turn in all of our Prestone. We used Prestone to cool the engines of the P-40s and all our vehicles. This was a crazy order. It meant draining all our trucks and jeeps each night and refilling them in the morning. This would be a difficult job especially when we flew early morning missions. We had no water on the field and had to haul it from a water point 15 miles away.

I talked with Tech Supply Sergeant Joseph Maolino from Winthrop, Massachusetts, about this crazy order. He told me not to worry. He had a good supply of Prestone and we would not have to drain our vehicles. Joe was the greatest. He was an old timer in the supply game. I believe they called him 'The Mooch" which meant he could obtain anything you wanted as far as supplies were concerned.

Lots of mail and packages this afternoon.

Monday, December 6. The boys were still trying out the new P-47s. They are scheduled for the first combat mission with them tomorrow. A USO show was scheduled at Manfredonia this evening but it did not go on. The lights in the theater failed so we all left and went back to the field.

Tuesday, December 7. Our boys were off on their first mission with the P-47s. They ran into bad weather and had to come home without reaching the assigned

We switched from our P-40s to the P-47 in December 1943.

target. The air seemed to be filled with B-25s today. This plane has been doing wonderful work since we started back in Egypt.

Thursday, December 9. Boys were off in their new planes this morning on a train-busting mission. They were all back safe. They love this ship.

Friday, December 10. This was one of the rainy days. The field was locked up for our missions. The bombers were out in force as they are every day.

Saturday, December 11. Lieutenant Frank, shot down over Yugoslavia on December 2, returned to the squadron. He had some stories to tell.

He reached the friendly island and was rescued after a gun battle. Unfriendly soldiers were on the island not far from where he landed. Friendly troops from the mainland proceeded to rescue him and were attacked. They lost two of their men in the rescue. He spent his days with the partisans and even went to a dance.

Frank stated these people were our friends and were very happy with the support we were giving them. It was good to have him with us again. He was a fine pilot and officer. He later commanded the Black Scorpion Squadron.

At the dance Lieutenant Frank attended, the partisans, who included men and women, had their weapons with them. In their belts, they had a knife and couple of hand grenades.

Sunday, December 12. We now have a Royal Engineer outfit on our field. They have set up a shower for all of us. This was a wonderful thing. We had been taking our baths out of a steel helmet for many months.

Our boys had no missions today, but the sky is filled with bombers on their way to give some spots the works.

Monday, December 13. A quiet day. Mr. Roy Degler visited us. This gentleman works for the U.S. Post Office. He was on his way to Sardinia to set up an APO (Army Post Office). Mr. Degler used to work out of Cairo. He followed us across the Western Desert. He would show up around pay day and issue money orders to all of us. This was a real service. It saved us from carrying around a lot of money. We had no place to spend money for several months and we appreciated the service Mr. Degler rendered.

Tuesday, December 14. B-17s and B-24s put up one of the biggest shows I have seen so far.

Lots of mail today.

Wednesday, December 15. Our boys were out over Yugoslavia this morning on a fighter sweep. They found a German airdrome and shot up eight bombers on the ground.

They saw a few German ME-109s for the first time in many months. They did not come near the formation during the bombing and strafing of the airfield.

As of this date, the 57th Fighter Group has dropped 2,329,300 pounds of bombs since we started in September 1942.

Red Cross girls were in the area with doughnuts and coffee. What a welcome sight.

Thursday, December 16. Boys were over to Yugoslavia again this morning with the 65th and 66th Squadrons. They did not get anything, but the other two squadrons shot a few ME-109s.

We lost Lt. Glen Johnson of Chicago, Illinois, when he had to bail out after being hit by flak. His parachute was seen. He was over enemy territory at 10:25 am.

Saturday, December 18. Boys were out again in the morning. Lieutenant Edward Liebing got an ME-109 over Yugoslavia. Major Carlton Chamberlain's plane was shot up, but he made it back to the coast near Manfredonia and bailed out. He made a good landing then swam to a small fishing boat which brought him ashore.

The evening after a show was always an interesting one, especially when we have a pilot shoot down an enemy airplane and a major being shot up and having to land in the ocean but making it back OK.

A group of American nurses were at the club tonight. It is not something we have had before. These girls came over from Africa to set up a hospital in the Foggia area, but the ship that brought all their supplies and equipment was blown up in the port of Bari, Italy, a few days ago.

The nurses were without a place to work. Some of the girls filled in at one of the established hospital units but there

Major Carlton Chamberlain. His plane was shot up and he bailed out on December 18, 1943.

Some of the nurses at the local hospital.

was no room for all of them. We were going to see a lot of these girls and that made the boys happy. Why not?

Wednesday, December 22. We have set up a Christmas tree in the enlisted club and in the officers' club in preparation. The boys went into the woods nearby and picked out a couple of nice trees. We did not have the decorations they would have liked to have but the tree let you know it was the festive season.

Friday, December 24. Bad weather held up the flying. That was OK by everybody. Who wants to be killing people around these days? We had a party in the enlisted club and in the officers' club. We visited the enlisted club and some of the tents of the enlisted men. The boys had the Christmas spirit. They had their tents decorated enough to let you know it was the season.

Everybody was in a happy mood tonight. We had enough beer, wine, and whiskey to help celebrate.

It was not the best place to celebrate Christmas so far from home.

Saturday, December 25. This was our second year away from home. Everybody hopes by next Christmas or sooner we will be all back home. Father Louge held Christmas service in the camp area for the Catholics. The boys of other faiths went into the bomber group area close by.

We did not have any mission scheduled for today, but the sky was full of B-17s. We kind of thought there would be a hold up for today but I guess the powers-that-be could not get together on a 24-hour truce.

The rations for today were outstanding. We had all the fixings.

Sunday, December 26. We had a mission scheduled but the weather held the ships on the ground. The only excitement in the area was one of our boys shot himself in the foot while cleaning his rifle. It was not a serious wound. This was the first such incident like this.

We had church services. The nurses were at the club tonight.

Monday–Thursday, December 27–30. Nothing doing these days on account of the weather. It was really cold and windy. The B-17s were out in full force. The weather does not bother them as they have their runways in top shape and fly above the bad weather, or they are going to Austria or Germany.

It seemed they were putting up bigger and bigger shows every day. We knew the work they were doing will help bring us home sooner.

For the first time overseas, we attend a dance given by the 845th Engineer Group in a hall in Foggia. How this building survived the bombing in Foggia was hard to understand.

Friday, December 31. The last day of this year. The boys were out on a bomber escort mission this morning. All but Lt. Charles Neese of Lynchburg, Virginia, returned safe. He picked up some flak and had to make a crash landing at another field in the area. He was OK.

On a field near us, an English officer was killed when a plane came in for a landing and his guns were blazing by mistake.

Here it is, the last evening of the year of 1943. We had quite a celebration at the club this evening and everybody let their hair down. Many of the pilots had never been away from home on a New Year's Eve. The ground officers of the squadron and a few of the original pilots that came over on the aircraft carrier celebrated their second New Year's overseas.

Last New Year's Eve we were on convoy in the Western Desert. We saved a can of juice and bottle of whiskey for the occasion. We were outside Alageligh, just a dot on the map in the sands of Libya.

Even with our celebration in this far away land, a big air raid took place just a few miles from where we had camped for the night.

The commanding officer, Capt. Art Exon, and I made the rounds to the club and tents of the enlisted men. They were in the best of spirits and had enough spirits to celebrate the occasion of the coming new year.

CHAPTER 31

Amendola, Italy

January 1–February 27, 1944

General Eisenhower's success in North Africa, and then leading the landings on Sicily and mainland Italy, meant he was assigned "other duties"; in this case it was to become the Supreme Commander of the Allied Expeditionary Force that continued the liberation of Europe on June 6, 1944, with the D-Day landings. As he left for even greater responsibility, he issued a farewell to the men and women he had led in the Mediterranean.

Saturday, January 1, 1944. Well, this day started off with a bang. Early this morning, we had one of the worst storms we have had since coming overseas. The wind was blowing a gale and the rains came down in sheets. Being on a hill did not help us as we took the brunt of this storm.

Sixty percent of the tents were down. One captured German plane was tipped over on its back and damaged beyond repair. This was used by Lt Col. Jere Chase of Durham, New Hampshire, the group executive officer, for many of his duties and to visit headquarters.

Many of the tents were beyond repair. We put a call to headquarters for more tentage which was promised by late in the day.

With this condition, many of the officers and enlisted men had to double up for the night. We had them sleep in the enlisted club and the officers' club.

Lieutenant Colonel Chase, 57th Fighter Group executive officer, and his captured German plane.

The special meal that was supposed to be served was postponed until tomorrow.

Sunday, January 2. The sun was out this morning and our camp needs lots of work. The replacement tentage arrived. The boys got to work putting things back in shape. At this point, our boys are experts in taking down and putting up tents. This was the 29th camp we have had to set up since arriving in Palestine in August 1942.

ALLIED FORCE HEADQUARTERS
Office of the Commander-in-Chief
1 January, 1944

Subject: **Farewell message**

To: **All men and women serving in or with Allied Forces in the Mediterranean Theater**

Soon I leave this theater to assume other duties assigned me by the Allied Governments.

I take my leave of you with feelings of personal regret that are equaled only by my pride in your brilliant accomplishments of the year just past. Although tempted to review again the many advantages that have accrued to the Allied cause through your bravery and fortitude, I believe all these will come to you if you will merely compare your present position and prospects in this great conflict with your position and outlook in the late Fall of 1942. The Eighth Army was making its final preparations to attack the enemy, who was standing only a short distance west of Cairo. Vast Allied armadas were approaching northwest Africa in complete ignorance as to whether good fortune or complete disaster awaited them. Battered Malta was being defended only by the bravery of her almost entirely isolated garrison. No Allied ship could transit the length of the Mediterranean. Our fortunes appeared at a low ebb.

All this is changed—changed by your skill, your determination, and your devotion to duty, Enemy action against our convoys in the Mediterranean is limited to harassing and submarine efforts. You have established yourselves on the mainland of Europe. You are still advancing.

You, along with the other Allied Forces fighting on many fronts, have already achieved the certainty that, provided every soldier, sailor and airman, and every citizen in our homeland continues incessantly to do his full duty, victory will be ours.

Altogether, you comprise a mighty fighting machine, which, under your new Commander, will continue, as a completely unified instrument of war, to make further inroads into the enemy's defenses and assist in bringing about his final collapse.

Until we meet again in the heart of the enemy's continental stronghold, I send Godspeed and good luck to each of you, along with the assurance of my lasting gratitude and admiration.

Dwight D. Eisenhower.

Monday, January 3. I am one year older this date. There were no parties as we were busy setting up our orderly room tent and trying to put our records back in shape. With the wind of the first day of the year, we have had a small problem on our hands.

Tuesday–Tuesday, January 4–11. The bad weather continued. Time was heavy on our hands. The field was in bad shape. The boys spent a lot of time playing bridge and cribbage.

The local theater at Manfredonia did a nice job of showing movies. The U.S. Special Services supplied the films. During the past week we have had some good shows.

We are getting some new pilots to replace the boys that went home. All they can do is sit around and wait for this weather to clear up.

Wednesday, January 12. The field was in good enough shape for the boys to take off on a mission to Yugoslavia with the other two squadrons. All boys returned safe. The boys from the 65th Squadron get a couple of ME-109s.

During the afternoon, a pilot from the 65th flew over the area in a captured ME-109 and ran into some trouble. He bailed out over the camp area. His chute failed to open. He landed in our camp area and was killed. A sad way for a young man to go.

A short time later, Major Lance Wade, the American officer who flew with the Royal Air Force and had 25 enemy planes to his credit, took off from our field after a visit with our group commander, Col. Art Salisbury. After he gained enough altitude, he came down for a buzz job as was customary when leaving. He did a tremendous buzz and came back to do a slow roll. Part-way through the roll, he spun to earth and landed in the middle of the bombs that were around the officers' area of our squadron.

When we arrived at the scene, we found him dead in the cockpit of his fighter plane. Two young Americans lost their lives on our field within a couple of hours.

Sunday, January 16. Took off for a couple of days and visited the Fifth Army front where my former CO, Col. Vincent P. Coyne of Boston, commanded an anti-aircraft battalion. It was quite different than back

Met my old boss, Vincent Coyne, at a granary cave near Monte Cassino.

with the fighter squadron. He was near the base of Monte Cassino. I spent the night in his headquarters, an old granary cave with plenty of protection. The sound of the artillery blasted all night long.

Started back to the Foggia area this morning and stopped off to do a little shopping. The prices have doubled since we were here a short time back. The Italians think we are all millionaires and jack up the prices on everything once the Americans take over an area.

Tuesday, January 18. Back in the camp area. It was still cold and raw. The boys have no missions. The only excitement was when our adjutant, Capt. Henry Mack of St. Petersburg, Florida, was rushed to the hospital at midnight for an appendix operation.

Thursday, January 20. Major Exon, our CO, took off this morning in the B-25 given to us to use for rest leaves and other errands. This morning he took a group to Cairo for a week's vacation. It was hoped that this will be a regular run.

The rumor of a few days ago was true. Colonel Salisbury was going to England. He talked to all the group at 6:00 pm. He told us as much as he could about his new job in England.

We hated to see this officer leave us. Everybody loved him. He was the tops in leading the 57th Fighter Group across the Western Desert, Sicily and now in Italy. The air group in England will have an expert to train them as Col. Art Salisbury know his business about fighter-bombers.

Captain Henry Mack had an emergency appendix operation. (57th Fighter Group website)

There was talk he wanted to take the 57th with him. He was overruled by the high brass at Fifth Army.

Friday, January 21. Still no flying. The weather, which was a good subject to talk about, left a lot to be desired. It stayed cold and the wood from Mussolini's forest was running out. We are in the process of installing our oil burner. It would never pass the fire marshal's approval back home.

We burned a mixture of oil and gasoline. It burns pretty hot, but it was cold outside.

Sunday, January 23. Boys have their first mission in days. They were out bombing some troops and trucks along the bomb line. All home safe.

Colonel Salisbury left for England. A large delegation of officers and men saw him off. Our new group commander will be Archie Knight, who came overseas as our weather officer with the original group. He had little to do as far as weather in the deserts, as the weather was the same about 99 and 44/100 of the time.

He did some flying. He will have his work cut out for him to fill the shoes of Colonel Salisbury.

Monday, January 24. The British Royal Engineers, who have been on our field for some time, have a lot of time on their hands due to the slack in the progress of the war. The weather played a big part in slowing progress down.

These boys wanted a project. We requested they put an addition on our mess and club. There was plenty of materiel, such as lumber, brick, cement, and tile, in Foggia. All you had to do was send a truck or two to pick it up.

The building was started today. As part of the deal, we had them build a shower for the squadron. Since those boys had moved into our area, we had been using their shower. It was getting a little crowded.

January 25–February 10. These were dull days without the boys flying. During this time, we had real bad storms and a few promotions. Joe E. Brown was in the Manfredonia theater and a few days later in comes Humphrey Bogart. It was nice to have these stars. We have had no shows to speak of since leaving the States. The Red Cross doughnut girls were back again. They are always welcome.

Just ahead of our area was a range of mountains. One of the B-24s crashed into it on returning from a mission. A few parachutes were seen floating down.

We had been very fortunate, since we came into the Foggia area, with so many bomber missions each day, that we had not seen many accidents near the base. We know many of the bombers we see taking off each morning fail to return.

The club was progressing. The pilots with nothing to do pay visits to the bombed areas nearby and pick up a few loads of furniture for the new addition to the club.

The shower has been completed. This was a needed asset to the outfit and was a 100% effort by the British Royal Engineers.

Working with the British has been very satisfactory. We found them to be excellent soldiers and most cooperative with us.

Finally received my orders promoting me to major. They were dated in October and bounced around a few APOs (Army Post Office) before I received them.

Friday, February 11. Even during the war there were problems with men other than military problems. A young man in another squadron was accused of stealing a camera from a local merchant. I was appointed investigating officer. This would take lots of time so the accused would be given a fair shake.

My first part of the investigation led me to believe the local merchant was an honorable gentleman. All he wanted was to have his camera back and to forget the whole matter.

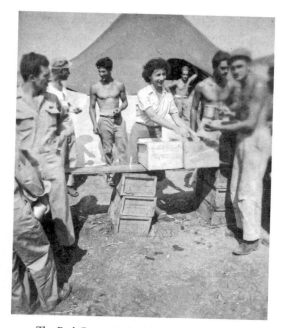

The Red Cross girls handing out doughnuts.

Monday, February 14. Boys were out early this morning on a bomber escort with B-25s. They have some trouble with belly tanks. Apparently, they tried to jettison them on this mission and the belly tanks failed to drop.

All returned safe but Lt. Joseph Kelly of Oakland, California. He went off the end of the runway but was not injured. His plane's undercarriage was damaged.

Tuesday, February 15. Nineteen months ago today, we left for Palestine. It looks like we have many more months to go before we return to the good old USA. A few more pilots went home today. They had finished their tour of duty.

Wednesday, February 16. The Air Force took over the hotels on the isle of Capri as a rest area. Each unit has a quota of trips to the island once a week. Captain Henry Mack, the adjutant, took off with a group of officers and enlisted men. This will be a real vacation as Capri is one of the top resorts in Italy.

Boys were out again on a bomber escort mission. These missions were called milk runs as there is not much action from enemy aircraft. They ran into a little anti-aircraft artillery, but nothing like the missions they flew in the Western Desert.

The Red Cross girls were around again today with the doughnuts and coffee. Gin rummy has become a great pastime in the club during the evening hours.

Saturday, February 19. The British Royal Engineers turned over the new addition to the mess and club. It is a masterpiece. It gave us lots of room for the great number of pilots that we now carry. With the continuous bad weather, we needed this added space for the pilots to spread out in to play cards or other activities to keep them busy.

Some of the pilots were given extra leave but we always have a large group on standby.

The bar room, which was just off the large dining room, had a counter finished off in green tile. On the wall above the counter, we had our Sgt Jack Sinclair of Brooklyn, New York, paint the cartoons and sayings that the pilots had on the side of their assigned aircraft.

I will list a few of them: *Maggie Hogan, Miss Army Jane, Sweet Stuff, Little Rhody, Frisco Flash, Dixie Girl, Jacqueline, Little Butch* and *Halliburton's Hellion.*

Our new officers' club with all the plane nicknames painted on the wall.

These names made a nice background for the bar. In the center, Jack painted the famous Black Scorpion insignia. These names meant a lot to the pilots. Some were from friends and sweethearts.

If a plane was shot up and the pilot assigned another plane, the plane had to be painted at once.

I know the plane carrying the name of Maggie Hogan *was the plane of Major Michael Christopher McCarthy. Both Michael and Maggie lived in the Dorchester area of Boston. They were married after the war. I was fortunate to attend the wedding of two of the nicest people that I know.*

Colonel McCarthy and Maggie went on to have 11 children. He served in Vietnam. I remember this young man when he reported back in the desert. He walked into the orderly room of the 64th Fighter Squadron, when I was the executive officer, and said, "I am Mike McCarthy from Boston, Mass." I replied, "I am Jim Lynch from Boston, Mass."

He was one of the best pilots that ever served the Black Scorpion Squadron. He was a real leader. Because Mike stayed in the service, the Air Force gained a top-notch officer and pilot.

Major Michael McCarthy, one of our best pilots.

Sunday, February 20. The area in back of the officers mess and club was being used for a bomb storage area. No one likes to eat and live so close to a lot of bombs. Most of these bombs are for the B-17 outfit on the field next to ours. This afternoon, another large load of bombs arrived. After they were on the ground, we found there was no passageway to the mess or club.

This meant we had to walk over these bombs at each meal. The bombs surrounded all the buildings of the mess, club, and a few of the sleeping quarters.

This was the doings of an ordnance group in charge of preparing the bombs for missions. I had a talk with the ordnance unit's commanding officer. He agreed to move some of the bombs so we could at least say we had an entrance to our property. It gave some of the boys peace of mind.

When you think about it, if a detonation set those bombs off, none of us would be around to talk about the subject of the storage of bombs.

The bombs had no fuses in them. The fuses were stored in another area. The fuses were placed in the bombs when they were ready to be loaded on the particular plane prior to a mission.

You could say they were pretty safe. When Major Lance Wade crashed a few days back, his plane landed in the middle of one of the many bomb dumps in this area.

A few months after we left this area for another part of Italy, one of our boys paid a visit to look over the old club and found that the ordnance company was using the whole building for the storage of bombs and ordnance equipment. It seemed a shame that some other group did not make proper use of those quarters. That was their business, and we were not involved so that closes out the club of the Black Scorpion Squadron.

Tuesday, February 22. If we were home this would be a holiday. We would celebrate George Washington's birthday. We were not home and were many miles from same.

Boys were out on a fighter sweep north of Rome but nothing much happened. They dropped their bombs on some bridges and they all came back home OK.

I watched the landing of Lt. Joe Kelly. It looked like he was going to be in trouble as he took a little more runway than the rest of the boys. The engineers had been extending our runway and making an all-weather job out of it. They had been working on it during the morning while the boys were out on their mission and failed to take a piece of grading equipment off the end of the runway.

Joe stopped just short of this piece of equipment. Had he run into it, it would probably be the end of a good pilot and a new P-47.

I talked with Joe after the briefing. I told him to be more careful as his bar bill was kind of high. I did not want to see a nice young fellow go out owing the club this money. Joe retorted, "Not to worry. I'll always come home." He did. He finished his missions and went home in good shape. We had a great laugh about this incident.

Wednesday, February 23. We now have metal strips on the runway (pierced steel planking). This should allow us to take off in bad weather, but the rumor of moving was around again. The boys were off on a long escort mission to Yugoslavia this morning although the weather was not the best.

The P-47, with larger gas tanks, can fly many more miles than the P-40 which we started out with at El Alamein.

Thursday–Sunday, February 24–27. These days were what we called non-flying days, on account of the subject that I have typed so many times, "weather." We all hoped the rumor of moving out of this spot was true.

We cannot move ahead on the east coast as the Germans have that area sealed off. The terrain was also in their favor. I would guess we would move over to the Naples area as they were moving ahead. Further moves ahead in that area were on the cards.

Our boys returned from the rest leave on Capri. The stories they told about this beautiful island made everybody want to move there at once. The hotel and food were superior. The Air Force is doing a good job. These officers and men that received the leave deserved the break. Many of our men have been on a long trek from El Alamein to this spot in Italy with very little time off.

Regulations call for the Articles of War to be read to the men. For the first time, we had a film on the Articles of War made up very well by some top movie people. They narrated this very difficult subject. In the past, the Articles were read and explained by an officer.

It was a very dry and uninteresting assignment for any officer. The film was well received by the men. We did it in two sittings.

We received a new table of organization (T/O) from Air Force Headquarters in Washington. I attended a meeting at group headquarters, and it was good news for many enlisted men and officers. The enlisted men will make out very well.

We will be able to promote a large segment of them. This is something we have been looking forward to for some time.

Many of the enlisted men have held important positions in the various sections of the squadron without, we thought, the proper compensation.

When the new T/O was announced to the men, they were very happy. This announcement meant more money to them each day they serve.

CHAPTER 32

Cercola, Italy

Wednesday, March 1. The rumors of a few days back came true this morning. We moved out with A Party to a spot called Cercola, not far from Naples. It has rained for many days. It poured this morning and that was not the best for the equipment, especially the tents. We had to roll them up and they will remain wet much longer.

We ran into a situation with a shortage of trucks and could not take as many men as we normally do. We have a lot of trucks that are really sick and should be replaced. We had been promised replacements.

Some days I was able to pull planes around.

The trek from El Alamein to this spot had been over tough terrain. The trucks have done very well. With our superior transportation section nursing them along, we were fortunate to have gone this far.

While we were assigned to the British Eighth Army, our big problem was we had no assigned depot to pick up parts for these American trucks. The British had no parts for us as they had none themselves. We have been parts beggars for a long time.

The road from Foggia to Naples to Cercola was through some rough mountain roads. The going was slow. The downpour made the move slower.

We passed through many small towns, some were untouched. Others had been damaged by the movement of war through their town.

Many children, even in the rain, lined the street with their hands out looking for candy and gum. The enlisted men and officers were always generous with candy and gum. We could always find something for the children. The smile on little children's faces, even in the war zone, made you feel that you have helped a little towards their comfort.

We arrived on Cercola Airfield at 4:30 pm and proceeded to set up our wet tents.

This was a picturesque spot at the base of the famous Mt. Vesuvius. There was a slight stream of white smoke coming out of the crater of this old and active volcano.

The first tent up was the mess tent. The meal would be ready for all after the camp area was set up. Our mess section was the best. They have been experts when it comes to serving a meal, whether it be on the road or in a camp area that has been going for days or months.

We had been told the Germans raided Naples most every night. Our first night was no exception. They were over just after dark. We were a few miles outside Naples. This raid did not bother us as the enemy planes worked over the port facilities.

The harbor had many transports and supply ships which made it a good target for the enemy. The anti-aircraft guns around Naples put on a good show for us on our first night.

It was the first time since Tripoli last year that we have seen so much action. I believe there are more guns protecting Naples than there were protecting Tripoli. This was a very important port in the plans for driving the Germans out of Italy.

Thursday, March 2. After a hectic night, we were sort of back to normal this morning. Spent some time in the town of San Sebastiano, which was one-and-a-half miles from the field, looking for a building we could use as a club for the pilots.

We found a former doctor's home that took care of all our needs. He must have been successful to own a spot like this. We could sleep all the officers and mess personnel here. There was also room enough to set up a mess hall as well as a living room for the pilots to hang around in while waiting for missions.

The population of the town was about two thousand five hundred people. It was the same as many of the towns of Italy except it was on the slopes of Vesuvius. It had a parochial school in the center of the town plus one other public school.

On the slopes leading up to Mt. Vesuvius were fertile vineyards where the finest of grapes are grown in the old lava that flowed down these slopes for many years. The last time Vesuvius erupted was 1906.

We were told these grapes produce the finest champagne in the world. The English name of the champagne is "Tears of Christ." Many of the townspeople own pieces of these vineyards and work hard to produce these famous grapes.

There seemed to be a little resentment from a few people who lived around this large home we took over. We informed them this building would be our home for a short time then we would be moving on. All Italy would be free very soon. We were told a German organization had been in this same building not too long ago.

We requisitioned this building in the required manner. The owner of same would be paid for the use of it.

Friday, March 3. The rest of our party from the Amendola field in the Foggia area came in during the day. By nightfall, we were all together again. A few of the pilots elected to sleep in tents in the camp area. The rest were very happy about the building we had selected in San Sebastiano.

We had our first meal in the new quarters this evening. There was no flying today because the bad weather was still with us.

Saturday, March 4. Still raining this morning and no flying today. This gave everybody a chance to look over Naples. This was the biggest city we had been near since Cairo. Many of the boys took tours through this old port. They saw a lot of sunken ships in the harbor; some the Germans sank before evacuation, others from the severe bombing this port took from the Allied bombers.

Most of the hotels along the waterfront were burnt out. This made for a very poor sight. There was some shopping to be done on the main street, Via Roma. The prices were high and the quality poor.

I visited the main Army hospital and had some of my teeth filled by my own family dentist from Boston, Col. Henry J. Carney. Not many soldiers could have their own dentist so far from home.

My family dentist from Boston, Col. Henry Carney.

Colonel Carney was also a plastic surgeon. I spent a long time with him at the hospital going through the wards. He showed me the various cases he and the staff of doctors worked on.

These were not very nice conditions to observe. Many soldiers had their eyes gone. Some had parts of their faces torn away from mines or bullets or other tools of war.

The work being done at this hospital amazed me. Many of the young men had been wounded in the Anzio area. The colonel explained they would go just so far with these young heroes' wounds and then fly them to the States for further medical treatment.

Sunday, March 5. Dull days again. Not much happens. Boys were still awed by the city of Naples. We received some new P-47s. They were going to be fixed up with bomb racks.

We expect to do a lot of dive-bombing missions. The P-47 wasn't built to do dive bombing, I don't believe, but our boys have had so much experience bombing with the P-40 that the powers-that-be felt they could do an outstanding job with this new plane.

Monday, March 13. The planes were ready. It looked like the boys will be off tomorrow morning on some kind of mission. We were just getting our camp down to a normal condition. We were told we will be moving on very soon.

Tonight was a hectic night. The German bombers were over in force. They dropped some heavy stuff around the Naples area. Early each afternoon, along the waterfront of Naples, an Army unit moved in special trucks. When alerted, the trucks would send up smoke that would look like a cloud over the city. To the enemy flying over, this would look like water, and they would drop their bombs on the edge of this cloud of smoke. Many times, the bombs would drop inside the city.

Tonight, some of these bombs fell in the 65th Squadron area. The damage was light with no casualties. An apartment house full of civilians was not so lucky. One of these bombs intended for the harbor landed in this house. Many were killed or injured.

Tuesday, March 14. Our boys finally got off the ground this morning on what was listed as a fighter sweep over the Fifth Army's front. This was the first time they have flown in this area. It was successful except our commanding officer, Major Art Exon, ran into some flak and came home with a bunch of holes in his plane. He was OK.

Wednesday, March 15. Boys were off this morning for the first time with bombs on. The mission was to dive bomb and strafe enemy troop concentrations just over the bomb line.

The reports were the plane acted very satisfactorily. They put bombs in the intended area with ease. The boys looked forward to many successful dive-bombing missions.

Thursday, March 16. No missions today but we did lose a good officer and a good enlisted man. Just after lunch, Lt. Edward Liebing of Hart, Michigan, and his crew chief, Sgt Harold Corey, took off on what was called a piggy-back ride. There was only room for one person in the cockpit of a P-47. Corey sat in first and Liebing sat on his lap. I believe there was a regulation against this situation, but they took off and we never heard from them again.

Late in the day, we received a report a P-47 had crashed south of Salerno. The serial numbers of the ship's engine in the report we received did not check with the numbers of our missing plane.

Sergeant Harold Corey was killed in an accident while ferrying a plane with Lt. Edward Liebing. (57th Fighter Group website)

During the night, we tried to obtain further information regarding this crashed plane, but communication broke down. We decided we would go to the site of the crash early tomorrow morning.

Friday, March 17. I was selected by the commanding officer to proceed to the site of the crash. I arrived in the area of the 96th Fighter Group stationed near Murcato.

Upon arriving, I reported to the group headquarters and was turned over to the chaplain who gave me the following report. He stated a P-47 was seen flying low in the valley. The plane seemed to hit some object that extended across the valley then bounced into the side of the mountain.

The plane broke into small pieces. The bodies were smashed into small bits. The only way they knew there were two people in the plane was because they found three hands.

He then took me to a tent where the clothing and jackets of the deceased were stored. The first piece of clothing was Liebing's jacket. Living with this young man for many months, I could tell the clothing at first sight.

In the case of Sergeant Corey, there were letters and papers found at the scene. They were presented to me by the chaplain. There was no mistake. Two boys of our squadron had been killed in this non-combat activity.

The serial numbers were checked again and confirmed it was the plane that Liebing and Corey took off in from our airfield yesterday.

I was very glad when told by the chaplain that he had already conducted the burial of these young men. From the story he told me, I don't think I would have liked to have seen the remains of these friends of mine.

They were both buried in the U.S. cemetery at Paestum, alongside many other fallen comrades.

I checked the valley where the crash took place. I found the plane had hit a cable that extended from one side of the mountain to the other. I was told this was used to carry charcoal from one side to the other.

We felt Liebing flew low in this valley and did not see the cable. He hit it and never had a chance.

The squadron was saddened by the news I brought back late on this day. These two young men were liked by all members of the squadron. They will be missed.

CHAPTER 33

Vesuvius

Saturday, March 18. Boys were off on an early morning mission to look over some enemy troop activity back of the front line of a German artillery outfit. They gave them the works. All returned safe and sound.

General Saville was in the camp to award decorations to the pilots of the group. Our squadron commander received a decoration.

On a hill not far from San Sebastiano outside Naples was a newly opened officers' club. A group of us went to see and hear a band appearing there this evening. We had our dinner at this club and afterwards there seemed to be some excitement out on the veranda. We wanted to be in on it, so we joined the group. We found, on the opposite hill, Mt. Vesuvius was acting up. The glow from the top of this famous volcano was alight. That was a sight I will never forget.

I was concerned as we had a tour arranged for the next morning to the crater opening at the top. Later, on our way back to the squadron, the red glow was very visible.

Sunday, March 19. Church services were as usual this morning. Afterwards, we proceeded with our Italian guide to the top of Mt. Vesuvius. It was slow going as we had to walk up this mountain. We talked with the guide about last night's activity, but he just shrugged it off.

On the way up the slope, we could see a little snow. That was the first snow I had seen in a few years.

Smoke rising from the crater of Mt. Vesuvius.

More evidence of Mt. Vesuvius eruption.

When we were about fifty feet from the crater, I noticed lava shooting up in the air and falling back in the crater. I turned around to question the guide and he was not there. Looking down the slope, I could see him running and yelling something in Italian.

We got the clue and proceeded to move off this slope. The lava action continued all day. It gave us something to think about as we lived just below this angry volcano.

Not knowing much about what we could expect, we started asking questions of the natives with one of our Italian boys who could interpret for us. We heard a series of stories from the natives. Some of them stated the lava would go down the ravines built many years ago to take care of a situation such as we had today. Other natives were concerned and thought this eruption would be serious and roll to Naples harbor.

We had to watch and see. The natives were not sure; who could blame them as the last eruption was in 1906? Who could tell how this one would wind up?

Late in the afternoon, one of the roads we went up in the morning was covered with slow moving, hot, molten lava. The Army had a plan. Trucks were assembled to evacuate the civilians.

Monday–Tuesday, March 20–21. Lava was still on the move. Some of the civilians had been evacuated. Others did not want to go. It was tragic to watch the natives climbing slopes to retrieve the stakes holding up their vines.

These civilians were losing their livelihood. Some of them had been working in these vineyards all their lives.

They were losing the only way of life they knew. Many of the men and women wept openly on the hill as they moved from row to row among the "Lacryma Christi" vines. That was all they could save.

I spent most of the day in the town. I watched a group of nuns outside their school praying in the street, hoping the flow of lava would stop before reaching their school. The school had been built on the edge of a ravine built to take care of the lava flow.

I supposed this ravine would take care of a normal flow, but this lava was starting to build up and could overflow the edges of the ravine.

I ordered enough trucks to take our luggage down to the field. I just had a premonition this lava would reach our living quarters.

We ate our supper. The pilots loaded all their belongings on the trucks except for their cots. I made an appeal to move out before night set in but was overruled.

The activities of the club went on as usual. The pilots retired without a care in the world. Captain Henry Mack, the adjutant, and I prepared to stand watch for the night. We played gin rummy through the night.

We would leave the house and go to the edge of lava about every half hour. The lava crawled slowly. It looked like it would take the town of San Sebastiano with it.

At about 2:30 am, Mack and I paid another visit to the lava. We decided to wake the pilots and move out of this home of ours. We had our trucks take the baggage to the field, return, and stand by.

We had quite a time waking up these young pilots. They slept soundly. I finally dragged one of them to the window to show him how the red molten lava lit the sky so he could see how close it was to his sleeping quarters.

He made a howl that brought all of the pilots out of their beds. At 4:20, we were clear of this home on the slope of the angry volcano.

We were down on the airfield at about 4:45. Just before leaving the house, we found the old man who had been acting as custodian of the property and lived on the lower floor of our building. We talked with him about coming with us.

Through an interpreter, we tried to explain to him the lava was just minutes from the house. He would not budge. He stated he was staying and kept repeating the lava would not touch the house. As time ran out for us, we left him there.

During the night, in our many visits to the edge of the lava, we witnessed real action by the Allied forces. With their trucks, they evacuated civilians from their homes. In many cases, the furniture was taken on the trucks along with the occupants.

It was not always possible to take all their belongings. Many people refused to leave until the last minute, hoping the lava would change its course. That did not happen.

The men of the Allied forces should be complimented to the highest degree. They worked diligently through the night. As far as I know there was no loss of life.

With such an activity as the volcano spitting lava all over the hill of San Sebastiano, I would say the people of this little town were fortunate the plan to evacuate worked so smoothly.

I understand, in some cases, force had to be used by soldiers during the last time around to pick up civilians. They were carried out of their homes.

Before we left our home on the hill, the squadron personnel that were living on the field at Cercola were alerted to us moving in. Some of the boys had to double up for the rest of the night.

As usual, the cooks were on the job. Upon arrival, we had a good cup of coffee which was really welcome at 4:30 in the morning.

Mt. Vesuvius overlooking the bay of Naples.

After a few hours of sleep, I had the problem of setting up some tents for the boys that lost their home on the hill. After breakfast, this was under way. Major Art Exon and I started up the road we had come down a few hours ago. We found, after about three miles, the road was blocked off as lava was still moving.

We had to turn around and go into Naples. We took the back road up to our home we had left earlier that morning.

Upon arrival, we found the lava had crossed the road, taken the house across from where we lived, then turned away from our house, went down the left side, and into our backyard.

All the homes on our street were covered by the lava. What a tragic sight. The lava continued down that hill behind our home and destroyed the public school. I can remember the red wall of the school. The red wall was all you could see of the school. Lava covered the rest and was still going down the hill.

The volcano sent up billows of smoke for miles in the air. Everybody in the area around Naples was concerned about the way this old monster acted. I would say rightfully so.

There was all kinds of talk by some of the old-time civilians. They predicted the flow would stop when it reached Naples harbor.

Milton Bracker, a news correspondent for the New York Times *filed the following story from San Sebastiano on March 21:*

At 12:30 … this morning a giant tongue of lava from Vesuvius crashed into the stone house where Giuseppe Battaglio has lived for years with his wife, Maria, and their six children. By one o'clock the house had been pulverized and was buried under the countless tons of molten stone.

The stream of lava continued inexorably on its way toward the main street of the town which has 2,500 inhabitants, and nestles on the volcano's northwest slope, eight miles from Naples.

Early yesterday afternoon, on orders of the Allied military government, San Sebastiano's inhabitants and those of the nearby Massa Di Somma began their pitiful evacuation, which was in full swing last night when the liquid avalanche, hotter than boiling, cascaded down the valley.

This correspondent stood within 50 feet of the lava stream when it demolished the first house in town. Another spectator was Lieut. Col. Charles Poletti, military governor of the Naples area. With his staff, he directed the civilian evacuation in Army trucks, and announced that the Allies were prepared to feed the refugees tomorrow.

Some were taken to Naples, others to Santa Anastasia and others possibly Ave Sa. The larger town of Cercola was next in line should the lava continue to flow after having inundated this doomed community.

Those who watched Vesuvius in action this morning will never forget it. The crater, from which alternately oozed or spurted the fiery volcanic matter, was forgotten in the presence of one prong of lava 100 yards wide and actually 30 feet deep. It was like the monstrous paw of an even more monstrous lion, slowly inching forward toward his prey.

The lava was white hot, it was orange gold with occasional black patches, undulating like waves. As the stream advanced, great boulders cracked off and tumbled down, setting fire to small fruit trees and causing onlookers to leap back in alarm.

The general sound was like that of an infinite number of clinkers rolling out of a furnace, but sometimes a great chunk of rock bent rather than broke. Its effect was like that of Devil's own taffy being pulled and twisted to suit his taste.

The rate of flow earlier had been officially estimated at 12 feet per minute. Last night and this morning the lava acted capriciously: here and there it leaped ahead with searing tentacles, and at other times it seemed to slow up, as if gathering weight to overwhelm a ridge in the valley.

At one side stood a peasant whose weathered face turned tawny in the glow. "Guerra, Fame, Distruzione (War, hunger, destruction)," he repeated, shaking his head ,"Guerra, Fame, Distruzione!"

But there was humor, too, An American corporal from Indiana squatted at a safe distance and muttered, "Gosh, when I tell them about this in Muncie!"

Gradually the stream spread out in the valley, the last few trees went up in flames, and then the crackling mass crunched down on an eight-foot wall and began to devour it. Giuseppe Battaglio's house was on the far side of the wall and for a while it seemed that it might channel the flow and save the modest stone dwelling.

But as the incandescent mass roared over the wall, it was plain that the house was fated. A spear of fire shot up to a corner of the building then it subsided, and the house seemed to be winning the battle.

(Continued)

The odds were too great, however. The lava ground into the base on the other side, and with a roar, the wall fell in. A few minutes later the surging flow literally cracked the house in half. What looked like an iron bedstead twisted into the air.

Thus the destruction of the town began. A few hundred yards back, but directly in the line of the flow stood the town's best houses, and the three-story yellow school that the inhabitants cherished. It was estimated that they were all crushed and buried within two hours.

A reporter from the Associated Press filed the following dispatch to his agency:

The Allied soldiers in San Sebastiano already had cleared out all the residents who would go. Some, mostly old and sick people, had refused to leave, cowering in their homes.

Once it became certain that the houses were in the path of the streams, the soldiers were told to remove everyone, regardless of their desires.

They smashed open doors with their rifle butts and went through the houses room by room for anyone left behind. As they went through, fumes from the approaching lava were already filling the rooms.

Lava poured over a gasoline dump and there was an explosion. Big, as explosions go, but trifling compared with what was happening inside Vesuvius. Then the lava poured over a well, sealing it, and at the same time bringing its water to the boiling point. The well exploded in a geyser, breaking through the crust of lava that had just covered it.

This was hard to believe but who were we to figure out something like this?

Some further information about this volcano. It has been called by many the best-known volcano in the world. It is about four thousand feet above sea level and stands on the site of an old volcano, called Monte Somma, which goes back to the Christian era.

Wednesday, March 22. This was another hectic day. One thing out of the way was our house in San Sebastiano. We are all through with this piece of property. As we awoke this morning, the first thing to do was look up the mountainside and see how the monster on the hill was doing. It was spurting clouds of smoke. Fire and lava still rolled.

We receive standby orders to move out of Cercola. The planes all flew out to Caserta for safekeeping. We still were not sure if the lava would reach us. We were in the path. We were ready to move at any time.

It was bad enough to be involved in the running of a war but to have to fight an eruption of a vicious volcano seemed to be just as bad.

At 6:00 pm, we received orders to move to a staging area at first light tomorrow morning, our destination was uncertain at this time.

This would be our last night at Cercola. During the night, we packed so that we could evacuate a spot we never will forget.

The lava still came out of the mouth of Vesuvius. The slopes were cherry red and made quite a sight during the hours of darkness.

CHAPTER 34

Naples, Italy

Thursday, March 23. This was the day to move. The rain came down. Vesuvius still pushed out clouds of smoke. We were told the lava had slowed down some. Professor Giouseppe Imbo, Director of the Vesuvius Royal Observatory, remained at his observatory on the slopes of Vesuvius and kept everybody posted on the flow of the lava during the four worst days of this eruption.

Went to Naples and selected a spot for our squadron to put up for the night. It looked like we were going to take a boat somewhere, but they were keeping where under wraps for the time being.

I went back to Cercola and moved out with the convoy at 2:00 pm to a place called Palace Gardens. It was a nice spot to set up the tents. As I have said many times, our boys are experts in setting up tents and taking them down. We were in a nice, grassed area and it would be fine for the duration. We had a good meal. The boys have passes to the city of Naples.

They enjoyed it, even though it will only be for a few hours.

Vesuvius still put on a gallant display. The bright red lava coming down the slopes reminded me of a steel mill pouring molten steel out of the furnaces.

Friday, March 24. We were all up early this morning. Breakfast was served at 6:00. After breakfast, the tents came down. The landing plan was the same one we have used since we started at Landing Ground 172 back of the El Alamein line 18 months ago.

Once the convoy was ready, we were put on a standby until 12:30 pm for movement to the dock area of the bombed-out port of Naples. On our way to Pier 5, we proceeded down the main street of Naples, the famous Via Roma.

Upon arriving at the dock proper, we got a good look at the damage inflicted by the Allied air forces. We were assigned to a British LST (Landing Ship, Tank), named HMS *Bruiser*, and by 7:30 pm we had all our equipment secure. A nice meal was served. We all had a chance to get a good shower. This was welcome as we had no showers since we left the Foggia area on March 1.

I was selected to be the officer in charge of troops. All the papers were turned over to me. Now I had the real information as to where we were going. The island of Corsica

Equipment packed in tight on our transport ship.

would be our destination. Since our planes were away from us, we did not have any information as to what they were doing.

I received a report later tonight they had been operating out of the airfield near Caserta. They ran into a bunch of German ME-109s and had a real dogfight. The Germans lost a few. Our boys just had a few scratches on their wings.

The LST was a crowded ship. We could not leave it during the night. Later that evening, the Germans came over Naples as usual. They dropped eggs around the town. And here we were locked up in a ship in the harbor. No evacuation plan was presented to us.

The anti-aircraft guns around the harbor put up a nice Fourth of July display. A couple of times, Jerry dropped some bombs close to the LST. It gave one an uncomfortable feeling, like being locked up in a cell.

We survived and proceeded to have a good night's sleep. Before going to sleep, I looked towards the slopes of Vesuvius. Red lava was still in attendance.

Saturday, March 25. We had a little extra bunk fatigue this morning as we did not have to get up until 7:30. These British boys were going all out by serving us a second good meal. We were to leave the harbor at 2:30 pm. After leaving, we were joined by another LST by the name of *Thruster*, another British ship. Also, we had a small escort vessel.

Once we cleared the harbor area, we knew we were in a for a rough voyage. These LSTs, when loaded with trucks and equipment, did not make for a pleasure trip. We started to roll. Before long, we had some seasick boys. After dark, we could still see the sky lit up by our friend Vesuvius.

CHAPTER 35

Corsica, France

Sunday, March 26. The ship rolled all night long. This morning, we were in the straits between Sardinia and Corsica. We proceeded very slowly and did not land until the afternoon due to the tide conditions. We were looking at a new spot this morning. The sight of Vesuvius was missing. This morning, we were anxious to see this island that had so much history. Many soldiers have passed through Corsica on their way to battles elsewhere.

We made the landing area and there seemed to be a lot of confusion along the disembarking area. Those in charge either did not have any experience or planning. Our group's arrival was not taken into consideration. It took until 10:30 pm before we had our group together. The evening meal was simply the good old standby C-rations.

Our area for the night was very crowded but we made out okay. I made some inquiries about Vesuvius during the long wait in the disembarking area. I was informed Professor Imbo issued a statement that the lava would no longer move and damage the towns they thought would be destroyed.

We landed in the small port of Ajaccio. The crowds around the dock were awed with all the activity and equipment coming out of the bow of this ship.

Getting ready to sail to our next landing ground.

The island of Corsica is south of Genoa, Italy. In 1954, the population was over 200,000. This spot was part of France. The capital of this island is Ajaccio.

Napoleon Bonaparte was born on this island and there were many areas of the island to remind you of this.

In reading some of the history of this island, I found that it had been inhabited back to about 600 BC. As for wars, they had their share of them with the French and the Italians. Of course, this island was populated by the Germans prior to our arrival.

I am not going to go into the history of this island, but I do want to say World War II brought a fighter squadron 20,000 miles all the way from Boston. We played a part in the history of this island that had wars for many years.

We never gave much thought about the history of some of the spots we set up on. We were busy in the assignment of defeating an enemy that had not made the world a very nice place to live in for the previous eight years.

Monday, March 27. We were up early this morning and on the road for our new home on the old island. The airfield was called Alto Landing Ground, a name that does not show on the map. I believe there was a small river nearby called Alto and that was where the name came from.

We traveled over very mountainous roads all day and put up for the night in a spot called Porto Vecchio. We were all tired and did not have to be rocked to sleep. The roads of Corsica were not built for heavy equipment. It made for slow going.

CHAPTER 36

Alto Landing Ground, Corsica

March 28–April 20

Tuesday, March 28. All were up early and out on the road for our 33rd landing ground since we arrived overseas in August 1942. Everybody was anxious to see what this new place was going to be like. We arrived at Alto and, for the first time, we had a service group already on the field. They had mess tents up for us and a meal already prepared.

This was a wonderful surprise. The boys were thrilled to think such a service was rendered. After this wonderful meal, prepared by someone other than our own boys, we had a job to do. We started laying out our camp area. This was accomplished before supper. We prepared our own meal and settled down for the evening.

There was planning to be done as we were only the forward party. The rest of the squadron and the planes would join us soon.

The tent area was not far from the landing strip, which was being completed by an American engineering group. This spot, we found out, was a swamp. The engineers had been working on it for some time. It had been filled in. The strip was not the longest, but they said it will take care of our needs.

There was plenty of room for dispersal of the planes. This was most important. We were in a spot where the enemy could hit us. We were not too far from southern France and were forward of the Allied troops on mainland Italy.

It was one of the best fields we had. It was all weather. The engineers had laid down the steel matting.

One other advantage we have at this field is that every tent will have electric lights. We gave the boys a briefing on the use of their mosquito nets and how important it was they cover their cots before dusk.

We were also told the island of Corsica, prior to the war, was the second worst place in the world for malaria. The Anopheles Mosquito breeds in the swamps, and they carry the malaria germ.

We had quite a few cases of malaria on the Edku airfield in Egypt. The boys remembered this miserable disease.

We were told an anti-malaria control unit had been set up on the island, made up of Italian and Yugoslavian soldiers. They were doing an outstanding job but by no means had they licked this germ-carrying insect.

Wednesday, March 29. We had first call at 7:45 am. We had had a rough time the last few days and the planes will not be in today. The engineers had some prefabricated buildings. They will set them up for us to use as mess halls and clubs.

The planes from the two other squadrons of the group arrived this morning. We found the boys we had left behind worked out of Cercola Landing Ground. We also received a report that Lt. Hermon Routh of Warren, Ohio, was killed on take-off from our old field. He was buried in a cemetery in Naples. Another fine young man gave his life for his country.

In this same report was the news the boys were on a mission in central Italy and were jumped by a group of German ME-109s. Lieutenant Loyst Towner of Chehalis, Washington, was missing in action. The report further stated that, when last seen, he was flying straight ahead and had three German ME-109s on his tail.

Other pilots caught in this attack called him to turn about but he kept on going straight. Some of the pilots felt he had already been killed. To the best of my knowledge, his plane was never found.

On the same mission, Lt. Robert Abercrombie of Stillwater, Minnesota, had lots of damage to his plane but made it back to the field okay. Captain William Nuding, of Morristown, Pennsylvania, shot down an Fw 190 on this same mission. This was a good day for Bill as the orders came through promoting him to captain.

Thursday, March 30. Received a report that our boys will do a mission out of the Italian field and will then come to our new field in Corsica. They put up a 12-plane mission. When they arrived over the field, I could only see 11 planes. During the war, we got into the habit of counting planes.

After landing and during the debriefing, we found out that Bob Abercrombie was missing. One of the pilots thought they saw a 'chute open but nothing definite.

They had been in some action. Only yesterday, Bob had been shot up but made it back to the field okay. Our squadron commander, Major Art Exon of Estherville, Iowa, shot down an ME-109. Lieutenant John J. Lineman of Manchester, Connecticut, shot some pieces off another one.

Lieutenant Robert Abercrombie, left, discussing his bar tab.

Later in the day, we received a good report; Abercrombie was picked up in his dinghy on the coast south of Rome. This was always good news. He will return to the squadron tomorrow.

All our planes were now on our new field. We also obtained eight brand-new pilots. The engineers were in the area putting up the fabricated buildings for the messes and clubs. They were nice buildings. They were appreciated by all.

B Party will pack up and join us very quickly as we need them on this field. It looks like some busy operations ahead.

With the pilots from the rear party coming in, we were getting some up-to-date news on our old friend Vesuvius. They told us the lava had practically stopped but the volcano was now pushing out ash like mad. Sometimes, in the middle of the smoke and ash, there was lightning.

If you look back in history, you will find Pompeii was destroyed by the ash after an eruption of Vesuvius. They didn't think it was going to be that bad, but a B-25 outfit stationed on the Pompeii side of Vesuvius was caught by surprise by the eruption. Many of their planes were destroyed. The fuselages of the B-25s burned from the hot ash from the eruption.

Friday, March 31. This was a nice day in Corsica. We were sort of getting settled after a busy week. B Party will not be able to leave Cercola until April 2. Our boys had a mission scheduled but it was canceled due to bad weather over the target area.

Bob Abercrombie, who dumped in the ocean yesterday, arrived back. He told us he picked up some flak over the target area and could not get his P-47 back to base and just had to bail out in the ocean. He told us he slipped out of his 'chute just as he hit the water. He inflated his dinghy and bounced around in the water for a couple of hours before being picked up by a British rescue plane called a Walrus.

They have set up an area near our camp for movies. Tonight, we all turned out, but the sound was no good, so we walked back to the camp.

The medics have a good set up at the entrance to this small field. They have a large bottle of bug juice that was supposed to keep the mosquitoes away. They have an attendant on duty who insists everyone use it.

Robert Abercrombie and his P-40.

Saturday, April 1. This was a clear morning. You could see for miles. One of the first things we saw from shore this morning was the island of Elba. It was about thirty-five miles away. It was still held by the Germans. Our boys have been briefed about passing over this island as it has some very effective anti-aircraft guns known as the 88mm.

One would think this island would be a good target for our boys. The powers-that-be have other plans for the taking of this spot just 35 miles away.

Our boys had a mission that took off at 10:45 am. The target, like all the targets from now on, will be in Italy. This morning, they went after a bridge and some railroad cars. The mission was successful. They all arrived back at the field in good shape except for Lt. Robert Brown of New York City.

After Bob dropped his bombs, he came back for the strafe job. He ran through a tree. Thankfully, the P-47 is a sturdy ship. Although he had a few holes and a bent propeller, he managed to make a safe landing.

When we say the mission was successful, we have proof in the pictures taken when the guns blast away (a gun camera that activates when the P-47's guns fire). The pictures were developed shortly after landing and printed for the boys.

Sunday, April 2. We had church services this morning for the first time on the island of Corsica. Being Sunday made no difference as far as the war goes. Our boys were off at 10:30 am on another bridge-busting mission and another one at 2:30 pm. They all returned safe. Just before the afternoon mission landed, we saw a 'chute coming down out over the water near the runway. A boy from the 65th Squadron had had his plane shot up. He had to bail out just when he thought he could make the field.

A British flying boat was soon on the scene; very little time elapsed between when the pilot left his ship and when he was picked up.

At Bastia, which was about twenty-five miles from our field, there were PT (patrol torpedo) boats and flying boats to take care of incidents like this.

Since we had been on the move during the last week, our mail was not taken care of. Our commanding officer, Major Exon, took our courier ship, the old B-25, and flew to Naples. Within a few hours, he was back with a load of mail and packages. This was a good tonic for all.

At 2:30 pm, our rear party in Italy boarded a boat in Naples. They will join us soon.

Monday–Wednesday, April 3–5. During these three days, we had one bridge-busting mission and played some softball. We had a couple of good movies for a change.

We received our March pay from the finance officer. This caused a lot of comment as we were paid in francs, which can only be spent on the island of Corsica. There was nothing here to buy. So, except for a few of the heavy gamblers, we saved our money.

Thursday, April 6. Boys were off on a 16-plane mission, which was out of the ordinary. They usually put up 12 planes. They were after another important bridge in Italy. They do their job and come home safe.

At 4:00 pm, Capt. Louis Frank of Louisville, Kentucky, Lt. John Linehan, Major Carlton Chamberlain of Olean, New York, and Lt. Richard Nevett of Indianapolis, Indiana, took off on a reconnaissance flight to Italy. Not very often did we have four-plane flights, but this was an order from wing headquarters so off they went. Shortly after they crossed the coast, they ran into 11 Italian transport planes. The boys had a field day. Linehan got three, Frank got two and Chamberlain got one for a total of six planes. Not bad for a recce flight.

These planes must have been flown by German die-hard fascists because Italy is out

Major Carlton Chamberlain receiving recognition for a job well done.

of the picture as far as fighting goes. The boys were not satisfied with their kill of the transports. On their way home, they ran into some trains and gave them some attention so they would not be able to supply the enemy with troops or materiel.

I made it a point to be at the operations and intelligence tents during these debriefings whenever possible. It was an education to hear the pilots explain the actions of a mission.

The operations tent on this field was a three-minute ride in my jeep so I attended most of them, especially when there was plenty of action.

With the arrival of B Party, we were all together again as one squadron. This made for good spirits among the men. They loved to work together.

Friday, April 7. During the past week, we have been having trouble with the planes' bomb racks. Some of the racks have not been releasing the bombs. The boys have had to do all kinds of maneuvers to release them. In a few cases, they have come home and landed without releasing them.

This afternoon, one pilot, returning from a mission, radioed the field and inquired whether or not his bomb was still on the rack as he thought that he had dropped it over the ocean.

He misunderstood the message which told him that he still had the bomb, and he came in for a landing. When his plane touched down, the 500-pound bomb let go and rolled towards our operations tent where there were always officers and men, especially when a mission returned.

Captain Henry Mack, our squadron adjutant.

Most of the officers and men saw this rolling bomb on a path towards the operations tent. They either fell on the ground or ran. Staff Sergeant Weinstock apparently did not see or hear the action. The bomb exploded not far from where he stood. He was killed by decapitation.

Captain Henry Mack, the squadron adjutant, was not far from Weinstock and saw something he will never forget.

After all the excitement, the medical section released the body. We buried this young man in the U.S. Army cemetery just outside the town of Bastia. This was the first time since coming overseas we had a burial conducted by the Grave's Registration Department of the Army.

In the past, we have had to bury our dead on the edge of the flying field or some spot along the road. In this case, the Army had a very competent officer running this cemetery. I complimented him on the splendid job he did and remarked that he must have had some experience in this type of work before coming into the Army. He informed me that he had none. He sold typewriters.

Sergeant Weinstock was our instrument specialist. There were not many around that would be able to fill his shoes for a while.

Sunday, April 9. This was Easter Sunday. I was on my way to church services when I was notified to report to the group headquarters. I was introduced to a colonel and a warrant officer. The colonel started by swearing me in. This was quite a surprise. They told me nothing about what was going on. I was finally told he was the inspector general. He was investigating the so-called captured civilian cars. In southern Italy, a few civilian cars showed up in the squadron. But, at this date, we had no cars. We had rendered a report some months back listing the civilian cars on hand. He had that report and wanted to know how and where those cars came from.

I believe there were four cars, and I could not remember where they came from. The boys that said they captured these cars, in each case, had returned to the States. This made it a little easier for me. I had my own idea on how some of the vehicles came into the hands of some of our boys, but I did not pass this information on to these officers.

I often wondered how the group headquarters explained some of the vehicles they had, especially the one that was written up in a national magazine after the war was over.

With poor weather over the target areas, most of the squadrons were getting in some softball games.

Monday, April 10. Our boys were out on two bridge-busting missions today. I spent most of the day with another inspector general. This colonel was in the area inspecting funds. I was very glad to see him as the squadron fund had not been inspected for almost three years and I was the custodian.

I still had the account back in the bank in East Boston and I had spent a lot of money for food back in the States. I had made some purchases in Egypt in which the bills were made out in pounds and piasters. Every purchase in Egypt had a King Farouk stamp for a certain percentage of the purchase prices of the item.

The colonel was very understanding and gave us a clean bill of health after a few adjustments, which were made in letter certificates by the former custodian and myself.

Just as the colonel finished and prepared to leave, our area was sprayed by .50-caliber bullets. We both fell to the floor and ended up under the small desk where we stayed for some time.

When it seemed that the action was over, we came out of the tent and found out a P-47 the French Air Force used on our field was on fire. The heat of the flames had reached the firing mechanism, which tripped the eight guns. Fortunately for all, the guns had not been refilled after a recent mission. The colonel wanted to see this plane sending up clouds of smoke through our area. We took off in my jeep and proceeded to the spot of the fire. Upon arriving, we could see this plane was doomed.

The flames at this time were starting to lick the two 500-pound bombs hanging from the bomb racks. I immediately turned and drove in the opposite direction. I wanted to be far enough away from danger if the bombs went off.

The bombs did go off and fragments from them were found all over the camp. There were no injuries as most of the men were on the flight line. It was like a battle front for about an hour. When it was over, we had a lot of tents with holes in the 64th tent area. The most important part of this affair was no one was hit by all the metal flying around for too long a time.

How no one was hurt I will never know.

The colonel felt like he had been in combat as he was about to leave the squadron area. He will remember the inspection of the funds of the 64th Fighter Squadron for the rest of his life.

Tuesday–Wednesday, April 11–12. During these two days, the boys were out several times on the same run. Railroads and trains. They were having a field day with the new assignment, specializing in railroad engines, freight cars and bridges. We have had lots of softball games. We seem to be building up a real competitive spirit between all the squadrons and group headquarters.

Friday, April 14. The boys were off this morning on a dive-bombing mission when they ran into a sky full of ME-109s and Fw 190s. There were 32 enemy aircraft in total. After the scramble with these enemy aircraft, the boys came home with a few victories and one loss.

Some of the pilots from the other squadrons on this mission with the Black Scorpion Squadron had a bigger share of victories. This was okay with us so long as they shoot these enemy planes out of the sky. Of course, our boys like to get them but, when you add the whole thing up, what difference does it make as long as someone gets them.

Lieutenant Paul Carl of Seneca, Pennsylvania, shot down two and Capt. Michael McCarthy of Boston shot down one. In the fracas these boys were in, all the planes covered a lot of airspace. When they formed up to come home, one of our planes was missing. Upon landing, we found Lt. Neal Gunderson of Cranford, New Jersey, had not returned. We carried him as missing in action.

Later in the afternoon, we had some trouble when a mission returned, and a couple of bombs rolled off the planes. We were lucky today. They did not explode. They were picked up by the ordnance boys to be used again.

Saturday, April 15. A few more missions and all our boys were back safe. More trouble with bombs rolling off planes. This afternoon, one of the bombs blew up just behind a P-47 as the plane landed. The good Lord was watching over this boy as it did not even damage his plane. A plane landing at about one hundred fifty miles an hour does not stay in one place very long.

The engineering and ordnance section of the squadron tried to correct these racks. This should have been taken care of before the racks were shipped to us.

The softball games were in full swing this evening. The 65th Squadron shut us out 7–0.

Monday, April 17. This was the first day since arriving at Alto that we have had any rain. This day made up for it. The rain came down heavy all day.

The day was brightened by a group of musicians from the 410th American Anti-Aircraft Battalion stationed on the island. A real splendid group of boys spreading cheer and doing something they no doubt love. Their usual job was manning the guns.

Tuesday–Wednesday, April 18–19. In these two days, we had a few more bridge-breaking and train-busting missions. We had some good movies for a change, and we had another concert by a group of American boys from the 817th

Engineer Battalion. These were the boys who built our field. They all come from the southern states.

Tonight, for the first time since we landed on this island, we had a few enemy planes overhead. Looked like they were taking some pictures. They may be planning things to come. Apparently, some of the night fighters or bombers were out over the island of Elba tonight. There was a great show of anti-aircraft fire and the sounds of bombing. This may be the prelude to the taking of this island by Allied forces.

A few of the boys were promoted today. That meant they bought the drinks this evening at the club. This was always a happy occasion as it meant more money for them. They don't mind spending a few dollars at their own bar where drinks are not too expensive.

Thursday, April 20. This was a bad day for the Black Scorpion Squadron. Captain Franklin, who was attached to the squadron from England, went out on the early morning mission. His plane was hit by flak. A direct hit in his belly tank full of gas caused an explosion. The last time he was seen, his plane was going down on fire. No open 'chute was seen.

On the afternoon show over Italy, our squadron commander, Major Art Exon, again received a direct hit on his plane. The plane caught fire and he bailed out. One of the boys had the opportunity to follow him down. He was seen to land okay and was seen running for cover.

The mission the boys were on when we lost Exon was dive bombing and strafing an ammunition dump. The boys had wonderful results.

Major Exon was hit during the strafing pass. This young man had been commanding the squadron since August 17, 1943, and doing an outstanding job. He was well liked by all members of the squadron. He was an outstanding pilot. It will be a loss to the squadron to lose the talents of this young man who came from Estherville, Iowa, and had been a high school principal in his hometown.

Normally, when a pilot is lost on a mission, activities in the evening go on as usual but tonight they seemed to be a bit subdued. The squadron will go on as usual but when the boys lose a pilot with the promise Art Exon had, it gives them something to think about.

Major Art Exon

Here is the report from Arthur Exon about his exploits after being shot down.

As many of the personnel of the 64th Fighter Squadron will remember, I was forced to bail out of an airplane that was on fire over Italy on Hitler's birthday, April 20, 1944.

On the evening of the 19th of April, the 64th Fighter Squadron was sent on a railroad bombing mission in the Florence area and on the way back we discovered a fairly new ammunition and storage facility near Cecina located on the west coast of Italy—just across from the island of Elba.

Our 16-aircraft formation strafed the area, setting off many fires and mild explosions. There was a certain area of the ammunition dump consisting of large bombs and other explosives which were not discharged as a result of machine-gun fire.

On the 20th of April, I led another 16-aircraft formation on a similar mission over Italy. However, the lead aircraft were loaded with thermite cluster bombs which were to be used on the remaining ammunition storage dump. At the completion of our dive run, I spotted a new frame building which appeared to have an adjacent concrete structure.

I ordered the remaining flight to higher altitude and attacked the build-ing myself. When the bullets struck the facility, there was an immediate intense flame followed by a terrific explosion. I was at tree-top level, flying at a high rate of speed, and unable to avoid the debris.

Major Art Exon was captured after bailing out over Florence.

I was forced to fly through the flying debris and, when I came out the other side, the aircraft was on fire and all power was lost.

I pulled up to gain altitude and bailed out at the first opportunity. My parachute blossomed in time to allow me to settle into an open spot in a local orchard. I immediately collected my parachute, disposed of it, and tried to look for cover.

Within a matter of minutes, I was completely surrounded by a German and Italian Coast Guard detachment and was taken prisoner. I was burned on the legs and had a minor bone fracture in the right ankle. I apparently had struck my leg on the empennage of the airplane.

I was forced to walk with hands over my head for approximately two hours until we came to a back road and subsequently picked up by a German jeep and taken to a dispensary for first aid treatment.

I spent time in various hospitals in Florence and Medina in the Po Valley in northern Italy. My hospital treatment was exceptional. I received X-rays of the broken leg and a number of plaster casts.

When I was cleared to leave the hospital, I was moved as a prisoner of war to an Allied POW camp in the Austrian Alps, where I remained until the D-Day landing in Europe in early June 1944. I was moved from the Allied camp to *Oflag 64* in Danzig, traveling by trains through Salzburg, Vienna, Breslua and into Danzig, where I found myself in a U.S. Army Officer POW camp.

This was contrary to German policy so, as soon as arrangements could be made, I was moved from *Oflag 64* to *Stalag Luft III* in Sagan, Germany, an Air Force POW camp 60 miles southeast of Berlin.

I was at *Luft III* and became the American senior officer immediately, and remained so until Lt Col. Ed Bland arrived and became the senior officer. I remained at *Luft III* as executive officer and chief of the athletic program until the end of December 1944.

In January, as the Russians broke through the Eastern Front, the Germans marched the prisoners out of *Luft III*. We walked for four days and nights until we arrived at a safe railroad station where we were loaded on cattle cars and transported to a camp near Nuremberg. We remained there from mid-January until mid-March.

At this time, Patton's Army broke through on the Western

Major Art Exon taking a break.

Front and we were forced to leave camp on foot, walking south and across the Danube River to a camp at Mossburg, Germany. We remained there until liberated on the 29th day of April 1945.

After approximately 10 days, we were flown to Camp Lucky Strike in France, where we were processed and boarded SS *Lejeune* for the United States, arriving at Camp Kilmer on 3 June 1945.

At various camps in Europe, I met many 57th Fighter Group pilots. Some that I recall are "Pug" Wheeler, 64th; "Spanky" Manda, 65th; Schwartz, 65th; Steve Turner, 64th; Schneider, 64th.

CHAPTER 37

Alto Landing Ground, Corsica

April 21–29

Friday, April 21. Major Louis Frank III took over this morning as squadron commander, another outstanding pilot who came from Louisville, Kentucky. We had no missions on account of the weather.

A group of officers and enlisted men departed for a seven-day rest leave on the island of Capri. There are many hotels on the island which can accommodate a few thousand men a week.

The officers and men were flown from the different organizations to Naples. Then they were taken by boat to the island paradise. The announcement of the leave went over with a bang when it was announced last night. We had no trouble filling our quota. We had a briefing this evening on how the situation on the Italian Front looked. We were told the picture was bright and all plans were moving on schedule. The air arm played a major part in the destruction of the German Army.

Saturday, April 22. Our boys had three missions today. They were routine and all returned safe. We had a little excitement this afternoon when a B-26 circled over the field as if he was in trouble just about the time our boys were returning from their second mission. The runway was cleared for him to come in and land. His approach was very good, and he landed okay but ran out of runway. Just before the end of our short runway, he nosed over.

There was quite a bit of damage to the front end of the plane. He had been shot up by flak on a bombing mission to southern France. His home

Major Louis Frank III, squadron commander, April 21–December 16, 1944.

base was in the Foggia area. He was sure he would not make it as one of his engines was not working. There were no injuries to the crew.

A few wreckers were put into play to remove this big plane from the middle of the runway.

The softball games were in full swing. The movies were held with a good selection of pictures. A new group of pilots reported to the squadron today. We were very fortunate in our replacement pilots. They were a great group of young men. They fit in the picture with the old timers in short order.

When I say "old timers," I should clarify these so-called old timers have only been around less than a year. But they are old in experience as fighter pilots. They were taught the rules of the game by the original pilots who came overseas in July 1942

The original pilots finished their missions and returned to the States.

The anti-aircraft guns barked tonight in the Bastia area. It can be assumed the Germans were looking over our island. At the present time, there are a lot of aircraft on the several landing strips the engineers had built.

Sunday, April 23. Church services this morning and the boys had two missions. They all returned safe. We had a few crack ups along the runway but no one was injured.

We received a few more new pilots to fill the gaps of the pilots going home and some pilots lost on missions.

Monday, April 24. The boys had two missions, one at 11:00 and another, kind of late, 6:30 pm. This will bring them back about 9:00 pm. It was still light as we are on British Summer Time. It does not get dark until about 10:15 pm.

All missions returned safe. The boys talked of their experiences shooting up of a row of trains.

For the first time since we came overseas, we put in a requisition for some lumber and received same. There was a lumber mill on the island. Good old Uncle Sam was doing business with the owners. We drew enough lumber to add sides to the mess hall tents, and a floor. Our carpenters were the best, Sgt Harry Axelrod from Brooklyn, New York, and Corp. Nicholas Detiberils of Astoria, New York.

These boys did an outstanding job. They even built a door to the kitchen so we could have some protection for the food during the night.

The natives were hungry; we lost lots of food. This frame and door to the most important department in the squadron gave us a little more security than just a tent.

We were also able to obtain enough wood to put a floor in the squadron orderly room. Later, we looked for some more wood to build a frame around this room. Some of the planes were parked pretty close to our orderly room and when they started up our records would have to be nailed down.

Tuesday, April 25. A report arrived this morning from one of the squadrons returning from a mission over Italy. They saw some enemy destroyers on the Italian side of the island of Elba. Our boys were excited when they were briefed for this type of mission.

At 8:00 am, off they went; they returned without finding any sight of the reported destroyers. A couple of hours had elapsed from the initial report. The ships were nowhere to be found.

The boys are unhappy as they have not had a target like this for some time. We had a few incidents of our boys working over some ships off the coast of Libya and Tunisia last year when they were pushing Rommel out of Africa.

Wednesday–Thursday, April 26–27. Two days full of heavy rain. The landing strip lacked combat activity.

We received some good American rations these days. We even drew some frozen chickens. Our cooks love to cook them as they get sick of the same old spam.

A plane came in with lots of mail. Our old CO, Col. Art Salisbury, all the way from England, paid us a visit.

Friday, April 28. This was a busy day for the squadron. First, we sent some pilots to pick up some replacement P-47s. In the courier plane (our old B-25), we sent home some officers and enlisted men who had finished their tour of duty.

Our pilots had three busy missions. They all returned safely. These missions, as I have written, were pretty much the same.

The targets were bridges and trains. On some of these missions, they fly a reconnaissance over a specified area and many times the information they collect is the target for another mission. They may receive this mission, or some other squadron will get it, depending on what headquarters thinks of the information.

The chickens we drew, for the first time since we have arrived on Corsica, were served tonight. It hit the right spot. I don't think we have had fresh chicken since we were on the streets of Messina waiting to go to Italy several months ago. Everybody felt we had a real supper tonight.

Saturday, April 29. Captains Michael McCarthy and Jim Novy, both of Boston, Massachusetts, went home this morning for 30 days. We will miss these two top pilots.

CHAPTER 38

Capri, Italy

Today was my day to start a week at the Air Force rest camp on the island of Capri. I needed a rest after the ride from Corsica to Naples. About fifteen of us from the group were in one of the old B-25s. Our pilot was Captain Benedict from one of the other squadrons.

When we arrived over Naples, Benedict started some crazy maneuvers with a group of P-39 fighters. He gave the group, crowded in the bomb bay of this old ship, quite a shaking. We were all glad when the plane stopped at the operations building.

We had quite a long wait for transportation and finally arrived at Capri at 5:30 pm. Supper at a nice hotel was out of this world. The Air Force did an outstanding job on our first day. There were several hotels on the island and the Grand Hotel Quisisana, where I stayed, was the best.

At the Quisisana, they had a big band and those boys put on a show. Dancing went on until midnight. It was good sleeping in a hotel room with nice and clean bedding for a change.

The next few days were a wonderful change from the activities on Corsica with the squadron. We had breakfast in bed and a show or a dance every day. During my week away, the squadron had

The isle of Capri. The Air Force turned the island into a spot for leave.

My hotel for my week on Capri.

their regular runs, beating up the enemy trains and bridges in Italy. The only incident out of the ordinary was on May 5.

Lieutenant Eliot Brown of Chepachet, Rhode Island, was hit but he made it back to near the field. He bailed out and landed in the water in an area not far from our field. "Johnny on the Spot," the PT Boat, was there to pick him up. Brown was wounded but not seriously and was taken to the Air Force hospital not far from our field. As always, he received super treatment.

On May 7, I returned from Capri. At the airport waiting to take us home was the pilot that gave us a bad time on our way to Naples Airport last week.

When I landed last week, I vowed never to ride with him. I was fortunate to find a friend from one of the bomber groups stationed on Corsica parked right next to the plane we were supposed to take back. He was kind enough to take a few of us back in his B-25.

We had some real bad flying weather. We had to get a fix from the Air Force control station on Corsica who gave us a good bearing. We came in for a good landing at Alto, the home of the 64th Fighter Squadron.

CHAPTER 39

Alto Landing Ground, Corsica

May 8–June 19

Monday, May 8. Back on the job this morning. The weather was so bad the flying schedules were all on standby until the weather cleared. Assigned to us were several French pilots of the Lafayette Squadron who will fly with our boys until they have enough planes to form their own unit.

The weather remained bad. By mid-afternoon, we were taken off standby with no further missions scheduled for this date.

The 41st American Engineer Battalion's band played a concert in the camp area. They were a splendid group of musicians. After midnight, the anti-aircraft guns opened up in the Bastia area. I believe these were after photo-reconnaissance ships looking over this island. There are lots of outfits and lots of equipment on this island at the present time. It would be a good target for the enemy.

We have been expecting some action since shortly after we arrived at this spot.

We had wonderful dispersal for our planes, but the camp area was a little crowded. Some of the units on other fields are more crowded and would be hurt if we had a good air raid.

Tuesday, May 9. The weather remains a problem, but the boys were able to put up one show this afternoon. They all returned safely.

Wednesday, May 10. Our boys had three missions today. They were of the regular brand. They returned okay.

One of the planes from the 66th Squadron came back with a big hole in its side and made a safe landing. These P-47s are rugged and can take it.

Our landing strip was near the water. The shoreline was guarded by a security guard unit made up of Puerto Rican soldiers. They did an outstanding job day and night.

This afternoon, one of the guards observed a rowboat off the shore. They managed to get the occupants to land near the end of our runway. They quickly put them under guard. They turned out to be some Italian soldiers who had slipped away from the island of Elba and wanted to be free.

They were taken to the island headquarters at Bastia. We didn't hear any more about them. I assumed that after the debriefing they would be freed and proceed to their hometown if it was free of Germans. This was what most of the Italian soldiers did after they gave up last year in southern Italy. I don't believe their hearts were ever in this business of war.

Thursday, May 11. The boys had three missions today. One of them was an early job that took them on a short run to the harbor at Elba. The boys reported severe anti-aircraft (AA) fire. We were lucky they came home okay.

Except Lt. Thomas Hannon of Torrington, Connecticut. Hannon received a direct hit in the wing of his plane and came home with a big hole in it. The Germans had 88-mm guns for the defense of Elba. They were well respected by all the Allies.

The hole in the wing of Hannon's plane was taken care of by our sheet metal men in the engineering section. These boys have been patching holes in P-40s and P-47s since we started this long trek from El Alamein in October 1942.

The sheet metal men take pride in their work. When they finished a job like this one, it was hard to find the spot that was damaged. The rest of the missions were of the same variety as I have been talking about all along.

Captain Crosbie from headquarters gave a talk this evening on the big show which will take place in Italy tonight at 11:00 pm. The combined Allied forces in Italy will start a big push. Prior to the jump-off time, the artillery will start the attack with 1,600 guns. This sounds like the start of the push back in El Alamein on October 23, 1942, when the British opened up their attack with over 1,000 guns.

Friday–Saturday, May 12–13. This was one of the days a soldier would not forget if he was with the 64th Fighter Squadron at Alto on the island of Corsica. We had a busy day with two missions in the morning and one mission in the afternoon. We had a nice supper with a group of French artillery officers who commanded the 40-mm gun battalion around our airfield.

Just after turning in about 10:30 pm, we heard a large explosion. We all headed for our slit trenches. As we did, the sky in the Bastia area lit up like a baseball field having a night game. An air raid was in progress. The first few bombs

Lieutenant Thomas Hannon came home with a hole in the wing of his plane on May 11, 1944. (57th Fighter Group website)

dropped knocked out the radar station at Bastia. The next series of bombs hit the high-octane gas dump which made for good lighting.

All the action seemed to be in the Bastia area. The Germans dropped flares that looked like a large chandelier. These lights seemed to just hang in the sky. I believe they had small parachutes attached to them to slow the drop to earth.

After about a half an hour of watching this tremendous show, if you want to call it that, Captain Mitchell of Nyssa, Oregon, our armament officer, and I got down in the bottom of the trench as the planes started to circle our area.

They never did drop any flares after their initial drop over the Bastia area. They kept the action up for almost an hour. Then they enlarged their circle and seemed to be working on the field south of us where the B-25 group, which had just come over to Corsica from the Pompeii, Italy, area, was based. This group had received heavy losses and damage from the ash of Vesuvius.

We could hear explosions in their area; we stayed in the trench for some time as all the anti-aircraft guns in our area fired away.

We were very fortunate no bombs dropped in our area. It was possible the photos the Germans had taken of the island showed our excellent dispersal. We had figured they would go after the other units who were not dispersed as well as we were.

That was okay with us, but we hated to see our comrades killed and injured by these night raiders of Adolf Hitler.

Brandon, Mitchell and Mobbs. (57th Fighter Group website)

Shortly after midnight, Pete and I decided it was safe to leave the slit trench and go to bed. The fires in the Bastia area were still lighting up the sky. We did not receive any information as to the losses at this time.

At about 3:30 am, the siren in our area went off full blast. We had another raid on our hands. Pete and I made for the slit trench. We heard lots of planes overhead. One of them sounded like he was coming into our runway for a landing. They still did not drop anything in our area except a lot of "window" (a material to jam the radar).

After an hour, we came out of the trench and went back to bed.

During the morning breakfast, all the conversations were about the two raids. Everybody felt lucky we did not get hit. From all the action, we felt these raids must have hurt someone. Shortly after breakfast, information started to come down to us about the damage and casualties. We had a couple of pilots in the hospital. They were discharged prior to the time we expected as the hospital needed the room.

The bomb group, which I believe was the 340th B-25 group, was hit hard. They had many wounded and 13 killed. They lost 52 B-25s to the enemy action. I was told they had few or no slit trenches and their planes were packed in close.

We also heard the Jerries strafed their area many times. These Krauts had a field day as our anti-aircraft artillery failed to be effective. I don't believe we had enough artillery to protect the number of troops and aircraft on the island.

B-24 destroyed as a result of German air raids.

The reports from the other end of the island in the Bastia area showed we lost a B-24 parked for the night on the British airfield which also had a large group of Spitfires. The report stated that 114 Spitfires were put out of action. The British field was in a shambles, but they went to work on the planes and the runway and put up a mission before the day was over.

The 340th Bomb Group, although hit hard, put up a mission and visited the field where the Jerries came from.

I learned later the mission the Spitfires put up strafed the Krauts' field. It was estimated the raid consisted of about seventy German aircraft. In the morning, no one claimed to have shot down any of the enemy aircraft.

There was no flying today. Picks and shovels operated all over the camp area. Although the boys had slit trenches, they were making them into different shapes and were also digging them deeper. This raid must have shaken up the brass at headquarters. Many AA units, along with searchlight units, were ordered to Corsica in a big hurry.

Monday–Wednesday, May 15–17. During these three days, our boys had three missions each day. We were very fortunate all our boys returned safe from these train and bridge-busting missions. On the 16th, our boys had two missions before noon, and all returned safe.

The 66th Squadron ran into a hornet's nest of anti-aircraft artillery and had two boys shot down; they also had six others shot up.

The line on the Italian Front started to move north and that was good news.

The softball games are in full swing these days although the enlisted men are busy boys, especially when we are putting up three missions a day. This meant lots of work for all sections. All the planes had to be gassed up, checked over by engineering, bombed up, eight .50-caliber machine guns rearmed, and any holes picked up from enemy AA patched.

As I have said many times, this outfit had the tops in officers and enlisted men. It was a happy team. We had very little friction in all the months we operated in the combat zone under very adverse conditions, such as sand, rain, and mud. They just

64th Fighter Squadron Maintenance Group. This photo illustrates the size of the P-47, the largest single-engine fighter of the war.

wanted to keep the planes flying. With this in mind, we always felt we had the top squadron in the group. The records prove this point.

Thursday, May 18. Boys were scheduled for two missions this morning. The Red Cross girls were in the area today with the coffee and doughnuts. What a treat.

We had a good movie this evening and the 41st Engineer's band played before the show went on. During the day, we saw many units of anti-aircraft and searchlights going up the road outside of our camp. They were heading for the Bastia area.

We felt the airfield needed more protection after what the Jerries did to them a few nights ago. I was very glad to see lots of 90-mm guns in the convoys.

On our field, we had the 40-mm guns. I don't ever remember seeing any 90mm on the outside of our camp area.

After the movie tonight, the boys at the club had a long discussion about the air raid of a few nights ago. Many of us felt we would be hit again.

Friday, May 19. Early this morning, we moved many of the enlisted men's tents to give them more dispersal. We had a storm in the area. This held up the morning missions. Later, it rained again. All planes were grounded for the day. The bright part of the day was when a courier plane got through from Naples with a bomb bay full of mail for us.

Saturday, May 20. The bad weather was still with us. All planes were still on standby.

Sunday, May 21. You would never know it was Sunday as the war goes on. The boys had an 8:30 am and a 2:30 pm mission. The same type as they have had for weeks.

What the boys wanted was to run into some German fighters for some action. With the hammering the airfields have been given by the fighters and bombers, it would be difficult for the Jerries to have any fighters in Italy.

Monday, May 22. Only one mission on the agenda today. The rest of the day was spent on a series of softball games after the group headquarters' inspection was completed.

The base at Bastia put out some wonderful rations. This helps make up for all the poor rations we have had in the past.

Tuesday–Wednesday, May 23–24. The missions of the 23rd were of the same caliber but, on the 24th, they had a very important mission. Their assignment this morning was to go into an area where intelligence claimed there was a nest of anti-aircraft guns. Their job was to silence these guns as they are protecting an important target that has been given to a bomb group to destroy. They did their job well. All came home to talk about it.

This afternoon was an important one for the 64th and the rest of the squadrons of the group. On the first mission after lunch, the boys ran into a group of trucks. Some were moving. Some were trying to hide. The boys went in for the kill and had a real field day, as one pilot described it. They strafed these trucks until they had no ammunition left and came home to reload.

This went on all afternoon and into the evening. Because the clocks were on British Summer Time, the boys flew until 8:45 pm. The total count in number of trucks destroyed ran to over 200 for the group. A destroyed truck was a burning truck. Many other trucks were put out of action, but I did not receive that count.

This was one of the busiest days we have had in a long time. When we counted the sorties, we found the 64th Squadron flew 49 sorties for the day.

It was a happy night at the club. All the pilots that flew today told of their experiences about the German truck targets. It was felt, with such damage to this equipment, the boys played an important part in the shortening of this silly war. It was further felt, with so much equipment moving, the enemy must be leaving the area they have defended for so long.

Thursday, May 25. Boys were off early this morning. They all returned safely except for Lt. Paul M. Hall of Salina, Kansas. He came in with his plane on fire. He made a good landing and was met at the end of the runway by medical and a fire truck.

He was taken out of the cockpit of his plane in a hurry. The medics barely got him out in time. Badly burned, he was close to the end. After first aid was given to him on a stretcher off the side of the runway, he was rushed to hospital. The flames were quickly extinguished, and the plane was towed to the service group at the other end of the field.

Hall, although badly burned, would be OK. He would not fly for a while.

On the afternoon mission, Lt. Myer "Bucky" Reynolds, of Washington, D.C., had to bail out over the water. He landed on a small island off the coast of Italy called Pianosa. He was back in the squadron for the supper meal and laughed it off.

There were lots of bomber shows today and we fueled the P-38s escorting them. These bombers come out of the Foggia area and pick up the P-38s on their way to the target.

The bombers had enough fuel to get home but the P-38s had to come into Corsica to receive enough fuel to get back to their base.

Captain Paul Hall after flying through some trees.

More damage to Hall's plane.

We fed many of the pilots and did not mind. We drew many extra rations for this operation. The reports from headquarters stated the Germans were pulling out of their positions in Italy.

Friday, May 26. The sky was full of B-17s and B-24s on their way to northern Italy and southern France with loads of destruction. The P-51s were the escort plane for the day. They came into Corsica for us to refuel them. I had lunch with a group we fed in our mess. They were another group of dedicated pilots. Our own boys had a busy day working over the railroad bridges and trains in Italy.

One of our enlisted men decided he did not like the squadron and took off for parts unknown. He stole some money and clothes from his tent mates and left a note saying try and find him. We were too busy these days to worry about one man that had been trouble since he joined us as a replacement a few months ago. We notified the Military Police unit and left it to them to take care of him.

Saturday–Monday, May 27–29. These days were repeats of the last few days. With the skies full of planes, you wondered how the enemy can take such a beating and still keep going?

Tuesday, May 30. If we were back in the States, this would not be a workday. Here on Corsica, the activities of the war just keep rolling along. The regular run of missions was on today. Nothing of great importance came out of them.

We know that someone is getting hurt with all the bombs and ammunition they dropped on these continuous daily runs. We were awakened tonight with the drone of what sounded like a German Ju-88. We got so used to hearing them back in Africa.

They came over the island and dropped an object which acted like a big flash bulb.

Wednesday, May 31. This was a normal day with a few missions; no one was hurt (except the recipients of the bombs dropped on Italy). Around the perimeter of our airfield, we had a French unit manning anti-aircraft guns and we had very good relations with these young men, especially the officer in charge of the guns in our immediate area.

The main reason was because he could speak English. We used him for an interpreter to communicate with the rest of the officers and enlisted men.

Our boys were very free with their candy and cigarette rations. It seemed the French force was dropped on the island and forgotten. They had no soap or toilet articles. Most of us had plenty so we fixed them up with their missing articles. This was for the best show of goodwill.

We also fed these officers and enlisted men. They thought we lived like kings. Our rations were wonderful compared to the days when the British fed us.

Perhaps sensing the growing frustration of the personnel under him, as the war seemingly dragged on, or perhaps feeling similar frustration himself, General Harold R. L. G. Alexander, 1st Earl Alexander of Tunis, acknowledged the progress the Allies had made and that victory was at hand if everyone maintained the effort and hung on for just a bit longer.

Soldiers of the Allied Armies in Italy

Throughout the past winter you have fought hard and valiantly and killed many Germans. Perhaps you are disappointed that we have not been able to advance faster farther, but I and those who know, realize full well how magnificently you have fought amongst these almost insurmountable obstacles of rocky, trackless mountains, deep in snow, and in valleys blocked by rivers and mud, against a stubborn foe.

The results of these past months may not appear spectacular, but you have drawn into Italy and mauled many of the enemy's best divisions which he badly needed to stem the advance of the Russian armies in the east. Hitler has admitted that his defeats in the east were largely due to the bitterness of the fighting and his losses in Italy. This, in itself, is a great achievement and you may well be as proud of yourselves as I am of you. You have gained the admiration of the world and the gratitude of our Russian allies.

Today the bad times are behind us and tomorrow we can see victory ahead. Under the ever-increasing blows of the air forces of the United Nations, which are mounting every day in intensity, the German war machine is beginning to crumble. The Allied armed forces are now assembling for the final battles on sea, on land, and in the air to crush the enemy once and for all. From the east and the west, from the north and the south, blows are about to fall which will result in the final destruction of the Nazis and bring freedom once again to Europe and hasten peace for us all. To us in Italy, has been given the honor to strike the first blow.

We are going to destroy the German armies in Italy. The fighting will be hard, bitter, and perhaps long, but you are warriors and soldiers of the highest order, who for more than a year have known only victory. You have courage, determination, and skill. You will be supported by overwhelming air forces. And in guns and tanks we far outnumber the Germans. No armies have entered battle before with more just and righteous cause.

So with God's help and blessing, we take the field—confident of victory.

H. R. Alexander
General,
Commander in Chief
Allied Armies in Italy

The battalion headquarters of this French unit had an area a few miles from our base. They had a club set up and this evening a few of the 64th officers were invited to a party, a thank you for the treatment we had given their men in our area. They had very little food, but they made this informal meeting seem like a banquet.

We had a seven-course meal, each course with a different wine. I thought they did an outstanding job with what they had to work with.

We left the area before dark and returned to our own, feeling there was nothing like a good American meal.

This evening, just after turning in for the night, the alert alarm went off and we were in the slit trenches for a while. It was Jerry back again taking some more pictures. No bombs.

Thursday, June 1. With 249 enlisted men and 60-plus officers, the paperwork at times piled up. That was what we had to clean up this morning. We had four missions today. All our boys returned home safe.

Friday, June 2. This was a busy day for the pilots. They had lots of missions on the schedule. During the afternoon, one of the flights went out on a routine run and were told to make a reconnaissance over an assigned area. This mission for our squadron was led by Capt. Robert B. Abercrombie of Stillwater, Minnesota. He was told if he saw a good target, he was to radio back that "Bananas are ripe."

When he reached the assigned spot after his bombing mission, he found what was thought to be the Hermann Göring Division going south to reinforce the beaten Jerries. Abercrombie called back on the radio and said, "Bananas are plentiful."

We had been tipped off something big was in the wind. All the gang was around the radio van at the base operations tent. Abercrombie's flight worked over this target of guns and trucks as long as their ammunition lasted.

In the meantime, every aircraft on the Alto Landing Ground was put at readiness. They flew for the rest of the afternoon and early evening. It was quite a sight to see the pilots, even those who had flown missions earlier in the day, pleading with the operations officer for a plane.

I would say this was one of the busiest days we ever had.

As soon as a plane came back, it was checked over, gassed up and bombed, and the eight machine

Captain Bob Abercrombie, "Bananas are ripe." Captain Abercrombie is shown in his P-40. (57th Fighter Group website)

guns were reloaded. The missions continued until about 8:00 pm as we were on British Summer Time. The planes came back at 9:45 and it was still light.

This was a happy day for all of us. We knew, with missions such as this, the war could not last. The convoy the boys worked over lost many vehicles and guns. I believe there were about eighty burning trucks. The guns and men destroyed made for a good day's work for the 57th Fighter Group and all the squadrons.

After many days of routine missions, this was what the squadron needed. This really made the pulse of these young men jump. The spirit of the squadron was at its highest peak tonight.

The enlisted men of all sections were tired boys tonight, but they were happy they played a major role in keeping these planes in the air. The mission was a major effort to shorten the war.

The club was a busy place tonight. Hearing these boys tell of their experiences was an evening of joy for all. The most important part of this whole operation was we didn't lose any pilots in one of the biggest operations since we arrived on Corsica.

Saturday, June 3. This morning started off with a bang. The first mission was assigned to the 66th Squadron and their first plane crashed into a grading machine parked too close to the runway.

The pilot was okay, but his plane was made worthless by fire and the ammunition burning up. This incident delayed the take-off of these early morning missions for a short time. These were important missions and were timed for take-off every 20 seconds. The boys were going after the remnants of the Hermann Göring Division they had mauled yesterday.

Our boys worked over the same area and were relieved at 2:00 pm for the day. Shortly thereafter, some good targets were found, and they flew two more missions after a busy morning dive bombing and strafing convoys.

Sunday, June 4. Just another Sunday with some church services. Two missions for the boys across the water in Italy to hit some Jerries trying to win a useless war.

We receive the good news this afternoon that American troops have entered Rome. For a change of pace this evening, our service group was the spot to go as the traveling USO (United Service Organizations) show would entertain us. A very good show was enjoyed by a large group from the units stationed nearby.

Monday, June 5. A routine day with three missions on targets in northern Italy on some bridges and trucks. All boys back safe. Our B-25 returned tonight with a group of officers and enlisted men from rest leave in Alexandria. It was always good to hear the various stories of the experiences of the boys. Movies tonight.

Tuesday, June 6. We had a pool on which day the invasion of France would take place and the officer who selected this date was the winner. We received the news early this morning.

We know, with this pressure on the enemy, the war in Italy could not last much longer. Our boys had a couple of missions. Lieutenant Richard K. Nevett of Indianapolis, Indiana, failed to return.

The report given at the briefing was he failed to come out of his dive on a strafing run. Some of our boys have shown up after a similar situation.

Wednesday, June 7. This was another busy morning for all squadrons. They were in the air early. The 65th and 66th Squadrons lost four boys. We lost Lt. Ernest Newhouse of Colby, Kansas. Newhouse was seen parachuting. He landed in enemy territory and seemed to be okay.

Thursday–Saturday, June 8–10. These days were about the same with lots of missions for all. The targets were trucks and trucks and more trucks. It was hard to believe how the Jerries can operate with the loss of so many vehicles. They seem to just pour them out on the roads and lose them to the airmen from many squadrons.

Sunday, June 11. When the 57th Fighter Group was back in the States, they built the group up to double strength and made two groups. The 57th and the 79th. We had many friends in the 79th as we were all one group back in the States.

Well, today, they were on the island of Corsica. They will be operating along with the 57th and many other outfits flying daily to Italy and southern France. The motto of the 57th is "The First in the Blue." The motto of the 79th is "Not the first but the best." A great competitive spirit exists between our two outfits. It all started when we operated together in the Western Desert towards the end of the push that

Major Louis Frank was awarded the Distinguished Flying Cross. (57th Fighter Group website)

put the Germans into the sea. With all the competition that exists, we had a nice reunion with our old friends and welcomed them to the slaughter of the Jerries on the mainland of Italy.

They would operate within a few days. For the first time, we had lots of rain today. This would not hurt the flying as we have a good runway. The runway has metal strips, and the boys operate under most any conditions.

Monday, June 12. A few missions today but the most important thing was Lieutenant Nevett was reported safe. He will be returned to the squadron in a few days. He was lost on the mission of June 6.

Tuesday, June 13. A few missions of the regular vein were in order today. All back safe.

A formation of all the squadrons was held at 8:00 pm. This formation was called to award medals to members of the 57th Fighter Group. Our squadron commander, Major Louis Frank, was awarded the Distinguished Flying Cross. Major Robert Brown was awarded the Purple Heart. Captain Louis Ruder Jr. of North Hampton, Massachusetts, was awarded the Air Medal.

Many other awards were given to the members of the other two squadrons.

Wednesday, June 14. A quiet day. We received word today that Lt. Neal Gunderson of Cranford, New Jersey, who failed to return from a mission on April 14, was a prisoner of war. This came through official channels. No doubt the Red Cross received the report and passed it on.

I remember one night we were listening to a German broadcast of prisoners of war and heard the name of one of our pilots who failed to return from a mission. We never thought he would make it as his plane was in flames at a very low altitude when last seen. We had Lieutenant Gunderson's report from the time he left Alto in Corsica until he was picked up in Italy by the Germans.

Monday, June 19. On June 6, Lt. Richard Nevett failed to return from a strafing mission. From the debriefing held after the pilots returned, it did not look good for this young man. One pilot stated he thought he saw Nevett's plane hit the deck (this is an expression that the pilots use when an airplane hits the ground). Well, whatever the reports stated, they had to be corrected. Nevett returned safe and sound to the squadron this afternoon.

It was a wonderful to see a man you thought you would never see again. I do not have the story of how Nevett came through the experience that he had. I know he looked good and went back on flying status shortly thereafter.

These young, dedicated men came overseas to fight the war with the Air Corps; nothing will stop them.

From this date to July 1, it was routine flying. The only important incident was the return of Lt. Ernest Newhouse of Colby, Kansas, who had parachuted over enemy held land in Italy. I believe he was picked up by Italian partisans and returned to our side.

The Italian partisans did an outstanding job of picking up men that parachuted over enemy territory.

CHAPTER 40

Two-year anniversary, Corsica

During the next week, a committee was selected to plan a celebration of our two years overseas. We set July 1 as the date for the party and did a lot of work. We went to Tunis to the brewery and obtained enough beer for about nine hundred men and officers. We had programs printed in Naples for the affair. The beer arrived a few days before the party. Our biggest problem was how to keep it cool.

There was not enough ice on Corsica to cool it. We scooped a big hole out of the ground near the party site and each unit had the assignment of filling the hole with water every day. This didn't do the job, but it kept the beer from going sour.

Beer for the 57th Fighter Group's two-year anniversary.

We tried to obtain ice from the various supply bases in Italy without much luck. A couple of days before the party, some good soul in Catania, Sicily, heard of our plight. We sent a B-25 down and it came back with the bomb bay filled with ice. We packed the ice down in the hole. On July 1, when we tapped that beer, it was like obtaining it from the local pub back in Boston.

The celebration for our second year overseas.

Climbing the greased pole to win a cash prize.

General Cannon stopped by the celebrations.

We had a lot of brass attend the anniversary celebration, including General Cannon who was our commanding general. We had many games for the enlisted men, including a greased pig chase. The man who finally caught the pig won 50 dollars. The grand prize was for climbing a greased pole. This was won by a trio who did a tremendous job getting to the top of the pole, which was about thirty feet tall. The trio won $135.00.

We were off flying for two days as a reward for the outstanding job the boys were doing, and many leaves were in order. A group of us were going to Rome for a week. The Air Corps had a nice hotel for the boys on leave. The highlight of the leave was our audience with the pope and a trip through St. Peter's Cathedral. It was amazing to see the crowds lining up for the audience with his Holiness.

It did not make any difference with the soldiers as to their faith. This prince of the Catholic Church made our visit a memorable one. The crowd was too large for the room we were to originally meet with him, so we were assigned to a larger room. At the appointed time, Pope Pius XII arrived. He gave us his blessing and blessed any religious articles the crowd had.

We also received a beautiful silver medal with the pope's likeness on it. The trip through the cathedral was an outstanding affair and, like the visit with the pope, I will always remember the cathedral tour.

July 11, I received orders from group headquarters to draw rations of food, candy, and cigarettes for 21 days to cover a trip to southern France. Our problem was we had no place to store this valuable merchandise other than a tent. This was not very good security. We had had some thefts of food and I didn't have any men we could

On the anniversary of the 57th Fighter Group's second anniversary overseas, 1 July 1944, General Alexander sent over this commendation to Lt Col. Knight, who added his commendation, which we shared with the men:

In a personal message delivered to the Command General, M.A.T.A.F., the Commanding General of the Allied Armies in Italy, conveys his best wishes on the occasion of the 57th Group's second overseas anniversary as follows:

"I SHOULD BE GRATEFUL IF YOU WOULD CONVEY TO THE COMMANDER AND ALL MEMBERS OF THE FIVE SEVEN FIGHTER GROUP CMA USAAF MY CONGRATULATIONS ON THE COMPLETION OF TWO YEARS UNBROKEN AIR SUPPORT OF THE ALLIED ARMIES PD I SHOULD ALSO LIKE YOU TO ASSURE THEM NOT ONLY OF MY PERSONAL ADMIRATION BUT THAT OF ALL THE GROUND FORCES UNDER MY COMMAND DASH PARTICULARLY THOSE OF US WHO SERVED AT ALAMEIN PD I TRUST THAT THE HAPPY ASSOCIATION BETWEEN THE ARMIES AND FIVE SEVEN GROUP SO FIRMLY ESTABLISHED BY ITS FINE RECORD WILL CONTINUE AND I WISH TO OFFER MY SINCEREST GOOD WISHES FOR THE FUTURE PD"

SIGNED ALEXANDER

During your two years of continuous air support, you have established an enviable record which has contributed in no small measure to the justifiable faith and trust which Army personnel have established in our Air Force. You have served as a keystone for the organization and employment of other units which have followed you—units which have gained materially from your hard-won experience. May you always enjoy the position of pacesetters for American support units throughout the world.

s/   Thomas C. Darcy
THOMAS C. DARCY
Colonel, Air Corps
Commanding

1st Ind AJK/c/il
Headquarters, 57th Fighter Group, AAF, 3 July 1944

To: All officers and men, 57th Fighter Group

No further comment is necessary on these birthday greetings from the Army Commander. To me, and, I feel sure, to all members of this command, this acknowledgement of our achievements and outstanding proficiency comes from the best possible source. To those of us who remember Palestine, Cyprus, Alamein, and the desert no more highly prized comment could have been forthcoming.

ARCHIE KNIGHT
Lt Col., Air Corps

spare to guard these items around the clock. This would be necessary if we expected to have these items when we left for southern France.

The candy and cigarettes were free to the troops as we were going to be very close to the front lines. I did not want to take these items. I fought with the adjutant who was a stubborn officer. He insisted I take the goods. He couldn't care less what happened to them after I drew them from the service group which issued this cargo.

I tried to figure out some way I could get out of taking the goods. I was very much relieved after a short talk with the commanding officer of the issuing depot. I explained my problem of a lack of proper place for storage of this merchandise. He informed me I could leave the items at this depot until 24 hours before departure to southern France.

It was nice to go back to the squadron with this off my mind.

Then the move to southern France was called off.

A day after I had made my deal with the colonel at the service group, I received a call from the group headquarters officer who gave me such a hard time when the orders came out to draw these rations.

I remember him saying "Jim, I am sorry to inform you that you must return all the rations you drew for the southern France invasion." My retort was "John, I did not draw the rations as I made a deal with the service group."

He blew his top and stated that I should obey the orders of his headquarters. After a few minutes of yelling and screaming, he cooled down. I guess he realized a good decision was made when we did not draw the rations.

Archbishop Spellman saying mass for the men.

Thursday, August 10. This morning we had a very important visitor, Archbishop Spellman, the military vicar of the church. The bishop said mass out in the open and met all the men of all squadrons. Being the senior Catholic officer in the Black Scorpion Squadron, I was invited to have breakfast with the bishop.

This was a very nice affair. The commanding officer did an excellent job in setting up the tables with linen and silver, something we had not seen since leaving home two years ago. We even had cantaloupe which we also had not seen since leaving the States.

My seat was close to the bishop, and I had a chance to talk with him during the wonderful meal. I could not let the

This was a public relations notice put out on the second anniversary of the 57th Fighter Group, July 31, 1944.

An attack against a railroad yard 25 miles northeast of Parma in north central ITALY has marked the 2,000th mission flown by the 57th Fighter Group of the Tactical Air Force. The mission, led by Richard O. Hunziker, 2804 E. Adams Street, Tucson, Arizona, cut the tracks in three places and destroyed three railroad cars.

Activated at Mitchell Field, New York, the group embarked for the Middle East in July 1942, and one month later flew its first mission while attached to General Montgomery's Eighth Army. By strafing and bombing its way through Egypt and Libya, the group expedited the termination of the African campaign. As a climax to their noteworthy achievements, they shot down 77 enemy planes at Cap Bon April 13, 1943.

From Africa, the group operated through the Pantellerian, Sicilian, and Italian campaigns. In August 1943, the group, commanded by Lieutenant Colonel Archie J. Knight, Fountain City, Indiana, was the first single-engine fighter unit to drop bombs on German-held Yugoslavia.

In December 1943, the group switched from Warhawks to Thunderbolts. They revolutionized the use of the P-47 by turning it into a low-level fighter-bomber carrying a 1,000-pound bomb under each wing.

Recently, while operating a separate task force, the unit was commended twice within five days by Major General John K. Cannon, commander of the Tactical Air Force, for the part it played in "Operation *Strangle*." A few days later, on July 1, at the conclusion of its second year of overseas duty, the 57th was again cited by General Cannon.

The outstanding month for the group was in May 1944, when it flew 255 missions, 2,760 sorties, dropped about 1,300 tons of bombs, and expended 616,400 rounds of ammunition.

To date the group has flown 21,992 sorties, dropped nearly 3,000 tons of bombs, and expended 3,090,882 rounds of ammunition.

Another commendation to be read out to all men of the 57th Fighter Group, and the rest of the Air Corps, for the job the Air Corps had been doing up to this point. Particular mention is made of Operation Strangle *which the 57th had a role in.*

HEADQUARTERS
57TH FIGHTER GROUP, AAF
APO 650

8 AUGUST 1944

SUBJECT: Commendation

To: Commanding Officers, All squadrons, & Hq Det.

1. The full message for ARNOLD signed BAKER will be published to your entire command.

August sixth marks the 37th Anniversary of the procurement of the first Army airplane. For this anniversary, General Arnold is having a roundup with Air Force Theater

(Continued)

Commanders throughout the world. This program will be broadcast over the Army Hour in the United States. General Baker's radio report to General Arnold is quoted for your information:

More than 2,000 aircraft of the Mediterranean Allied Air Forces attacked the enemy today. Our Coastal Air Force Fighters protected every Allied convoy and searched for U-Boats on all the sea lanes from Gibraltar to Cairo. Our Tactical Air Force B-26s destroyed bridges in the Po Valley, while P-51s, P-38s, P-47s and Spitfires strafed and bombed German troops, transports, tanks, and artillery all along the line from Pisa to Rimini. Our Strategic Air Force heavy bombers have just returned from a heavy attack on vital enemy targets. The enemy's main effort was less than 1/10 ours today. That is normal. We have broken the once proud and arrogant *Luftwaffe* in our area. We have complete domination of the air above our armies, harbors, ships, supply lines, and bases.

This spring, our Tactical Air Force under Major General John K. Cannon, smashed enemy supply lines in preparation for the great Allied ground offensive which started May 12th. Operation "Strangle" we called it. It cut all railway lines and the principal roads down the Italian Peninsula and reduced the German supply position so radically that he was unable to resist the Allied advance. In the disorganized retreat that followed, the Tactical Air Force had a Field Day, destroying more than 10,000 German tanks and trucks fleeing north on the battered Italian roads.

The Strategic Air Force under Major General Nathan Twining did its part magnificently in the destruction of German Air Force factories in Europe. In our campaign to sweep the black crosses from the sky, we destroyed 685 enemy planes in April, 500 in May, 541 in June and more than 600 in July. The Strategic Air Force then turned its terrific power on the vital German oil supply, robbing the enemy of about 2/3 of his petroleum supply from the Balkans, Hungary, and southern Germany.

General Arnold, I am delighted to report that your two (2) US Air Forces, the Tactical 12th and the Strategic 15th have been superior organizations through the Italian campaign. Their leaders have been bold and decisive: their ground crews have been highly skilled, thorough, and energetic; their combat crews have been skillful and courageous. They have defeated the German in every air battle: they have never been turned back from any target by the best the German could throw against them. I do not believe there are better fighting men anywhere in the world.

By Order of Lt Col. KNIGHT.

J. H. MILLER II
Major, Air Corps
Adjutant

opportunity go by and told the bishop we had not had such a fancy meal in our two years overseas.

The commanding officer overheard my conversation and gave me a dirty look. The bishop stayed around until the pilots, who were off on a mission when he said mass, returned. It was a wonderful sight to see these boys lining up for the bishop with their flying clothes still on. Many of these boys had some very interesting conversations with him about their missions.

The boys were now flying over a new territory, southern France. Major Michael Christopher McCarthy of Boston, our operations officer, led a mission to southern France and had a field day shooting up gun positions. It was quite an experience to be in the operations tent to listen to the debriefing of the boys when they returned from a mission when there was lots to report.

The USO brought Joe Louis to entertain the troops.

These boys got excited. Each one wanted to tell his story first. Major Mike normally debriefed the boys but, in this case, he was on the mission. He reported firsthand on this show. Of course, with a flight of 12 P-47s, he could not see all the action and the boys gave their reports.

We also had another celebrity visit the group area this evening. The USO (United Service Organizations) presented Joe Louis, heavyweight champion, with a group of fighters who put on a good show.

Bad weather kept the planes on the ground for a few days. We had some lightning like I had never seen before.

Monday, August 14. Some of our boys were going home today as they had finished their tour of duty. They had done an outstanding job. We hated to see these boys go but they deserved the change of station to the good old USA. One of them was Capt. Robert Abercrombie, who we will always remember as the pilot who reported "Bananas are plentiful" when he sighted what turned out to be the Hermann Göring Division moving down from northern Italy. The division was on the move to try to help the Jerries who were having a hard time from the constant hammering our boys gave them daily.

This was one of the most important missions of the war.

Going home with "Abbie," as we called him, was Capt. Louis Ruder of North Hampton, Massachusetts, and Capt. John J. Linehan of Manchester, Connecticut. Three wonderful young men left the Black Scorpion Squadron. This afternoon, we were all briefed on the invasion of southern France, which would start early tomorrow morning.

Tuesday, August 15. Our boys took off this morning in the dark. All the crew chiefs and all the men of the squadron were up very early this morning. The cooks had hot coffee and toast for all. The cooks prepared a good breakfast later in the morning.

The air was full of fighter planes. Later, the bombers from Italy and Africa filled the sky. This went on for hours. We repeated the remark, "Thank God they are our planes" many times.

Early in the war, all the bombers were of an olive drab color. This morning, there were many planes up there with no paint at all. I believe this was true with the B-17, a beautiful sight that awed us all. Hundreds of these unpainted planes passed over Corsica with the sun coming up in the east. The reflection of this red ball of fire shining on the aluminum B-17s made a picture I would love to paint.

For the next few days, it was around-the-clock planning and flying missions to southern France. Some were fighter sweeps and others were bomber escorts.

Thursday, August 17. On a return flight from Naples after attending a court-martial, we had an experience that I will always remember. A short time after take-off in our own B-25 we used as a courier, we flew over a piece of land that jutted out of the mainland called Gaeta Point.

All of a sudden, the area in front of us was full of black puffs. This told us some anti-aircraft guns were firing at us. Many things ran through my mind and one of them was that a German plane must have been in the area and our own anti-aircraft tried to shoot it down. The pilot stated he couldn't see any aircraft. He started to look for some flares. After finding them he stated that he did not have the colors of the day, which were necessary to let the ground know we were not the enemy.

The puffs continued to fill the air ahead of us. Our pilot made some radical changes in his course and departed the area. We found out, when we landed, this piece of land was not to be flown over by anyone.

I never did find out what was so important about this piece of real estate far removed from the front lines. We were very happy to be able to put the wheels down on Alto, home of the Black Scorpion Squadron on Corsica.

Friday–Saturday, August 18–19. The boys still pounded the area of the invasion in southern France. From the after-mission reports, the Germans will be out of this

The powers-that-be made sure we did rifle drills.

part of France within a short time. The most important thing was all our boys came home safe from these missions.

For the first time in a year, we were all ordered to the rifle range not far from our field. The powers-that-be wanted the boys to keep their eyes sharp in case they ever have to use their weapons. It was quite a problem arranging times for shooting as the missions still went on.

We worked a shuttle system and by nightfall everybody had fired the prescribed course. The officers and men enjoyed this activity as it was a change of pace from the regular run of things.

Monday, August 21. Called to group headquarters for a meeting pertaining to the move which will take place within the next three weeks. Before the meeting started, I had a short session with Lt Col. Jere Chase, the group executive officer. He stated he was having a hard time running his office with all the dust flying from the jeeps passing his office. His office was a trailer without any windows. This was a homemade deal. He had open holes instead of windows.

He showed me all the dust in his office. I told him I had briefed all our jeep drivers about keeping clear of his trailer. As I told him it must be drivers from the other squadrons, a jeep comes down the road by his trailer. Dust flies in all directions. My face turned red when the driver turned out to be our own doctor, Capt. Lester Wall from Baltimore, Maryland.

After the meeting, I told the doc about the cloud of dust he left behind. He promised this would never happen again.

Back at the meeting, the colonel informed us we would go to Italy. Although we had been told we were not going to France earlier, we hoped the plans would change. We had been to Italy before coming to Corsica. We thought a change of scenery would be good for all.

Wednesday, August 23. Routine flying. All returned safe. The good news of the day was the Allies had moved into Paris.

For the rest of August, things were normal except a terrific heat wave hit the island. All of us took a licking from this unexpected change in the weather.

Thursday, August 31. This was a pay day and a day I will always remember. Shortly after lunch, about half of the officers and men of the squadron passed out, most of them in the camp area, and we had a couple of hours of concern.

We obtained every doctor within reach of our area. The men complained of dizziness and stomach pains. The doctors treated the men right on the ground where they fell. Most were able to get up and make for their tents within a half hour of receiving medication from the doctors.

We had missions scheduled for the afternoon and, with a skeleton crew, we were able to meet our commitments. We had had canned turkey for the main meal and bread pudding for dessert. The doctors thought it could have been either one of these items which caused this sudden attack. The main thing was by supper time most of the boys were feeling okay.

Late this afternoon, Lt. Edward M. Nelson, from Chicago, Illinois, returning from his first mission, crashed his plane on the approach to the runway. He was killed instantly, and his plane caught fire. He was pulled from the plane, but he was beyond help. This mission, scheduled to dive bomb in southern France, was called back a short time after they left Corsica.

We assumed, on his approach to the runway, he did not take into consideration the fact he still had two 500-lb bombs on his wings and a lot of gasoline. Not having had to cope with such a situation before could have been the cause for this tragic accident.

We gave this brave young officer a military funeral at 7:00 pm this evening in the military cemetery at Bastia, Corsica.

Friday, September 1. Today, one of our enlisted men, who had been suspected of many acts of thievery since we came overseas, was caught stealing a bag of sugar from the kitchen. There was no mistake this time. Three men saw him take the sugar and it was found in his own tent inside his barracks bag. The act was a small one. A 5-lb bag of sugar costs 49 cents.

We always felt he was involved in selling stolen food for his own profit. This same man was outside the kitchen one morning at 2:30 am when a few cases of bacon were stolen. A case of bacon would bring $30.00 on the black market.

When questioned about the missing bacon, and what he was doing around the kitchen at that hour, he stated he was nervous and arose from his tent for a smoke. With this theft, we could try him under summary court-martial, which was done. He was found guilty and transferred from our squadron.

The weather remained very hot and there were no missions for this date.

Saturday, September 2. Weather remained the same. The only action on the field today was our good friends, the French anti-aircraft unit, received orders to move out. They had been giving us protection around the landing ground.

There were many goodbyes as we had built up quite a friendship with these dedicated soldiers. They were going back to France. This made them happy as many of them had not been on their own soil for a long time.

Sunday, September 3. Church service early this morning and the missions started. The targets for the day were railroad engines and freight cars. The boys had a field day. They had become experts in this type of operation. Each engine and freight car destroyed denied the enemy troops, food, or equipment for their war effort.

Some of the stories about how the train engines blew up or freight cars exploded made for good conversation when the pilots were debriefed after the missions.

Monday, September 4. Two more of our pilots left this morning as their orders arrived. They had done a good job and deserved to go home. Captain Charles

Sawicki of New Bedford, Massachusetts, and Capt. Jack Wilson of Benton City, Washington, were happy boys when they boarded the B-25 courier plane for the short trip to Naples.

The boys were off on an early mission. One of them did not return: Lt. Edgar Peters of Pleasant Valley, New York. One of the pilots saw him bail out over the target area at a very low altitude. We never did receive a report on this outstanding pilot.

Tuesday, September 5. Our flight surgeon, Capt. Lester Wall, gave a lecture to all the officers on marital relations which enlightened all of us. This officer was always working, day or night. The health of our squadron was the most important thing on the mind of Doc Wall.

He also cared for the civilians stationed near our area. I know Doc spent many nights caring for the sick in the hills not far from our camp. It was said he had even delivered children for some of the Corsican natives. He was the most dedicated doctor I have ever met. He was an asset to the Black Scorpion Squadron.

Wednesday, September 6. We drew our rations today. All the men were back from leave as we prepared for the move back mainland Italy. The rains came to the island of Corsica today. There were only training flights for some of the new replacements.

These new men received their training in the States but the real test for them was to fly with some of the veterans of many combat missions. This was real training. Most of the new boys got acclimated very fast to this new kind of flying and landing on a field such as Alto Landing Ground.

Thursday, September 7. This morning, the boys had some more training flights. Captain Pete Mitchell, our armament officer, and I had to leave the field. As we traveled down a road not far from our field, I noticed a P-47 flying at a very slow speed. I mentioned this to Pete. The words were barely out of my mouth when this aircraft spun out on the end of our runway.

We rushed back to the area and found the plane was from our squadron. The pilot was killed instantly, and the plane demolished. He never had a chance. When this plane dropped to such a low altitude, and with its tremendous weight, there was not much chance for survival.

Our flight surgeon, Captain Lester Wall.

The pilot killed was one of our new replacements, Lt. John C. Noeges, of Chicago, Illinois. He was the pal of Lt. Edward O. Nelson, who was killed on August 31, only seven days before.

I understood they both went to school together, joined the Air Corps, went through flight school at the same time, came overseas, and both reported to the Black Scorpion Squadron together.

A rough fate for two brave young men. We gave this young man the same military burial we gave his buddy. Grave Registrations arranged for them to be buried side by side.

CHAPTER 41

Grosseto, Italy

September 9–October 22

Saturday–Sunday, September 9–10. This was moving day, and this made our 35th move since we left East Boston over two years ago. Our boys were experts when it came to moving. All you have to say is "Boys, we are on the move again" and you will see a precision action take place.

We moved from Alto Landing Ground, Corsica, with A Party, which was about half of the enlisted men and about half of the ground officers. Most of the pilots will join us later with their planes after we establish our new base in Italy.

We proceeded to the staging area on the northern end of the island. Our transportation to Italy was an American LST (Landing Ship, Tank). Loading was a slow process. The top deck had to be loaded first. The trucks and jeeps on the top deck had to be chained down securely before the men and equipment went into the lower area of the ship.

We finished this task sometime after midnight. The orders to proceed to Italy were given about 2:30 am. As we left Calvi, the wind played games with the water. As the ship made its turn around the end of the island, it started to roll even with all this heavy equipment top side. We were like a cork on top of the waves.

We had some men stationed top side with the trucks and jeeps. They were all ordered below deck. I talked with some of the crew of this craft about previous trips with gear such as ours and how this ship stood up in rough seas.

I was informed they had lost some equipment overboard on one trip when some of the chains broke. We did not have much sleep as we rolled all night.

In the morning, the seas were calm and a good breakfast was on tap. We had a nice day and landed at Piombino, Italy, about 4:30 pm. The unloading was a slow process. By nightfall, we were clear of Piombino.

We made a temporary camp for the night not far from our home for the next six months in Grosseto.

We slept in the open. It was 10:30 pm. We didn't feel it was worth it to put up the tents. The area had been a cornfield and it worked out very well.

On our way from Piombino, we passed through a small village. In this village there was a store that only sold glassware. We marked this spot for a future visit as we needed glasses. We had not seen a glass since leaving East Boston over two years ago.

This morning, after we got settled at Grosseto, two of us returned to the small village of the day before. We purchased a couple hundred drinking glasses. They were very cheap, something like two lira a piece, about two cents in American money.

I am sure the price went up later. When we arrived for the first time in any new area, the price was always cheap. When merchants found out the Americans were big spenders, and would pay any price for any item they wanted, prices went up.

That evening, we had a party in the little house that would be our home for the next six months. It had a small living room and, of course, no furniture.

After the party was a few minutes old, one of the boys decided it would be a good idea to break glasses after each drink. Since the glasses were cheap, the idea of breaking them caught on with great rapidity. Before the evening was over, we had a fireplace full of glass fragments.

The next morning when the old Italian civilian who cleaned our house each morning saw the broken glasses, he scratched his head and began mumbling in his native tongue. Through one of the Italian soldiers, I explained what had happened. The civilian thought that was a strange custom of celebration and went about his chores.

Monday, September 11. We were assigned to an area called Marina di Grosseto. We loaded our equipment back on to the trucks at the cornfield where we spent the night and proceeded to our new area. We set up camp in a pine grove behind a school built by Mussolini. We spent the day going over this area. There was a beach about five miles from the airfield.

The area looked like it would be a nice place to live. We spent most of the day requisitioning buildings and houses we would use in the operations of the squadron and for the housing of enlisted men and officers.

Most of the men were assigned to the schoolhouse, which was a modern building. Some of the men requested to live in tents in the pine grove in the rear of the school. They felt they had been out in the open for so long that living indoors was not for them.

We set up a kitchen in the school along with some recreation rooms. We were fortunate in finding a barber. We set the barber up in the lobby of the school. He had a good business going within a short time.

My one problem with this native was he did not want to conform with the health regulations we laid out for him. It took a little while, but finally he became a real asset to the squadron.

We found one house to take care of the 10 ground officers. Most of the pilots had small houses along the beach which would take care of about six of them.

Our P-47s ready for battle.

We were very fortunate having a house large enough for a club and a mess hall for the officers.

This proved to be a wonderful building. It had plenty of room for the pilots to lay around on their off time. We set up a ping-pong room. This room saw many hot games between the ground officers and the pilots.

This building was right on the beach and was good for morale. The enlisted men only had a two-minute walk to any part of the beach.

We didn't have any lights in the building tonight, but they were promised for tomorrow. Until the rest of the squadron arrived, we were all going to eat with the enlisted men.

Tuesday, September 12. We had a lot to straighten out this morning, taking over of our buildings and making sure the other squadrons did not try to take possession of our buildings for their own beach house.

Headquarters and the two other squadrons had been assigned to some nice buildings in the center of Grosseto. After seeing our area, they had ideas about spending some time in the beach area.

We took a trip into town to see what they had to offer in the way of supplies and rations. We had a well set up service group which was a great asset to the needs of our squadron. They even had an icehouse under their jurisdiction. This was wonderful. We didn't have electric refrigerators and we were supposed to get a good ration of beer. Beer without icing was not beer.

The 316th Service Group also took care of having our lights hooked up this evening. We had a report from the B Party still on Corsica. Lieutenant Paul E. Rawson of Hillsdale, Michigan, failed to return from a mission this morning. One of the pilots stated at the debriefing he did not think he made it.

We never gave up on these boys as so many of them returned even when it looked hopeless for them at the time of their loss.

Wednesday–Saturday, September 13–16. A visit to the service group proved to be very fruitful. We had a good ration setup, and they had a supply of furniture in their warehouse we could requisition for the clubs and buildings in our living area. The officer in charge of seeing to our needs turned out to be Major Chester Dolan, a state senator from Boston. As a squadron from Boston, how could we lose? Major Dolan really went out of his way to see all our needs were taken care of.

At the meeting with the service group, we found out we could have civilians help work in our living area. This turned out to be a real asset as the area was badly in need of a real cleaning. When the Germans left, they did not clean up.

The area was about one-and-a-half miles by a half a mile. With the civilian help, we could keep the area spotless and use our men for what they were trained for.

We even found a few Italian civilians able to work in our two kitchens. Starting tomorrow, all of the squadron will be together again.

For the first time since we left Africa, we drew a ration of nice steaks. We had sort of forgotten what that kind of meat was like.

In the beach area, we lived among a lot of civilians. Most of them were very cooperative, especially the families who had people working for us. There were some hungry families, and we did our best to take care of them.

We had resentment from a few. We found they were the dedicated fascists and still had faith in the Hitler/Mussolini operation and would not give up. At one time, they set up a parade through our area that failed to prove much.

Sunday, September 17. First church services were at our new area this morning. We were fortunate this little area had a chapel.

Most of the pilots arrived this afternoon. The mad scramble for rooms started. We had a good plan for them. It worked out very well except a few boys who wanted to switch around. It's an easy fix. We let them move around to their liking.

After the pilots arrived, we opened the club for the supper meal. They were happy with the layout after being in tents for so long.

Lots of bridge and ping-pong games went on this evening. B Party left Corsica. They should be along in a few days.

Tuesday, September 19. Getting settled down. The boys flew a couple of missions out of our new field, a routine strafing job. All returned okay.

Wednesday, September 20. The rains came during the night, and I mean rain. When we moved into the house for the ground officers, we never thought to look at the roof made of red tile. This area had been strafed and the tiles were full of holes. We took in so much water most of the ceilings need to be repaired.

We went to the 316th Service Group for a tarpaulin large enough to cover the whole roof, as the rains came down all day. In fact, it got so bad all the missions were canceled. The airfield was deep in water. The club was a busy place with all the boys driven indoors by the elements.

Thursday–Friday, September 21–22. The weather was beautiful this morning, but the rains had left their mark. The runway was under water and no plane could get in or out. The club was in full operation. We received the necessary furniture from the service group, and we were in good shape.

Saturday, September 23. The only incident of the day was one of our pilots tried to take the top off a 20-mm shell with a pair of pliers. It exploded in his hand. What a mess. He lost a couple of fingers. We all thought he was pretty lucky. This piece of ammunition can do a lot of damage. He won't be flying for a long time.

Monday, September 25. Planes were moved to Grossetto Main, which had an all-weather strip. The rains have left our field a quagmire.

October 12–22. The gap in the reports was due to the fact I was in hospital with some poisoning, and rest leave. During this time, I have one thing to report about an evening in the Excelsior Hotel in Florence, Italy. We had a few cocktails before dinner. Just as we were about to leave, the hotel went into complete darkness.

We stayed under candlelight and people moved around near our table. After the lights went

I took the volleyball team to Florence.

on, we found ourselves sitting next to Brian Aherne and Katherine Cornel, the movie actor and actress.

We had a very nice visit with these famous people and attended the show they presented the next evening, a remarkable presentation of *The Barretts of Wimpole Street*. We were invited backstage before and after the show. This occasion will always remain in my memories, such down-to-earth people.

Before leaving Florence, I made arrangements with Vincent P. Coyne, of Boston, whom I served with for many years, to show Katherine and Brian around this beautiful city. He commanded an artillery unit just outside of Florence. He would be around the city for a while.

The acting troupe saw more of Florence and its treasures than they would under normal circumstances. The report I received from Coyne was they were very appreciative of the time he spent with them.

On this date, on a mission to northern Italy, Lt. Billy Adams of Fort Worth, Texas, and Lt. George Dorval of Waltham, Massachusetts, failed to return. Other pilots reported they saw Dorval's plane on fire. They did not think he had a chance as he was at a very low altitude.

A few nights later, while some of the boys listened to a German radio station, they heard that Dorval was a prisoner of war (see Appendix 4 for his story of survival). We never did hear about Adams.

CHAPTER 42

Home on leave

October 23, 1944–January 27, 1945. During these days I was fortunate to obtain leave to the States. But, before getting to the States, there was lots of work to do turning over my duties as executive officer to another officer who would take care of things for the next couple of months.

My trip to Naples was a pleasant one. My good friend Major Michael McCarthy flew a group of us in our B-25 courier plane. I spent a few days around Naples with some of my old buddies from Boston, Col. Walter Gleason, port liaison officer for the Air Force, and Lt Col. W. M. Hagerty, the port transportation officer. Both men were from the Massachusetts National Guard in Boston and, like me, were called

Christmas in Grosseto. (57th Fighter Group, Carl Lovick Collection)

Staff Sergeant Jack Sinclair was one of the resident artists of the 64th Fighter Squadron. He would frequently add cartoons to the letters I sent home to my sons. He made this drawing when I was going home on leave and asked the men of the squadron to sign it.

Major Michael McCarthy and his plane.

to active duty with their own units back in Boston. The three of us were many miles from home doing a little different work than when the three of us joined the Guard in the 1920s.

On the ship I was assigned to, I was very fortunate. I was made the ship's security officer. I had a crew of soldiers who were going home like myself. In case of an attack, our job would be to man the life-raft stations and make sure, on a given signal, these rafts would be released into the water. We worked in teams around all the decks. Each morning we had a drill at 10:00 am. All the troops would report on deck. The crew I had would report to the assigned life rafts. After the first morning, the crew did a nice job.

This ship was *Athos II*, a former German ship now run by the French. My position as ship's security officer gave me a stateroom, which I appreciated very much. There were very few staterooms available. Most of them had been made over into rooms for sick patients going home to a hospital in the States for further treatment.

The doctor in charge of these patients lived next to me and I was very interested in the stories he told me about them. I accompanied the doctor one morning on a visit to the area of the ship where these young men were locked up. I saw something I have never forgotten. These young mental patients were all acting up this morning. They were given treatment just before we arrived. Most of them had been given jabs to quiet them down. I saw some fine-looking young heroes of World War II that had just cracked up under the terrific pressure of a crazy war.

Heading to Boston on leave.

One of the boys I saw had all his clothes taken away. All he had in his room, which was once a stateroom, was a mattress. It was hard to take.

The doctor informed me most of these mental patients would be returned to a normal life with the treatment given to them at the various hospitals in the States.

On the third morning out, I woke up and thought the ship was pretty quiet. When I arrived on deck, I found we had stopped. The rest of the ships in our convoy were not around. All we had was a destroyer circling around us. Our electrical system had broken down. We were a sitting duck for any German submarines in this area, off the coast of North Africa.

After many hours we were on our way again. It took us 24 hours to catch up with the rest of the convoy. We had a nice trip. The sight of the Statue of Liberty at the entrance to New York Harbor looked very good. It brought back memories of some two-and-a-half years ago when we left New York for Egypt.

After a couple of days at Camp Kilmer in New Jersey, we were all sorted out and sent to the camp nearest our home. I went to Fort Devens. I arrived at 6:00 am. We were all escorted to a mess hall for a super breakfast. They had German prisoners for waiters. I never saw such a clean mess hall.

After a day of processing, I was off to Boston and home. It was good to see the family after being away a long time. My two boys had grown quite a bit and they had a lot of questions. I learned a lot about ration books and coupons after a few days at home.

I wanted to have a turkey for the family, but you couldn't obtain a turkey in Medford. I called my old chaplain, Col. David Hickey, at Fort Banks. He was assigned to us when we were called to active duty with the 241st Coast Artillery (HD) in 1940. Colonel Hickey saved the day when he drove up to the house in a staff car with a nice 15-lb bird. The family was very happy. We had a nice Thanksgiving together for the first time since 1941.

Time went by fast. My orders read to report back to Fort Devens on December 21. This was changed when President Roosevelt allowed all members of the Armed Forces returning overseas around Christmas time to report after January 1.

I received a telegram to report to Fort Devens on January 5. This gave me Christmas, New Years, and my birthday home with my family. I never expected to have that when I first received my orders with the December 21 return date.

We left Fort Devens for Newport News, Virginia, on a cold night. The next morning, we were in the railroad yards outside Richmond. The cars of our train were all frozen up.

It was a cold morning, and the food service was not the best. The railroad had not planned correctly for the large number of troops traveling on these trains. After a delay of several hours, we proceeded to our destination, Camp Patrick Henry just outside Newport News.

They kept us on this post until January 13 with only 12 hours' leave to go to Newport and Norfolk. We received all kinds of lectures on how to behave when we arrived overseas.

We left Newport News on January 13. Our destination was Naples. Twelve days later, we arrived in Naples without incident. I stayed overnight and was back with the Black Scorpion Squadron the next morning.

CHAPTER 43

Grosseto, Italy

January 27–April 26, 1945

January 27–February 17. These were days of getting back to the old grind of fighter squadron life. I met a few of the new pilots who came to join the Black Scorpion Squadron while I was home on leave. The squadron had been busy during my absence going about the same work, knocking out bridges and strafing convoys.

Movies and USO (United Service Organizations) shows were more plentiful. This was always welcome to the squadron. Most of the movies were pretty old but the shows were well attended.

In our area, we also had the 84th Squadron from the 47th Bomb Group. The 84th Squadron and our squadron had become a friendly group. It was nice to hear the stories of a different outfit other than fighters. These men crew the medium bomber known as the A-20. Their mission was different than ours. They do most of their work at night.

The bombers fly up to the Po Valley at the base of the Alps and drop their bombs on troop movements. Many times, they drop bombs in the path of a convoy expected to pass a given area later.

The bombs dropped have delayed-action fuses. The detonations are set for a given time when the suspected convoy will pass. The Po Valley these days is a busy spot. This was about the only marshalling yards the Germans had left.

Many nights the bomb squadron would go north on a mission and be unable to drop their bombs. They would return and drop them in the water not too far from our beach area.

With all this activity, and the sound of the detonations, we couldn't sleep. This action was necessary, they told us, as the orders were to not land in the dark with bombs on board. Of course, our young pilots did not like to be awakened. When they returned from their missions during the afternoon, when the bomber pilots slept, they gave their sleeping quarters a real buzz job. Sometimes this would go on for quite a while.

This was against orders, but we were quite far from headquarters, so they got away with it.

During this time, we received orders promoting a group of officers. This was always good news. This meant more money for those promoted. It was also the custom for all the promoted officers to buy drinks. In the evening, after a receipt of promotions orders, there was always a gay time at the club.

During this time, we found we had several boys in the squadron who could play musical instruments. We tried through the special service to obtain a set of instruments but all they could give us was a trombone and a cornet.

It takes more than two instruments to make a band. We appointed a committee to see what we needed. This committee was headed by M/Sgt Joseph Maiolino, of Winthrop, Massachusetts, who was a violin player from his days in the school orchestra.

We felt this band would be a great morale booster and help create good relations with the civilians in the area. We had a large hall in the area where a few dances had been held. The music was supplied by the limited number of records we had collected in our two-and-a-half years overseas.

This system helped but what we wanted was real live music. One of the first things we did was to approach the Red Cross for a piano. They had been very good setting up the hall for the dances.

The squadron was busy daily with fighter sweeps and bridge-busting missions. We had quite a few pilots replacing the boys that had gone home on rotation. They all looked for enemy aircraft.

Flight Surgeon Lester Wall.

By this time, the enemy had very few planes left in Italy. Our boys had not seen any of them for some time. Back in Egypt, we were outnumbered on every mission, sometimes by 10 to 1. It was believed the Germans had moved their planes back to protect the homeland, if they could.

Sunday, February 18. We had been very lucky with all the missions flown. We have not had a loss for some time in the air or on the ground. This bright, sunny Sunday morning made up for it.

As our squadron formed up over the field for a mission, we lost two brave young men.

Lieutenant James T. Knight of Effie, Minnesota, and Lt. Royce J. Maier of Plum City, Wisconsin, collided in midair. Both planes landed in pieces in a farmer's field not far from the airfield. These boys never had a chance to get out of their planes. When they collided, the planes just plummeted to earth.

One of the boys' cockpits was in one piece. He was taken out dead after a short time. The other plane nosed into the soft earth and caught fire. The task of removing this brave young pilot was not an easy one. The amount of fuel on board and the plane's position in the earth made the recovery a difficult one.

We had firefighting equipment on hand, but the gas soaked into the earth around the area. As the boys put out the fire, another group would start digging and the flames would start up again.

Flight Surgeon Lester Wall was in charge of the mission to recover the body. He worked with great effort and even had his shoes burned. It was some time before the body was removed.

We have seen many young men make the supreme sacrifice during our years overseas. Each one makes you question why these men have to die.

The mission to northern Italy this morning went on as planned, short the two boys who did not make the formation.

Monday, February 19. The plane still burned this morning. The doc still worked. Later this morning, they reached what was left of the pilot. The remains were moved to the cemetery. We made plans this evening for the burial of these two Black Scorpion pilots.

Tuesday, February 20. This morning, Lieutenants Knight and Maier were given a full military burial at the U.S. military cemetery at Follonica where many fallen soldiers were buried.

Wednesday, February 21. The missions were still going at full swing. The boys buzzed the beach this afternoon as the bombers dropped a lot of bombs in the water off our area during the night.

We had a little trouble with a few die-hard fascists in the area. We were notified some of the civilian workers had not been cleared before coming to work for us. Yesterday, something showed up in the records that was not favorable to a few workers. We had to let them go.

I remember one man, who worked in the officers mess, asked to talk with us. He was one of the best workers we had. We did not want to see him go. We had a long talk with this fellow and he told us of the troubles he had with the Germans. He stated unless you were a fascist, you did not receive any food.

This man had a large family, he was not a fascist, and did not believe in their theory. But in order to obtain food for his family during the occupation by the Germans, he told them he was a fascist. We believed his story and we paid him from a donation taken from among the officers.

Monday, February 26. We had an inspection of the records this morning. The colonel making the inspection was not very familiar with the records. I believe this was his first inspection. He needed a lot of help. When he went back to his headquarters, he made the remark that he went to inspect Lynch's records and was shown how to go about an inspection.

Not many of the flying officers knew much about records. The important thing in the 1940s was to fly. Leave the administration to the ground officers.

Wednesday, February 28. We called this a day of donations to two worthy causes. One was to the Air Force Aid Society. The other was to the enlisted men's band fund. The boys located some instruments we could buy. The officers were glad to cooperate.

Friday, March 2. Off to Florence to obtain some musical instruments. Some of the enlisted men went to Rome for a few instruments. I was fortunate. I obtained a nice violin from the Twelfth Air Force for free. This will make Jo Maiolino, our orchestra leader, happy. He has not had a violin in his hands for many years.

After I did my business on the violins, I looked up my old commanding officer, Vincent P. Coyne. He was stationed in the mountains outside Florence, and I decided to spend the night with him.

Found my old boss, Vincent Coyne, in the hills outside Florence.

I was glad to leave in the morning. The temperature fell during the night and a snow-storm came in. The area looked beautiful with the new fallen snow all over this mountain range.

Sunday, March 4. Returned to the squadron just in time to see Lt. James L. Harpe of Quincy, Illinois, bail out of his plane over the field. He landed okay. His plane crashed away from town. Nobody was hurt.

Tuesday–Friday, March 6–9. Took off this morning on a booze run to Malta. We were not obtaining our liquor ration. We had paid the Italians $14.00 a bottle for poor brandy. We had a contact in Malta for some scotch whiskey, although the price was $13.00 a bottle. Anything would be better than the Italian varnish, as the boys called it.

We used our courier B-25 for the trip. It had a good bomb bay and could handle the shipment with ease. I remember, when I arrived, I had four thousand dollars in Italian lira. Before you spend any money on Malta, you had to exchange the lira for Maltese pounds.

I had to go to the British officer in charge of the exchange of money. I went to his office, and I remember him saying to me, "May I help you?" I said I would like to exchange some Italian lira. He said he would be glad to assist me. I dumped the four thousand dollars of Italian lira on his desk. He remarked "What the hell are you going to do? Buy all the scotch on the island?" My answer was, with the price of scotch at $13.00 a bottle, I could not buy much.

He made out the necessary papers. I had to certify I was buying merchandise for our organization. It took a couple of days for my supplier to round up the 250 bottles of scotch.

We found a musical instrument store and I purchased a base violin for the orchestra. Being a musical instrument salesman for many years, it hurt me greatly to pay $90.00 for a bass that could be purchased back in the States for about $50.00 (and $150.00 for a trombone worth $45.00).

The owner of the store said, "If you don't buy them, someone else will." We also purchased strings for the guitar and reeds for the clarinets and saxophone, paying top prices for everything.

I had a very pleasant trip to the factory on the island that made all the official desks and chairs for the government. They only used solid mahogany. I wanted to obtain a plaque we had planned to have for the officers' club with all the names of all the officers who served the squadron and a plaque for the enlisted club with the same idea.

They made up one for the officers but could not get one for the enlisted men on account of the size to take care of all the names.

On the morning of the 9th, we loaded the scotch, the plaque, the bass violin, trombone, and the musical instrument accessories into the bomb bay of the B-25.

The last item that went aboard was a couple of cases of milk we purchased on the way to the airport. We had not seen any fresh milk since we left Fort Dix two-and-a-half years ago.

A couple of hours later, we were over Grosseto airfield, the home of the Black Scorpion Squadron. The only thing wrong was it was raining and, in between the rain squalls, it hailed. Hail stones bouncing on the airplane was not the most pleasant sound.

The pilot of the booze run was Lt. John Glaws of Long Island, New York. John kept calling the tower on the field for a clearance. They kept saying "Go to Pisa, the field is not safe for a landing."

Our booze run pilot, Lt. John Glaws. The attachment on top of his goggles is a flip-down sun visor.

We circled the field for a long time as we had a valuable cargo on board. We did not want to put down on a strange field. John watched a mission of P-47s land, and he contacted one of the pilots by radio. "Of course," the pilot said. "The field is okay, come in."

The pilot knew what we had on board. A party had been planned for both clubs for the evening. We did not want to disappoint them.

Glaws said to me "Jim, I think I can make it," and he made the approach pattern and started in. I held my breath but had faith in this young man's ability to handle a plane. We made it and a happy group of enlisted men and officers greeted us as we taxied to the Black Scorpion area of the field.

The truck was waiting. It did not take long to unload our precious cargo. We had quite a night at the club. I was surprised to see Col. Henry Carney, my own family dentist from Boston, was at the squadron when we arrived.

Henry enjoyed the milk and drank a couple of pints with his supper. Doc Carney was in the area to help the local remount station (a unit in charge of looking after beasts of burden like mules) operate his metal detecting device. He perfected this device based on the detector used in the field for locating enemy mines.

This machine was used in all the hospitals in the theater. It could locate any metal fragment in the body by the same method it located mines in the ground. It was a compact device that weighed about five pounds.

We had a lot of fun talking about the dentist working on donkeys. The doc had quite an evening watching our young fighter pilots in action at the club. He planned to spend a few days with us, and we put him up.

Saturday, March 10. This morning we made our way to the remount station only a few miles from our field. It took the doctor a few minutes to show the attendant at the station how to operate the machine.

They had many donkeys in the station hit by shrapnel. With this machine, they could locate the metal and remove the shrapnel. Then the donkeys could carry on the important tasks assigned to these animals. Many loads of ammunition were carried on the backs of donkeys over the hills of Italy.

Monday–Tuesday, March 12–13. The boys had many missions today. We lost a wonderful young man on a strafing run. The loss of Myer Reynolds (better known as "Bucky") of Washington, D.C., bothered me. He went home on leave with me and did not have to return. He had done his tour.

He elected to return. On his first mission after returning, his plane hit the ground on the approach to an assigned target. We had become very friendly. He loved all kinds of music.

He had a great collection of records that friends had sent him. When he returned, he brought a large batch of records with him.

Bucky's wife, who I believe was with the Red Cross, arrived in the Naples area the day after this fateful mission. One of Bucky's close pilot friends went down to break the news to her. Not a very pleasant task but it had to be done.

Lieutenant Leroy Hill crash landed on March 21, 1945, and required surgery.

Wednesday, March 14. An accident over the field took the life of another pilot from the 65th Squadron. He had to bail out from the plane he could not bring in for landing due to some difficulty. He bailed out and, apparently, did not clear the tail of his plane. He hit the stabilizer and never pulled his 'chute ripcord.

Wednesday, March 21. Lieutenant Leroy Hall of Hillsboro, North Carolina, took off from our field in an L-5, a small reconnaissance plane, for a trip up to Futa Pass in northern Italy to visit some friends. The area where he had to land was on the side of a hill and the approach was one that had to be handled with great care.

The lieutenant made his landing but, before he brought the plane to a stop, he flopped it over on its back and was badly hurt. He had his face banged up. He was lucky to be alive and plastic surgery would be necessary.

Friday, March 23. Our boys flew some escort missions over Austria today. I believe this is the first time they have had a mission to this country. All home safe.

Our squadron's volleyball team won three straight games. This qualifies them to participate in the Twelfth Air Force tournament held in Florence.

Saturday–Thursday, March 24–29. The British Broadcasting Co. broadcasted some recordings made at the site of the Rhine River crossings in Germany.

The way the Italian Front and the German Front are moving, we should be on our way home soon.

Volleyball practice for the upcoming tournament.

The rain closed all operations. We caught up on our paperwork and read the Articles of War to the command.

We had to cancel a recreation trip to Alexandria, Egypt, due to the condition of the runway.

The volleyball team will go to the tournament in Florence very soon. After some practice in a gym in the town of Grosseto, I took the volleyball team to Florence for the championship.

Friday, March 30. We were in Florence this morning and the volleyball team had a practice session. They took this tournament very seriously and wanted to win. The practice must have helped. We won six straight games.

During the evening, I received a report from the squadron that Major Michael McCarthy, our operations officer, and Flight Surgeon Lester Wall were injured when their L-5 crashed at the same spot where Lt. Leroy Hall crashed a few days ago. In fact, Doc and Major Mac were going to see Hall. They received facial injuries but not as bad as Hall received.

Saturday, March 31. Our volleyball team made the semi-finals, but the competition was too tough, and they went down in a gracious defeat. They were very happy to get as far as they did.

They were awarded a volleyball for their efforts.

We stayed around for the finals. The 21st U.S. Engineers defeated the 321st Bomb Group for the Championship of Italy.

Picked up the parachutes and other equipment from the two wrecked L-5s that crashed just north of Florence a few days ago. The three patients were recovering. Lieutenant Hall will need some plastic surgery to fix up his face. Doc Wall lost two of his front teeth and received small facial injuries. Major McCarthy was very lucky. His facial injuries were within less than half an inch of his eye. They all will be in the hospital for a while.

Monday, April 2. Our boys did a special escort mission to northern Italy this morning. A C-47 had to land on a field not far from the enemy. The mission was a successful one. A look at our operations map shows the enemy does not hold too much real estate in northern Italy.

Tuesday, April 3. Lots of mail from home today. I received a nice collection of the latest hit records which the young pilots enjoy. A back injury caused me lots of pain and the local field hospital set up a series of infra-red treatments for me. What a relief from this treatment. We were fortunate having this hospital with a wonderful staff of doctors and nurses.

Piping music into the rooms to entertain the men.

Thursday, April 5. Our boys were off on a mission this morning. All returned safe. John P. Anderson of San Francisco, California, came home with a plane full of holes, but the important thing was he was safe.

More records and orchestrations for The Black Scorpion Orchestra arrived with lots of mail. With this new music, the orchestra held a rehearsal this evening. The boys sounded good.

One of our men set up the equipment to pipe music to each man's bunk.

Saturday, April 7. Drove to Leghorn (Livorno) this morning to pick up our flight surgeon. Lieutenant Hall and Major McCarthy will have to stay in hospital for another while.

After picking up Doc, I took him to see my own family dentist, Colonel Carney. Doc Carney was stationed in the field hospital. He gave Doc Wall a good examination and set up an appointment for the work to be done on his mouth. Wall wanted two buck teeth to be pulled and a partial plate for the four front teeth. Carney said no; he did not believe in pulling teeth, except in hopeless cases.

Sunday, April 8. In the schoolhouse, we had a room we used for a studio. One of our boys set up all the equipment to feed to each boy's bunk. He piped the

I'm getting ready to make a broadcast to the squad.

We lowered the flag to half-staff in honor of Franklin D. Roosevelt's passing.

recreation room radio programs through the equipment. We also had a record turntable and a pretty good selection of records. We piped music to the bunks and rec room.

We took a series of pictures today with the idea of submitting them with a recommendation for the Bronze Star for this young man. The young man set up this studio on his own time and it was a real morale builder for the squadron.

We also had a mic we could use for announcements to the men. The whole set up was called "Black Scorpion Station."

Monday, April 9. On my visit to Malta, I purchased some fine mahogany and had it shaped for a plaque. On it we had painted the names of all the officers who served in the squadron. We tried to obtain a piece of the same wood for the enlisted men's plaque, but we needed a much larger piece, and it was not available.

In Grosseto, we obtained the correct-sized plaque. The project was started to paint all the names of the officers (187) and enlisted men (325).

We had a pilot who was an expert with the brush and oil, as long as he had a bottle of gin.

Thursday, April 12. We received the news late tonight of the death of President Roosevelt.

Friday, April 13. Flag at half-mast this morning. Lieutenant Zane Amell of Lansing, Michigan, returned from an assignment up on the front lines. He acted as the liaison officer for the Air Force with the infantry. This was something new. He told us tonight how he directed air strikes on the enemy troops and equipment from the information supplied by the boys right up where the action was.

During the day, we had a mad dog in our area. The dog was killed and its head sent to Naples for a rabies test. One man, in the depot in Naples waiting to go home, was ordered back to our hospital for injections against rabies. He had been close to this dog before leaving for home.

He was very unhappy but. after listening to Doc Wall give a talk on what happens to anyone infected with rabies, he was grateful he was called back.

During my correspondence with my former commanding officer, Vincent Coyne, I requested, if possible, a couple of German helmets for my sons, James and Gregory, back in Medford.

Lieutenant Zane Amell was a liaison officer with the infantry, performing ground-based forward air controller duties.

I had plenty of these helmets when we rushed through Egypt. At the time, I did not think to keep any of this equipment.

Coyne and his driver, Corp. Francis Cuchick from Quincy, Massachusetts, with the 71st Anti-Aircraft Artillery Brigade were conducting advanced reconnaissance near Pietramala when a group of planes passed over the position they observed. They witnessed a P-47 being shot down.

Shortly after they saw the plane hit, a parachute popped open. A pilot was on his way to earth. Coyne drove to the spot where they figured this boy would hit the earth.

Within about ten minutes, Coyne and Cuchick were on the scene and a young American fighter pilot was happy to see them. Coyne questioned him and found he was a pilot from the 57th Fighter Group. Coyne said, "Your troubles are over, get in the jeep." Sometime later, this airman was on his way back to the 57th Fighter Group. This young man delivered two German helmets for the two boys back in Medford.

Saturday–Sunday, April 14–15. Many missions were sent up. They all came home safe except for Lt. William F. Berry of Decatur, Illinois. He was seen bailing out and landing safe about ten miles inside the enemy lines.

Wednesday, April 18. This was a quiet day but a wild night at the club. We had four officers promoted to captain. As was the custom, when one was promoted, one must buy the drinks for the gang. The new captains did and more. You could say this was a successful promotion party.

Thursday, April 19. Back home in Boston, April 19 would be a holiday. This was Patriots Day, celebrating the midnight ride of Paul Revere through the villages and towns of Middlesex County, alerting the countryside of the coming of the British.

Here in Italy, the war goes on. We had a celebration this evening at the officers' club for the unveiling of the plaque by Col. Robert Barnum, our squadron commander from Lake City, Michigan.

We also gave out a card with a picture of Marble Arch on it. We passed under this arch on our push through the Western Desert in 1942.

This card was a gag and presented to anyone still in the squadron from that trek after General Rommel, the "Desert Fox."

Our band gave a wonderful performance this evening. Everybody was happy with this outstanding musical unit, organized only a few weeks before this party.

The boys had a few missions this afternoon and one of our boys bailed out. It was thought Lt. Arthur Goettel of Miami, Oklahoma, landed on our side of the lines.

The Fifth Army would occasionally put out books about their history. This book 19 Days from the Apennine to the Alps *details the action in the Po Valley in Italy at the close of the war. This excerpt is from the chapter "The Bell and the Opening rounds."*

It was 4:00 in the morning on the 14th of April, and in the small tent he used for a mess sat the Fifth Army Commander. With him sat his Chief of Staff, Brigadier General Don E. Carleton, and Brigadier General Thomas Darcy, commander of the Twelfth Tactical Air Force [The Black Scorpion Squadron and the two other squadrons of the 57th Fighter Group were under the command of the Twelfth Tactical Air Force] The Chinese boy was serving black coffee; General Darcy's ear was glued to the telephone. As he listened, he repeated what was coming to him from his Air Bases at Pisa, Florence, and Grosseto [Black Scorpion Squadron was at Grosseto]. He says the clouds are banked up over the south slopes of the mountains and the fog is rolling in from the sea.

General Truscott turned to the Chief of Staff.

"Call Critt (General Crittenberger, Commanding IV Corps) and tell him the planes are not yet able to get off the ground and we may have to delay George's attack. I won't let him go without air support." (George was Major General Hayes, 10th Mountain Division Commander)

The hours ticked slowly by; many cups of coffee were consumed; the receiver remained glued to General Darcy's ear.

Florence blanketed with heavy fog, Pisa visibility one half mile, Grosseto broken clouds of fog rolling in from the west.

On all fields sat row after row of Fighter Bombers, warmed up and armed, their pilots at the controls waiting for the order.

The attack was delayed to 8:00 am. It was 6:45 and the planes had not yet left the ground. 7:15 and it was set back another half hour to 8:30, when General Darcy's face broke with a grin: "57th Fighter Group is in the air!"

General Truscott said: "Get Critt. The show is on. We attack at 8:30."

The last great battle of the Fifth Army had begun, and the Black Scorpion Squadron played a leading part as it had from El Alamein to the Po Valley.

The 64th Fighter Squadron Band.

Robert Barnum unveils the new officer's plaque in the officers' club.

Friday, April 20. Many missions this morning and one of our boys had a narrow escape when one of his tires blew out just as he came down the runway, and before being airborne. Lieutenant Robert Neilson of Chicago, Illinois, did a masterful job in keeping his plane from crashing.

Saturday, April 21. Good news this morning: Lt. Arthur Goettel returned. Goettel bailed out on the 19th. He told us about his descent to earth after bailing out of his plane, which had been hit by enemy action.

Everything went well except he landed in a small village which had many houses close together. He came down between two houses and his face took a real beating. He left some skin on the walls of a home of the village where he landed. He will not be flying for a while.

The good Doc Wall will have him under his wing for a few weeks.

Sunday, April 22. We had many missions today, more than have been flown for some time. Our boys had 58 sorties. The targets were Germans fleeing towards the Po River in the north. There was not much more room for them to run to.

Lieutenant Robert L. Hubbard of San Antonio, Texas, failed to return. One of the boys at the debriefing said he was pretty sure he saw him parachute on our side of the front line.

Had a call from my former commanding officer, Vincent Coyne. He called to inform me he was promoted to colonel. He never thought he would make colonel as his commanding general was a West Point officer and the rest of his staff were graduates of West Point. Coyne was the only National Guard officer on the staff. He was elated.

Monday, April 23. The Germans fled like dogs in the Po Valley, made for lots of targets. The boys from the Black Scorpion Squadron bombed and strafed these poor unfortunates all day long.

When you put up a lot of sorties as we did today, some of the boys will get hurt. This day was one of them. First Lt. Robert H. Reichelder of Philadelphia, Pennsylvania, bailed out of his plane after it was hit by anti-aircraft fire. His 'chute failed to open. One of the pilots stated he thought Reichelder hit the tail of his plane.

Bob Hubbard, who failed to return yesterday, returned to the squadron this morning. It was always good news to see one of our boys returned all in one piece. We received more good news; Lt. William Berry, who bailed out of his plane on April 15, was safe. He would be back with the squadron soon.

Major Carlton A. Chamberlain of Olean, New York, was hit by enemy fire. He belly-landed his plane 15 miles inside our lines and was able to walk away from his P-47. A busy day for all.

Wednesday, April 25. Another busy day with lots of sorties in the air. After the missions were over, Lt. Albert B. Nichols of Bourne, Texas, failed to return. At the debriefing, it was recorded his plane hit the ground on the strafing run. The prospect of him coming out of this action did not look good. All we can do is hope.

Lieutenant Charles E. May of Courtland, Ohio, also failed to return. One of the pilots stated he saw an open parachute in the area of the target.

Thursday, April 26. The weather was poor this morning but there were lots of Germans fleeing with their equipment, trying to get out of Italy. They made good targets.

We sent a mission up with Lt Col. Robert A. Barnum, our commanding officer, as leader. After the boys did their work, both Barnum and Lt. Paul M. Hall, of Salina, Kansas, got caught in a thunderhead over Florence and had to bail out.

Hall made it OK, but Barnum hit the tail of his plane and took a slice out of his rump. Both wound up in the 24th Field Hospital. They will spend a few days there resting and recuperating.

CHAPTER 44

Villafranca, Italy

April 27–May 1

We had been on this base for six months. I figured this would be our last field. It was a surprise when I was called to headquarters at 6:00 pm and informed that A Party would move out tomorrow morning.

I went back to the squadron and had a meeting with all the section chiefs. I broke the news. This meant working through the night for everybody so we could move to a new base and be ready to operate as quickly as possible. The new base would be in the Po Valley in an area called Villafranca. The boys were happy. They liked to move and see new areas.

Friday, April 27. We left Grosseto at 8:45 for our trek to the Po Valley. Everybody was excited. Our first stop was for lunch in a town called Rosignano. We saw thousands of German prisoners moving south, some on foot and some in trucks. This was evidence this messy war was coming to an end.

We passed through a town called Vergato, south of Bologna. This was one of the targets the boys of the Black Scorpions worked over a couple of weeks ago. From the ruins we saw, I would say our boys did their work well. What a shambles.

Our stop for the night was in Bologna but, by mid-afternoon, we were slowed down by heavy rains. We arrived in our assigned area at 10:00 pm and the area was a sea of mud. Many of our trucks sank in the loose mire. We spent a miserable night there but that was part of the game and very little grumbling was heard.

Saturday, April 28. Everybody was up at dawn. It was still raining, and the German prisoners were still moving south in droves. They were a sad looking lot. From their appearance you could tell these fellows have not had a bed of roses for a long time.

Despite the heavy rain, our cooks prepared an excellent breakfast for over one hundred men and officers. After breakfast, we thought we would move out, but we found out we were under the control of the Fifth Army's traffic control. They told us we would move out tomorrow morning between 3:40 and 4:40 am.

This was the first time, since we came overseas two-and-a-half years ago, we were told when to move. We had always been told the area to move to and away we went.

The 64th Fighter Squadron also had the following incident with pilot Lt. Albert Nichols. I am not sure of the exact date.

On April 25/45, Lt Albert Nichols of Bourne, TX, failed to return from a strafing mission. At the debriefing it was recorded Nichols's plane had hit the ground.

Sometime after this action, we received an order from a hospital of the award of the Purple Heart to Lt. Albert Nichols and we assumed this medal was presented posthumously as we had received no reports "Nick" was alive.

A few days later, according to the orders from headquarters, I prepared a condolence letter to the next to kin of this young man, in his case, it was his mother. These letters were not easy to write when you must try and explain to a mother what has happened to her son.

Well after a long time, I pieced together a letter I thought would break the news to this boy's parent. The letter was forwarded to our headquarters where it was held for five days, just in case we had been misinformed or there was a chance this young hero had escaped death which would be hard to believe after the story that he hit the ground on a strafing run doing over 150 miles per hour.

Five days after the letter was forwarded, I received a call in the evening and the voice said "Jim, this is Nick. Send me some clothes."

I thought I was hearing things and said, "Where are you?"

"I am in the hospital and ready to come back to the squadron."

It took me a long time to return to normal as this call really shocked me. When I informed the boys about the call, they were all amazed just as I was.

The clothes went off the next morning and Nick came back to the squadron with the most amazing story I ever heard.

He told us he hit the ground after his plane was shot and skidded along and when the plane came to a stop, all that was left was parts of the wings and cockpit and he was bleeding from the mouth and ears and his plane was burning all around him.

He tried to get out one side and was driven back by the flames and then he tried the other side and the same condition existed.

He finally fell out of the plane and rolled away the best he could to avoid the flames. He lay on the ground for some time when a German came by and fired a shot at his head which grazed him. The German left and Nick was still on the ground. A short time later another German came to him and fired two shots into the ground not far from his head.

This soldier took his watch and ring and left the area.

A group of Italian civilians watched this whole affair and, when the second German left, they picked Nick up and hid him in a barn until all the enemy had left.

After dark they placed him on a bicycle and brought him through the American lines and from there he was rushed to a hospital. Nick said when he was in the cockpit of the plane, he figured his time was up and little did he know what was ahead of him after he rolled away from his P-47.

This young man I thought looked very good considering what he had been through since leaving from Black Scorpion headquarters for a routine mission into the Po Valley of northern Italy.

The mark from the pistol shot along the side of Nick's head will be there for a long time. I would say in closing out this incident that it was not the time of Lt. Albert Nichols to meet his maker.

I can understand this arrangement. We were in a country with narrow roads and lots of traffic moving towards the enemy.

The rain continued. We moved out of the large mud pie we had been assigned to and stayed in a bombed outbuilding for the night. It was good to be under cover. The rain made us look like drowned rats.

Sunday, April 29. Not much sleep as we were all wet during the night. We were told we would move out at 3:40 and we did. We arrived at our new base, Villafranca, at 8:15 am. This was the first time we moved during the night. It was interesting as we checked in at the various check points along the road.

We set up a temporary camp on the edge of this large airfield and started looking for buildings

The partisans were well armed and helped us find housing.

to house our 300 officers and enlisted men. There were plenty of nice buildings in the area, but we found the service group had them all tied up.

A group of cooperative partisans took us around the area. They wanted us to have good quarters and they showed us some beautiful villas which would take care of our needs.

The sky was full of C-47s bringing in supplies to end this foolish war. With our supply lines extended, these planes had a lot of work ahead of them. I know they don't mind. They have been flying this type of mission for years.

The new area has flat ground for many miles. But, as you look north, the great mountains of the Alps, with their snowcapped peaks, awe you.

Our squadron commander, Lt Col. Robert A. Barnum, was released from hospital. He arrived later this afternoon and assisted us in the search for a home for the Black Scorpion Squadron.

We lined up quite a few buildings and planned a meeting tomorrow with the service group people to release one of the many buildings we inspected. We had a long talk with the partisans who escorted us around this new area of Italy. They were decked out with guns and knives. Some of the stories they told us would turn your blood cold.

One story they told us was that a friend of one of the partisans wanted a certain German artillery outfit insignia. He told us how he snuck into an artillery position during the night and cut the throat of a soldier and stripped him of his insignia.

We had great respect for these dedicated partisans, which included men and women, young and old. Many a downed pilot had been rescued by these young men and women, sometimes at great risk. They also hid many American and Allied pilots who had been shot down on missions in Italy during this war.

Benito Mussolini and his mistress, Clara Petacci, were executed and their bodies hung by their feet in the center of Milan. A story came to us that after Mussolini's body was cut down, it was left in the square for the partisans to kick around. A woman approached the body of *Il Duce* and fired five bullets into his face. She was heard to remark that it was "for the five sons of mine you killed."

Monday, April 30. We are still trying to get the service group to release a building for us to set up our squadron. The strange and foolish part of this whole thing was there were more buildings than all the troops will ever use.

Our group commander, Col. Archie Knight, set up an appointment with the commanding officer of the service group. After the meeting, we felt that some progress had been made. A decision will be rendered tomorrow morning.

We are not hurting. We have lots of tents set up. The weather is okay but on the cold side. The breezes from the snowcapped Alps cool the area.

Our pilots came in this afternoon; this was always cause for commotion. I can hear them say, "Jim, what kind of quarters have you obtained for us?" or "I don't want to be in the tent with that so and so" or "He wants his tent entrance moved around." We try to make them all happy and do most of the time.

Lots of excitement around the field this afternoon. A special plane came in to collect Italian General Graziani and one of the German leaders. They were taken prisoner a short distance from our field.

And to add to the excitement, a group of Germans was holed up in an area not far from our field. By early evening, they were convinced their number was up and they were taken away.

Lieutenant Charles May, reported missing in action on April 25, was back with us. He bailed out and was picked up by some front-line troops.

Barnum is back in the hospital for treatment for the injury he received when he bailed out of his plane in the thunderhead over Florence a few days ago. This young man must make up his mind; he had a bad injury and must relax. I was surprised they let him out of the hospital.

These pilots want to fly and that is all they are interested in. It was hard to convince these men injuries must be taken care of first and then fly.

Tuesday, May 1. The service group made a big decision this morning. They gave us the okay to move into the big house on the hill. The house was close to the airfield in the town of Valeggio and would take care of 50-plus officers. The house also had a dining room that could seat them all.

This was a beautiful spot, and it had a lot of history which I do not have. It was called Villa Ghiradini. I suppose that was the name of the family who owned this mammoth piece of real estate.

We had the same trouble with the boys we had when we set up a tent camp. We had to allocate the rooms according to rank. That was the only way to try to keep them happy.

We found, in the same village, a wonderful place for the enlisted men. It was a fairly new schoolhouse; they were satisfied to be away from the tent camp in the field. There was lots of activity all day and night bringing in supplies.

Our first night in town was a cold one. There was no heat in this old villa. After a cold night, we started thinking about building stoves similar to the ones we built in southern Italy last winter.

CHAPTER 45

Villafranca, Italy

May 2–5

Wednesday, May 2. This was moving day from the field for all. With no flying, everybody pitched in to the move to Valeggio. The sky was full again today with C-47s with their loads of supplies, equipment, food, and all the necessary items it takes to keep thousands of troops going.

We received word that Adolf Hitler was dead this morning. This, of course, was good news. It was hard to believe a guy like this little paperhanger could cause so much trouble throughout the world.

For the first time in a long while, we had a snowstorm. It did not last long but it left its chill in the air.

Our rear party from Grosseto were on the way to join us. It will be nice to have the squadron all together again. There were a few missions in the air today but, according to the map, there were no targets left. The bomb line shows we had all the territory in Italy sewn up.

The best news in a long time was that the Germans gave up in Italy at 2:00 pm today. This was hard to believe but true. We had been chasing them since September 1942 when we first started flying missions out of a landing ground in Egypt.

This Black Scorpion Squadron has covered approximately 30,000 miles since we left Boston on July 5, 1942.

Thursday, May 3. With the thought of another cold night, a few of us started to build a stove out of an old gas drum. Our fuel would be a mixture of diesel oil and gas.

Friday, May 4. The Black Scorpion Squadron was all together again with the arrival of our B Party from Grosseto.

Saturday, May 5. Went to Verona to visit my old commanding officer, Colonel Coyne. During our chat at Fifth Army Headquarters, I found out the colonel was involved in the capture from the Germans of the airfield at Villafranca, which was now the home of the Black Scorpion Squadron and the 57th Fighter Group.

He went further and explained he was task force commander in the 4th Corps under Maj Gen. Willis Crittenberger. The operation to take the airfield was made up of a combined anti-aircraft artillery (AAA) force of the American battalions plus three British AAA regiments.

One of the British regiments secured this field where we now operate. He went on to state the Villa Ghiradini that we now lived in was supposed to be the 4th Corps' AAA command post.

I took him back to the villa. We had lunch and lots of laughs over the turn of events in this crazy war.

I must go back a few years to get to the meat of this incident. On April 10, 1928, I enlisted in the 241st Coast Artillery of the Massachusetts National Guard (Battery L). A few months later, a young officer was assigned as the battery commander. We had a talk one evening about the battery clerk who was leaving the unit. Lieutenant Vincent P. Coyne offered me the position.

At that time, I did not know how to operate a typewriter but agreed to think it over until the next drill. There was extra pay for doing this job. In 1928, money was tight so I told the lieutenant that, if he would put up with my one-finger typing, I would give it a try. I stayed with this officer for 12 years as battery clerk and later as his sergeant major when he became battalion commander.

When we were called to active duty, the regimental commander separated us, and I went to another battery of the battalion. On December 6, 1941, I was separated from the service for being over age in grade (I was a 2nd Lt. at that time).

Less than 60 days later, I was back in the service but with the Air Corps as it was called in 1942. I kept in touch with Coyne and later, in 1942, we were both in Africa but many miles apart. We got together once down in Kasserine Pass, later in Rome, and this day, May 5, 1945.

I just had to write about this incident as I think it is something out of the ordinary the way we bounced around since 1928. This officer, who I served for many years in Boston, and I wound up together many thousands of miles from home when his outfit captured the field where my outfit was going to work.

Captain Earl D. Lovick of Libby, Missouri, and our Doc Wall found the grave of Capt. Myer J. "Bucky" Reynolds of Washington, D.C. This was the young hero who failed to return from the strafing mission of March 12, 1944. They also found the grave of Lt. Billy Adams of Fort Worth, Texas, who failed to return from a mission over northern Italy on October 12. Another young hero who gave his life for his country.

CHAPTER 46

Grosseto, Italy

May 6–26

Sunday–Monday, May 6–7. Our short stay in northern Italy came to an end when we received orders to move back to Grosseto, the spot we left on April 25. The orders called for a convoy to move out at first light on the morning of May 7.

We made a hurried trip to the hospital to see our CO and explained our plan. He okayed it. Captain Pete Mitchell and I took off at 6:00 pm with the idea of getting to Grosseto before anyone else to claim our old buildings and any others we needed.

We came down Route 65 which gave us a chance to see the damage our boys and the rest of the Air Corps inflicted on the road the Germans held for so long.

We drove all night and arrived back in our former home at 3:30 am. We still had a rear detachment of a few enlisted men who had work to do on some planes that were out of action.

We woke up these boys and obtained some paint. At 4:00 am, we started painting 64th Squadron logos on all the empty buildings we could find.

We found the bomb group which had remained behind had taken some of the buildings we occupied before moving. A breakfast with the commanding officer of the bomb group was fruitful. He understood our problem on housing and turned over many of our former buildings to us.

By 9:00 am, we had new requisitions for these buildings in the hands of the service group in Grosseto. When some of the other squadrons returned later on, they were quite surprised to find us already in the area.

On the afternoon of the 7th, we received word the Germans had surrendered. The war was over in Europe. This was the best news we had heard in a long time. We had been expecting this news for days as the reports coming in indicated the end was near.

As reported earlier, we had a few die-hard fascists in the area. They put on a parade with the red flags flying. We paid them little attention and they broke up without any incident.

Tuesday, May 8. This morning was a busy one with housekeeping and the arrival of many of our trucks and equipment. The talk all day was when would we go home.

This was a natural reaction after the news of yesterday that the enemy in Europe no longer existed.

Captain Lovick reported he found the graves of a few more boys of our squadron: Lt. Edwin S. Frierson of Shreveport, Louisiana; Lt. Charles R. Newmann of Cheyenne, Wyoming; and Lt. James A. Graham of Beaver Falls, Pennsylvania. I had no record of when these young men were lost.

Wednesday–Sunday, May 9–13. Most of the boys arrived this morning from Villafranca. We were told to prepare for a VE (Victory in Europe) party for all. Meetings were held and a committee started planning at once.

The pilots were kept on their toes with lots of training flights as they may have another mission planned for them in the Pacific.

Lots of paperwork as many of the men will be rotated back to the States very soon. We still had a large percentage of men who had been with us since 1942. I received orders today for two more battle stars. This meant the officers and men who were with us all the way from Palestine to the Po Valley will be permitted to wear nine battle stars.

Monday, May 14. A report from 57th Group Headquarters this morning stated the Black Scorpion Squadron had flown 1,615 combat missions, with 11,924 sorties, since starting to operate back in Egypt in September 1942.

We felt this was quite an accomplishment. It was a proud moment when this report was read to the members of the 64th Fighter Squadron during supper.

Thursday, May 17. After much pressure on the Red Cross, they agreed to open a club on the beach for the enlisted men and friends. The Red Cross had a club 8 miles away in town and felt that was enough.

We convinced them the travel back and forth would not be a good idea. They saw the light that this was good for morale as the boys had more time on their hands now the war was over.

The enlisted men's plaque was finished and will be unveiled at the party on the 21st. The completion of the plaque was delayed due to the fact the officer painting it went home.

A civilian artist was called in. He did an excellent job completing what someone else had started. The names, as on the officers' plaque, were in oil.

The squad celebrating VE-Day.

Monday, May 21. This was the day for our VE-Day celebration. We set up tents this morning on one of the blocked off streets. We obtained two hospital tents from the service group so everything would be under cover.

The cooks went all out with the meal. And the beverage committee did a superb job. We had a head table for the brass. The unveiling of the enlisted men's plaque was the hit of the afternoon.

Group commander, Col. Archie Knight, and the service group commander, Lehman, congratulated the squadron on their outstanding efforts during the almost three years of overseas duty.

Our squadron commander was still in the hospital, but he was ably represented by Major Michael McCarthy, our operations officer.

The party went on through the night. I know there will be many big heads in the morning.

We found plenty of refreshments for the VE celebration.

Tuesday–Wednesday, May 22–23. These were happy days for one of our enlisted men. I went to Florence to witness the wedding of Sgt George W. Lutton Jr of Jackson Heights, New York, to a WAC (Women's Army Corps) sergeant by the name of Balish from Brooklyn, New York.

I think George started courting the young WAC back in Foggia in 1943. We did not spend too much time in this area before we moved to the Naples area and then to Corsica.

George had frequent passes when we were in Italy. But passes to Foggia were not as easy to get when we moved to Corsica. When we were alerted to move to Corsica, the passes were clamped down on. This young man, however, stayed over his leave after the clamp down and we were required to punish him.

I unveiled the plaque with all the enlisted men's names on it.

George Lutton and his beautiful bride, Sergeant Balish.

George Lutton, his bride, and her parents.

The direct punishment was reduction in rank. He did not like this but, being a good soldier, he took the reduction. Within a short space of time before the wedding, he was back to his original rank.

Tuesday night, the bride's parents, Mr. and Mrs. Balish, who came over from New York for the wedding, gave a dinner party. After the party, we witnessed the wedding rehearsal. On Wednesday, George Lutton married Miss Balish at a very nice wedding, although both were thousands of miles from home.

The wedding reception was a gala affair attended by many of the members of this squadron.

When George told me of his wedding plans, I knew there were villas on the island of Capri assigned to the Air Force where some honeymoons had been held. I made inquiries and was fortunate to obtain a villa for Mr. and Mrs. George Lutton for a 10-day period.

I know this couple will always remember their honeymoon in a beautiful villa on the beautiful isle of Capri.

Saturday, May 26. Our squadron commander, Col. Robert Barnum, reported back to the squadron from hospital. We also received a letter from Mrs. Arthur Exon of Estherville, Iowa, about her husband Art, our former squadron commander who was shot down on a mission from Corsica on April 20, 1944.

He was seen to parachute and land in a field in Italy. This was the first word the squadron received as to the condition of Art Exon.

CHAPTER 47

Final days

May 28–August 6. These last days in Italy, there was not much to write about; I am just going to roam through the notes. Each day a few men were rotated home and they were happy. They all could say "I did my duty."

I remember one boy, Sgt Lynn S. Pang of Marlis, Michigan. The doc found this young man had some knee trouble and the States was the best place for him. He had done an outstanding job as a crew chief.

When I called him in to tell him he would leave very shortly for the States, tears came to his eyes. He pleaded to stay with the squadron. We told him he needed treatment and must go.

The final condolence letters had to go out. This was one task I disliked very much.

On June 7, General Israel from the Twelfth Air Force came to the group with the final decorations for officers and enlisted men. I was awarded the Bronze Star. I don't know why as all I did was the work my job called for.

We received lots of lumber for the crating of Black Scorpion property. The area around our headquarters looks like a lumber yard. It was surprising to find out how many fine carpenters we had in the squadron.

I believe the boys felt if they helped out with the crating they would get home sooner. The same *esprit de corps* was in effect as it had been in the Black Scorpion Squadron from the beginning.

General Israel from Twelfth Air Force awarding me the Bronze Star.

On the evening of June 11, I had a meeting with all the enlisted men to give them the straight story about what was going to happen to members of the squadron. There had been many rumors making the rounds that most of them would remain with the squadron and be shipped to the Pacific.

Colonel Barnum and I had worked through the late hours last night and set the stage for those that would go home and those who would stay. Believe it or not, we had a few boys who did not want to go home and agreed to go wherever the squadron went.

When we finished with the list, there were 18 members of the original group that came overseas in July 1942 who agreed to stay on.

During our trek from Palestine to the Po Valley of northern Italy, we had very few inspections by higher headquarters. But in the days since the war ended, we had our share. It seemed every headquarters from our own on up had sent in teams to look us over.

June 23 and 24 were the days most of our men took off for the depot in Naples where they would leave for the States. There were a lot of goodbyes, many of them did not want to leave.

We received many replacements. I hoped the squadron did not have to go into action soon. It looked like poor planning went into the selection of replacements.

I remember one young man who was to be a replacement for a radio man. This was a very important job in a squadron of P-47s. During my interview, I asked him what he had done in the radio field. He informed me he had been a guard around a radio station in Africa when he was selected for replacement in the Black Scorpion Squadron.

In most cases, we received poor replacements.

On July 12, I was transferred from the Black Scorpion Squadron to the 62nd Fighter Wing at Leghorn (Livorno), Italy. This ended my three-and-a-half years with a wonderful outfit. It was not hard to leave as most of the pilots were new and all but 18 of the original enlisted men had been shipped out.

From July 12 to August 6, my assignment with the fighter wing was as information and educational officer. Most of my work was to send officers and enlisted men to the various rest areas assigned to the command.

Venice, Switzerland, France, Rome, Capri, and others had wonderful facilities for these officers and enlisted men. We had a quota for each week. Believe it or not, we had a hard time filling it out of the 2,000-plus men we had in the command.

My office had to keep the command informed about what was going on all over the world. We had many charts supplied to us. A sergeant, my assistant, and I tried to visit the headquarters of the units assigned to us as often as possible.

On the morning of August 6, my duties ended when I received orders to go home. I departed from this short assignment with the 62nd Fighter Wing. I was packed and on a plane to Naples before noon.

Tuesday, August 7. This morning I found out I would stay around Naples for about a week. They put me up in a small hotel near the dock. Fortunately, the troop movement officer was from Boston. Colonel Wm. A. Hagerty informed me I would go home on SS *Wakefield* on August 13.

I made the rounds of Naples. I went to the opera and visited the island of Ischia. This was the island where Benito Mussolini's daughter had her home.

I visited the repo depot (replacement depot) where the Black Scorpion Squadron awaited loading orders.

On August 11, the Black Scorpion Squadron, along with many troops, was loaded on a ship. No one seemed to know where they were going. I went aboard and said my goodbyes. As I left the top deck and came down to the main deck, where a group of GIs sat around, one of these young men got up and said "Hi, Mr. Lynch."

From his remark I figured this young man must have been from home. After a short conversation, he informed me he had played a trombone in the Chelsea High School, one of the many schools I serviced before the war.

I promised to call his mother and tell her of my visit. I saw this ship leave the dock and was informed later the boys were on their way to Lingayen Gulf in the Pacific.

Two days later, I left Naples. On August 14, the war in the Pacific was over. The ship with the Black Scorpion Squadron on board was diverted to Boston, the spot where the squadron left from on July 5, 1942.

The unit moved to Drew Field in Florida. Here ends this episode about the Black Scorpion Squadron.

What I typed during the past four years from the notes I made daily during my three years overseas, with a tremendous group of officers and enlisted men, was what happened.

It is all truth without any fictions mixed in. The incidents listed happened and I have tried to write them in the best manner that I know how. When I made the notes in the four memo books I kept during our overseas tour, I had no intention of putting the actions and incidents of this famous squadron to print.

I have read a few books by officers and enlisted men of their experiences during World War I and II; these gave me the inspiration to start this long project.

Appendices

Black Scorpions Commanding Officers

Major Clermont E. Wheeler	1942–43	Retired as colonel, 1964
Major Glade B. Bilby*	1943	
Major Arthur E. Exon**	1943–44	
Major Louis Frank III	1944	Out of Service
Lt. Col Robert A. Barnum	1944–45	Out of Service

*   Killed in aircraft accident after World War II
**   Became Brigadier General Air Force Defense Supply Agency

Miscellaneous Statistics

October 14, 1942 to December 31, 1943

In a little over a year, from its first combat operations to just after its conversion from the P-40 Warhawk to the P-47 Thunderbolt, the 64th Fighter Squadron accumulated an impressive record. The subsequent 17 months, with the more heavily armed P-47s capable of carrying greater bomb loads on each mission, more than likely at least doubled most of the statistics listed below and certainly set new records.

Total number of missions flown	405
Total number of sorties flown	4,360
Approximate number of combat hours flown	7,072
Approximate number of gallons of gasoline consumed	3,909,450
Total number of enemy aircraft destroyed	63
Total number of enemy aircraft probably destroyed	10
Total number of enemy aircraft damaged	27
Approximate number of vessels sunk or damaged	23
Total number of locomotives destroyed or damaged	12
Approximate number of railroad cars destroyed or damaged	133
Approximate number of motor transport vehicles destroyed or damaged	840
Number of 500-lb bombs dropped	832
Number of 250-lb bombs dropped	1,204
Number of 40-lb bombs dropped	2,425
Number of 25-lb bombs dropped	820
Total weight of bombs dropped in pounds	894,509
Total weight of bombs dropped in tons	446.09
Total number of rounds of ammunition expended	412,930
Month that greatest weight of bombs was dropped: August 1943	152,415 lbs
Month that most ammunition was expended: November 1943	54,316
Most combat hours on any plane	426.25
Total number of engines changed	75
Squadron serviceability in Africa	72.1%

Squadron serviceability in Sicily	70.8%
Squadron serviceability in Italy	69.2%
Number of days operated in Africa	221
Number of days operated in Sicily	62
Number of days operated in Italy	105

In addition to the above, numerous gun positions, supply dumps, and personnel have been destroyed or damaged.

Remarks of the commanding officer, Col. Arthur G. Salisbury, when this report was submitted: "The above statistics have been worked out very carefully and speak for themselves. Behind these figures are many hours of hard work, and very often under the most trying climatic conditions of sand, rain, cold, and mud. Behind these figures lies the legend of a Fighter Squadron whose exploits and accomplishments will go down in history and which will occupy a prominent part when the story of this is written."

George Dorval's Survival

In correspondence with the author, Lt. George Dorval shared what happened to him after being shot down over northern Italy during October 1944.

We took off with three flights that afternoon to strafe an airfield in northern Italy, in the Bergamo area. Unfortunately, the flight leader (a fellow by the name of Nall, as I recall, who later became CO) did not take us in on the raid properly. I had been to this area about three days previously and knew there was a dummy field set up a few miles east of the target field. The plan was to strike from the west out of a late afternoon sun, shoot up the airfield, and then lay low on the deck to a dry riverbed and follow the bed out of the anti-aircraft gun range.

Unfortunately, Nall led us in between the active target field and the dummy field. With the sun coming from the west (left), all he noticed was the dummy field on our right (east) and gave orders to peel off. I radioed that it was the wrong field, but everyone went in anyway.

As soon as he strafed the dummies, he realized what I was talking about and then headed for the real field under the worst possible conditions.

1. The enemy field was well alerted by now.
2. We were flying into the low afternoon sun, instead of out of it.
3. We were not in the best shooting position or at top strafing speed out of a dive because we were already pulling up from the other field.

At about this time, to make matters worse, propeller oil started spraying across my front glass which made it very difficult, if not impossible, to see ahead of me and, more particularly, because of the sun glare also coming in.

I called my wingman, I think it was Anderson (who I believe came from San Francisco), and told him to move as I was afraid we might collide with my limited vision.

I was trying to see what was ahead, where the planes were to shoot up, by pressing my face against the side glass when, all of a sudden, I looked down and ahead, straight at an 88-mm cannon with three or four Jerries around it. It was too late to fire at them. Suddenly there was a "WUMP" in my plane and smoke began pouring into the cockpit. I called the *Hitchhike* leader and told him, but Red Boyd, from Montgomery, Alabama, answered and said, "Drop your auxiliary gas tanks." I did but it did no good—the fire was roaring in the cockpit, and I was burning. I knew we couldn't have been over 200 feet off the ground, but I had to get out of the plane. I pulled back on the stick and opened the canopy. This just created a draft and a roaring inferno. I quickly moved to throw myself out but forgot to loosen the safety belt. I slapped it open and tore myself out of the cockpit—plugs, wires, oxygen lines, everything—and threw myself over the left side.

My right hand was pretty numb and stiff from the fire as I blindly clawed for the parachute release handle. I was expecting every instant to strike the ground as I knew we were right on the deck when it started. Finally, however, a white streak went by me, and the chute jerked me to a halt.

What a relief!! I was still only 200 or 300 feet off the ground but at least I didn't bounce! I could hear shooting going on around and some rifle fire (maybe at me), but it seemed very quiet and peaceful after the hectic seconds previously. I could see the trees coming up and, luckily, a cornfield under me. Also, I looked down and saw my legs blackened and my pants burned off at the crotch. My face felt all cracked and there was smoke still trailing from me.

I hit the ground in good form, took off the 'chute, and the yellow Mae-West which I threw into the corn patch. An old Italian man was working in the field about 150 feet away and he waved at me. I waved back. I could still hear shooting and shouting as I must have landed close to the enemy field's dispersal area. Just as I turned to decide which way to run, I saw two young men in helmets with rifles come running up to me, so I stood still and waited. One of them excitedly raised his rifle, cocked it and, what's worse, fired it!! But over my head. For a second there, I thought I was a "goner" again with no chance to say a prayer or goodbye to anyone.

The two young Italian men (probably 18 or 19 years old) were apparently soldiers or militia and they were most excited and panicky. After the first shot, they looked at me and seemed to be very concerned about my appearance. They couldn't speak English and I couldn't remember one damned word of Italian. About this time, I became conscious of the painfulness of my burned condition and my fingers steaming inside the leather gloves. I asked them to take my gloves off and finally they did—skin and all came off on my right fingers—particularly the little finger and ring finger.

The Italian soldiers led me to a gun emplacement and two German soldiers and an introduction to the Nazi swastika. I was questioned but by this time was in quite a bit of pain and kept asking for a doctor. After about an hour of lying on the ground, a civilian doctor came and gave me a shot of morphine. A crowd of civilians, mostly women and children, had gathered by this time and from the exclamations and wails as each one came up and looked at me, I imagined that I must have looked pretty awful. After a while, the morphine began to take effect and I felt more relaxed. Just about the time I was drowsy, someone came up with an old door and a mattress. I was placed on it and carried out to the nearest road where a motorcycle with a cab attached was waiting. I was placed inside the cab with a German medic and took off. I don't know how far, or where we were, but it seemed I was in the cab for about an hour. I can't remember much of how I got out of the cab or into a bed but the next thing I remember was being in a small bunk in a small, dark wardroom with many other men in beds. It was dark, cool, quiet.

After a couple of hours, I noticed the men eating. I didn't receive anything—they must have been on a budget or rations—and I wasn't included. The fellow next to me said something—I don't know what—then handed me a stogy. I made the best of it but didn't feel much like smoking for I still had a terrible smell of smoke in my nose from my clothes.

Later that night, a doctor came in and asked me to come to his office. This is when I got a real shock; I couldn't move my legs out of the bed and couldn't stand to walk.

Somehow, we got to an operating table and the doctor cut off my trousers, and then I got a look at the legs. What a mess! Skin hanging off and blisters as big as teacups. The doctor took a pair of small scissors and began cutting off the loose skin and the bulging skin covering the blisters. Fluid poured out. Without anesthetics, it did sting but by this time I guess I was used to it. I finally convinced him that I could use a little morphine and he managed to get me a shot. Back in the bunk, I spent the longest, most nightmarish, night I can remember. The next day I was taken into Bergamo to a large hospital, run by the German military with civilian employees. The doctor I got turned out to be a skin specialist and took very good care of me. I was delirious for about three days, so the doctor told me we had a very close call due to the large percentage of burns. I couldn't eat for several days as nothing would stay down. Finally, about the fourth or fifth day, they scrounged up two soft-boiled eggs and some boiled rice and green salad which did stay down. After that, I was able to eat and began to feel better. The civilian women in the hospital were very kind and the German and Italian soldiers were curious to look at me, particularly since they heard I was a lieutenant; this seemed to perk up their ears and they would remark, "Ach! Lieutenant!" as though I was a big catch.

I was questioned on several occasions during the first few days but fortunately the interrogators believed me when I found it easy to act delirious and in pain and they would depart.

A Polish soldier in the German Army was placed in the room with me in the next bunk. He was there both to guard and to assist me as I could not help myself to a restroom. Although he could not speak English, or I German, we got along quite well. He did indicate that this was a very unusual circumstance for him; in all his training, he had been taught to stand at attention with a lieutenant and had rarely ever talked to one and now suddenly he was not only talking to one but also assisting in bed pan detail. We both got a laugh out of that.

While lying in bed nights, I could hear planes taking off from a nearby airfield. I had always wondered why we rarely saw any enemy aircraft on our missions. Apparently, they did most of their flying after dark and before full daylight.

It was the rainy season in late October and it seemed that, every day, it would just pour off and on. It got pretty lonesome and at times I wondered what the war was all about and if anyone knew I was alive.

One morning about three weeks later, about 6:00 am, I was hustled out of the room on a stretcher and shipped to another hospital in Mantua. It came with such suddenness that I did not get the opportunity of saying goodbye to anyone or even get names and addresses of any of those who had shown me any kindness except for an older Italian woman.

From this point on, I was really "back in the war," an enemy in hostile territory. I was lugged around on a stretcher, hid in cellars during air raids, and sometimes left on the sidewalk when everyone else ran inside. One day during the trip, the truck stopped, and everyone jumped out, they pulled me out and ran, leaving me on the side of the road. Looking up, I saw a group of P-47s attacking something nearby. A couple of them zoomed up and pulled away right over me and in the glisten of sunlight against the side of the plane as it turned, I saw the Black Scorpion insignia of my own squadron! Oh, how I wished they could see me, or by some magic, reach down to pick me up. I sort of smiled and said nothing when the German soldiers and Italian civilians came out of hiding. While I felt helpless lying there, knowing full well that by an ironic twist I might have been killed by my own flying buddies, it suddenly made me realize the terror that we all put into these people when we raided a railroad yard or shot up a truck convoy. I began to realize, too, that as an airplane pilot, I was a *persona non grata* as far as these people were concerned; that I should not admit that I was a pilot. Airmen were not very well liked by the majority of the population—"Luft Gangsters" they called us—and from my helpless position on the ground could see what they meant. The trouble was that, because of my burned appearance, it was pretty obvious that I must have been in a plane as most everyone guessed it immediately upon looking at me until one day, a young German boy said, "You vas Panzer?" meaning "in a tank?" I could see he was sympathetic with a tank driver that had been caught on fire and I took the lead. From then on, if any civilian or soldier asked me about the burns or inferred that I was an airman, I simply said "panzer" and they all nodded and seemed satisfied. Some were even sympathetic with my burned appearance.

Eventually, by cattle car, through bombed out RR stations, and raiding P-47s and Spitfires, up through the Brenner Pass and over into Austria, I was taken to *Stalag 18A* at Spittal an der Drau. By this time, several other wounded prisoners were on board and about sixty of us arrived at the camp. This was my first taste of prison camps as such. I had lost all track of time, but I had now been down about six to eight weeks.

Stalag 18A was located in the mountains, not far from the Austrian Alps. The camp was run pretty much by the British—there being many South Africans, English, Scots, and Australians who had been taken prisoner in the early days of the war in North Africa. Some of the fellows had been taken in Crete and were about to spend their fifth Christmas in prison. The latter group were quite bitter about their long incarceration and refused to recognize Christmas, rarely laughing, or finding anything to be cheery about.

It was at this camp, about one week before Christmas, that I finally walked again. What a wonderful feeling to be mobile again, to walk to the bathroom, to stand up and shave, to go down the hall to visit with someone. I enjoyed my prison comrades very much at this camp and, generally, I think they had very good spirit. We had Russians, Yugoslavs, English, French, Australians, and a few Americans. All were different enough to make it interesting. The Germans had little to do with us except guard the camp. Internally, the prisoners ran everything. Every night, someone would come around with news from Dicky Bird. I soon learned that Dicky Bird was a radio, hidden somewhere in the compound, and the BBC broadcasts were picked up almost every night. In this way we could follow the progress of the war. I was amazed at the presence of a radio but none of us ever spoke of it as such and its location and the distribution of the news was a closely held secret by a tiny few.

I had always hung up my sock at Christmas and this Christmas was to be no exception. So, before going to midnight mass on Christmas Eve, I hung a sock behind the potbellied stove in our room. Everyone got a kick out of it, particularly the two South Africans and the three Englishmen. The three Americans, of course, thought it was a little silly. Even I felt a little foolish, but I was so happy with everything, being able to walk about, Santa Claus came anyway. Upon my return from midnight mass, I came back into the room to find most of the fellows still up, with a humorous glint in their eyes. They asked me how the service was with an amused look on their faces. I realized something was up and I glanced around at their faces. Out of the corner of my eye, I caught sight of my sock. It had bulges in it! I thought for a moment someone was playing a joke but then went ahead with the bluff and opened up the sock. It was real enough! Nothing fancy, of course, but the items I found looked like the treasures of the world at that moment. There was an empty devilled ham can that had been washed and wrapped in toilet tissue. Inside were two gleaming cubes of sugar. Another wrapping disclosed a cube of chocolate. One slim package had three cigarettes. Another soft bulge turned out to be a small wool scarf someone had knitted. Another reach brought me a pencil, another a notebook rolled up, and two soda biscuits came out. My eyes were moist when I realized what these fellows had done and they in turn were a little red around the eyes. One of the fellows piped up that "Santa's sleigh couldn't make it this year because the flak got him." This broke the spell, and we were all glad to have an excuse to laugh. Tea was brewed from leaves only used about four times and we all sat down to enjoy my sock.

A show was planned for New Year's Eve, and I was coaxed to play a guitar and sing a couple of numbers—dressed as a cowboy—only, instead of a 10-gallon hat, the best we could dig up was one of those Aussie hats. I turned out to be a big hit singing *El Rancho Grande* with the big, loud "yippies," particularly with the Russians in the audience. If I had any doubts about getting through to these people in my get-up, they were soon dispelled as I heard the Russians clap and shout with glee "Kovboy, Kovboy, Americansky Kovboy"—at least that's what it sounded like. I think my roommates got a big kick out of it and were quite proud of me.

A couple of days later, the other three Americans and myself got some sad news, we were to be moved out of *Stalag 18A* up into Germany; first to Frankfurt for interrogation and then to a permanent camp somewhere. We tied our few belongings up in a box and left one night about 5:30 pm to catch a train. It had just snowed so we were loaded aboard a horse-drawn sleigh and taken to the RR station. The trip to Frankfurt is another story but it took about three or four days. At Frankfurt, we were grouped together with four or five hundred other American airmen and shipped across Germany and up to Barth—near the Baltic Sea—to *Stalag Luft I*. There we were placed in large compounds of approximately 2,000 men per compound. About 200 men per barracks building and, believe it or not, 24 men to a room not much larger than 15×10. Because I had been back on my feet for only a couple of weeks, the trip was difficult for me. Although we rode the train most of the way, there were long stretches of blown-up track to the next train. Fresh snow continued to fall, making footing very difficult for me and there were times when I was so weak and trembling that I was happy to have an air raid to make the guards stop and we could rest.

As I said, Jim, there is much more story and details to tell but I suddenly realize I've been carried away here and gone into more detail than you wanted.

Suffice it to say that we were liberated by the Russians just about May Day. After much negotiation, the Russians finally permitted some American planes to fly in and pick us up. We left *Stalag Luft I* about May 8, 1945, and were flown to Belgium and then Camp Lucky Strike near the French coast. That Army chow sure looked and tasted good. At first all I wanted or cared to have was that beautiful white French bread, that the Army cooks learned to make, and plenty of coffee. It was only a few days, though, before I was eating most everything. I had dropped in weight from 175 pounds to about 130 pound and, while I was thin, as were most of the other fellows, the doctors and dentists were amazed at our good health and lack of cavities. My burns had healed very well. Most of the scaly appearance on my legs had disappeared and my hands and face only had a nice pinkish look from new skin. "Rather Hollywoodish" as one Englishman said. We were anxious to get out of

Camp Lucky Strike and do something, go somewhere, or get back to our squadrons. This we found was impossible, particularly for me since my squadron was in Italy.

One day we heard that, if we had relatives in England, we could get a two-week pass to visit. I borrowed someone's aunt in London, gave the address and got the pass. New uniforms were issued, pay was advanced, and off I went with one of the fellows I had bumped into from *Stalag 18A*.

It was quite a thrill to be in fresh clothes and barging around London, drinking at a fancy hotel bar, and looking at well-dressed soldiers and civilians. What a hodgepodge of returning Recovered Allied Military Personnel (RAMPs) trying to locate buddies, telegram, or telephone, or write home. Heroes, newcomers, rough guys, gentlemen. The paratroopers who had seen service were, for the most part, much more civil and less boisterous than when they were getting ready to go overseas, and much more appreciative of front-line tactical air support fighter pilots than they had been on the way over.

On the first night out in London, we met a couple of American nurses who were on their first leave in London from an Army Recovery Hospital in Midlands. We all went out dancing, four guys and two girls. As the evening wore on, two of the fellows left and my friend from *Stalag 18A* and I remained. I made a date with one of the nurses for lunch the next day. She kept it. That afternoon, we strolled around London and went out that night. She told me that the Midlands around Malvern were quite pretty and so when she left the next day to go back to duty, I went along too. To make a long story short, I married her almost a year later. We're still married and have five children—four girls and a boy.

I'm now running my own mortgage-loan business here in Martinez, California. We like it here and we like the mortgage-banker business. It's the only way I could get to be president of the company; start my own!

Jim, I'm so glad that my folks still live in the same old house and don't move around as much as our generation has, otherwise I probably never would have heard from you. Now that I'm into putting this down on paper, I may have to write the whole story someday just so my kids can read it.

You know, they look at me kind of strangely when they learn that I was a fighter pilot in that old WWII and ask if there really was any shooting and did I do any shooting. It's hard for me to believe myself. Many of the names I've forgotten and some of the places and most of the 45 missions. But some of it still stands out when I think back. It almost seems unreal, even as I write. Almost like fiction as thoughts and memory returns in my daydreaming as I write.

I'd like to go back for a visit to Algiers, Casablanca, Naples, Capri, Rome, Corsica and, as much as anything, to the area where I was shot down and to the hospital where I first recovered—somewhere near Bergamo. I still send a Christmas card to one Italian woman that brought me a piece of Italian bread most every morning before she started mopping floors.

I think it does me good to reflect on all that has happened. By comparison, I live like a prince with everything anyone would want in the way of a comfortable life. I guess I'm just lucky at that. Of course, I always jokingly tell my family that the Lord saved me for bigger and better things.

Kindest Regards,

George Dorval

Index